THE MEANING OF EVIL

The Meaning of Evil

CHARLES JOURNET

Translated by Michael Barry

P. J. KENEDY & SONS—NEW YORK

This book was originally published in French under the title *Le Mal* by Desclée de Brouwer in 1961.
The quotations from Scripture are taken from the Revised Standard Version, published by Thomas Nelson & Sons Ltd.

Library of Congress Catalog Card Number 63-10457
© translation, 1963, Geoffrey Chapman Ltd.

Nihil obstat: ROBERTUS CAN. MEAGHER, S.T.D.
Imprimatur: DIONYSIUS MCDONNELL, *Vic. Gen.*
Liverpolii, DIE 4A DECEMBRIS 1962

MADE AND PRINTED IN GREAT BRITAIN

CONTENTS

v

CHAPTER THREE
The Forms of Evil

CHAPTER FOUR
God and Evil
The Metaphysical Aspect of the Problem

CHAPTER FIVE

The Evil in Nature

CHAPTER SEVEN
The Punishment of Actual Sin

II. THE TEMPORAL PUNISHMENT OF SIN 214

CHAPTER EIGHT
The Trials of the Present Life

FOREWORD

The mystery of evil is considered in this book from the theological viewpoint. There is no question more urgent for Christians, none which they are more frequently called upon to answer. It might seem surprising that the manuals of theology do not contain any treatise on evil. It can be replied that, since evil is present everywhere, it is mentioned in all the treatises, whether they deal with God who permits it, with the creation in which it has so large a part, with angels, man, human acts, law, grace, the redemptive Incarnation, the Church or final ends. This is true; but it might just as well be said that every theological treatise is implied in all the others without dispensing with the necessity of separate treatment. The same holds true for evil. Every treatise touches on evil under some particular aspect, but it can well be looked at on its own, so that fundamental points can be dealt with: its nature, its origins and its forms. There is a short treatise on evil in St Thomas's *III Contra Gentiles,* and another is inserted into the treatise on creation in the *Summa Theologica.* Evil in general is approached in the *quaestio disputata: De malo* (between 1269 and 1272). There is no reason why this example should not be followed today when the problem of evil faces us. We do not need to trespass on the ground covered by other, different theological treatises. Leaving aside anything coming under particular sciences like biology, psychology, etc., evil will here be treated in general, in its theological and philosophical aspects.

First of all the problem will be set out (ch. 1), and then there will be a discussion of its nature (ch. 2) and its forms (ch. 3). Then comes the central question of its relation to an all-powerful and infinitely good God (ch. 4), followed by a consideration of the different forms of evil: the evil in nature (ch. 5); the evil of sin, where the central truth to be established is that all free creatures are by nature liable to sin (ch. 6); the evil of the pains of hell and purgatory (ch. 7); and the trials of the present life (ch. 8). After a short section on evil in history (ch. 9), we will come back to our

13

point of departure in order to see what attitude can be taken to evil (ch. 10).

A consequence of the phenomenon of inward questioning which characterizes our modern age is the directing of attention to the mystery of evil and the obligation on Christians to take up the traditional answers, study them closely and develop them. It has been written : 'The Middle Ages kept their eyes fixed on the luminous points revealed by St Augustine in the mystery of grace and freedom, which is concerned with the divine depths of the mystery. The vast regions lying in shadow, concerned with its created and human depths, in particular with all that relates to God's permission of evil acts and the production of evil by the creature, as also the whole significance and proper value, that is, in the orders of philosophy and of theology, of the temporal and secular activity of human beings : on the threshold of these regions, the Middle Ages laid down boldly the principles of solution; but they advanced only a little way into that obscurity and these problems, and left much land in fallow and a whole field of complexities unexplored.'[1] Maritain, the author of these lines, has made the problem of evil one of the constant preoccupations of his philosophical enquiries. An apology must be made for the constant quotations from his works—but we consider these to be rich and coherent, traditional yet full of innovation, and containing the most penetrating teaching on evil written in our own times from the Christian viewpoint.

In the task of extracting the teaching on evil revealed in Holy Scripture, especially in the New Testament, our principal guides have been St Augustine and St Thomas Aquinas, the masters who are loved now as at all times, whose great contemplative intuitions we hope not to have misrepresented. The aim of the theologian dealing with a mystery is to do away with phrases which diminish the mystery. His fear is that he in his turn may remain a prisoner of a deficient phraseology lacking simplicity and clarity, and run the risk of clouding the issue and preventing the reader's mind being led on to silent adoration of the depths of God. This fear has been with me all through the course of this work.

Fribourg, January, 1960.

[1] J. Maritain, *True Humanism,* trans. M. R. Adamson (Geoffrey Bles, London, 1938), pp. 4-5.

CHAPTER ONE

The Question of Evil

I. REASONS FOR HESITATION

To avoid a whole series of misunderstandings, it must be realized from the beginning that the question of evil is difficult and limitless, not to say dangerous.

a. *A difficult question*

Its difficulty must never be forgotten. This does not mean that the answer does not exist, nor that it is confused or vague, but that the answer does not appear unless the search is started from a point from which everything is clear. It is often said that objections are easier to grasp than answers. If this is true the mind would seem to be made more for destructiveness and chaos than for constructiveness and truth. Certainly there is a lazy and misguided way of tackling any important issue, a low-level perspective, in which everything is reduced to objections and no solution is possible. But there is another way, a high-level perspective, where everything starts to fit into place of its own accord, where what immediately strikes the mind is the truth of the answer and the hollowness of the objections.[1] The first and only difficulty—and it can be a big one—is to bring ourselves from the first visual perspective to the second, and then to draw others the same way. What answer can ultimately be given to someone who reproaches God for treating his creatures as no good family man would treat his children, except to say that God is not a good family man and that his providence is unfathomable? When Dostoyevsky paints

---

[1] 'Listen to a discussion between two philosophers, one of whom believes in determinism and the other in liberty: it is always the determinist who seems to have reason on his side. He may be a novice and his opponent experienced ... It will always be said of him that he is simple and clear and speaking the truth. He does this easily and naturally, having only to pick on prepared thoughts and ready made phrases ... Criticizing an intuitive philosophy is so easy and so sure of being well received that it will always tempt the beginner. Regrets may come later . . .' Henri Bergson, *La pensée et le mouvant* (Paris, 1934).

an unbearable picture of evil for us and brings to a climax the
scandal that this causes some who want to believe in God, he makes
us see that in the hearts of certain men there exists a more penetrating vision of the world, where the perspective is reversed,
where all scandal subsides, and his concern is to know whether
he has succeeded in convincing his readers of this.[2]

b. A limitless question

The question of evil is immense and in a sense limitless. Evil
extends to the whole of creation, to angels, to man, to material
things.

On one particular point the existence of evil seems to enter into
direct conflict with the Christian message. How is it to be reconciled with the dogma of divine causality? God has created all
things, he has made them what they are. Is evil a thing and has it
a nature? Has God created things which are bad by nature? For
instance, material things among which conflicts and destruction
pile up? Is he the author of evil? Or must we give up the dogma
of God's universal causality and imagine, perhaps, two antagonistic first principles, one good, author of all good things, the
other evil, author of all bad things? Christian preaching has been
preoccupied with such questions from the earliest times, yet it has
always proclaimed without hesitation the omnipotence and infinite

[2]'Dostoyevsky plainly comes up against the ultimate problem, that of evil.
This problem constantly obsesses him, in both general and particular
questions such as the child martyrs, for surely the most unjustifiable evil
is the suffering of innocent people. This lies at the heart of *The Brothers
Karamazov*. The author made this clear in several letters: "My hero (*i.e.
Ivan*) deals in this with a subject which for me is irrefutable: the sense-
lessness of the suffering of children—and he deduces from this the
absurdity of all history." Ivan's complaint against God is irrefutable,
Dostoyevsky thinks, on the level of reasoning. He has, he goes on to say,
developed in it the arguments for radical atheism, which denies not only
God, but the very meaning of creation, and that with a forcefulness
which has never been attained *even in Europe*. His readers, like Pobie-
donotsev, with whom he was at the time in regular contact, and he himself,
wonder how he is going to reply to it (the novel was appearing in
instalments in a review while it was being written): "I myself feel that
atheism seems the stronger.—I am in fear and trembling to know whether
the answer is sufficient." The answer is not a point for point refutation
of the arguments for atheism, but leads up to a shifting of one's viewpoint
. . . The answer lies in the person of Zosima, in his life, preaching and
practice of love.' Pierre Pascal, 'Dostoiewski et la foi chrétienne' in
Istina, 1954, no. 2, p. 237.

goodness of God. It has never denied the immense part played by evil in the universe and in history, and has striven to form clearer ideas about it. God may indeed seem to sleep when storms break on his creatures, but he knows everything and will at the crucial moment awaken, like Christ in the ship. Moreover it should be realized immediately that if the co-existence of evil and an all-powerful, infinitely good God poses a problem, this problem does admit of a solution and does not throw the mind into chaos; it should not be imagined that by rejecting the Christian message and making appeal to the impotent pagan gods or the conflict of two rival principles, one good, one evil, let alone to atheism, the scandal of evil is diminished : the problem is not suppressed but simply rendered insoluble, and the mind is thrown back upon the contradictory and the absurd.

When the medieval theologians treated directly of evil, they devoted themselves to clarifying these very questions. Is evil a thing, an essence? Can it be created by God? If God does not create it, why at least does he permit it? By permitting it does he will it? Could he not prevent it, being all-powerful and infinitely good? Does he meet with resistance and is there, set against the absolute Good, an absolute Evil which is the cause of all other evils?[3]

[3]These are the main subjects considered by St Thomas when he deals directly with evil. In *III contra Gent.*: Every agent acts for the sake of some good, ch. 3; evil is not sought for its own sake, ch. 4; evil is not a thing, not a nature, ch. 7; it is by accident that evil, physical or moral, can result from something good, ch. 10; evil has good for a subject, ch. 11; it attacks good without being able to destroy it completely, ch. 12; in what sense has it a cause? ch. 13; in what sense can it be a cause? ch. 14; there is no supreme Evil, cause of all other evils, ch. 15. In the *Summa Theologica*, I, qu. 19, a. 9: Does God will evils? Qu. 48, a. 1, has evil a nature? a. 2, does it exist? a. 3, does it have good as a subject? a. 4, does it completely destroy good? a. 5 & 6, division of human evil into evil of sin and evil of punishment. Qu. 49, a. 1, can good be the cause of evil? a. 2, is God, the supreme Good, the cause of evil? a. 3, is there a supreme Evil, cause of all other evils? In *De Malo*, the first question is kept for evil in general: a. 1, is it a thing? a. 2, is it in good? a. 3, does good cause evil? a. 4 & 5, division of the evil of rational creatures into evil of sin and evil of punishment. Question 2 is a study of sin. Question 3, the causes of sin: a. 1 & 2, is it God? a. 3, 4 & 5, is it the devil? a. 6, 7 & 8, the part played by ignorance; a. 9, 10, 11, the part played by weakness; a. 11, 12, 13, 14, 15, the part played by wickedness. Questions 4 & 5 bring us back to original sin. Questions 7-15, venial sin and the deadly sins. Question 16 deals with devils.

Nonetheless, however necessary explanations of these topics may be, they will not suffice to calm the soul tormented by the question of evil; they give a partial answer. The full answer lies in Christianity as a whole, accepted, understood and lived without reserve. It opens with a message of joy : 'And an angel of the Lord appeared to them, and the glory of the Lord shone around them, and they were filled with fear. And the angel said to them "Be not afraid; for behold, I bring you good news of a great joy which will come to all the people" ' (Luke 2, 9-10). It is rich enough to give an eminently satisfactory answer to the spectacle of the world's tragedy. It tells us that God is a God of love; that the creation of the universe is the effect of a free outpouring of this love; that man's first condition was a privileged one; that the fall was certainly followed by a condition of affliction, but one in which God continued to love us to the point of sending us his only Son in the Incarnation and Redemption; that the Holy Spirit bestows Christ's riches on men who do not refuse them, calling them all, from far and near, to constitute in this world a kingdom which is not of this world; that this kingdom and the universe itself will give way to an unimaginable transfiguration which free creatures are invited beforehand to consent to, but which they may also beforehand, by a fearful mystery, deprive themselves of. There is no element of the Christian message which is not to some extent an answer to the question of evil; it is this which makes this answer immense and limitless.

c. A dangerous question: the risk of deception

It is dangerous to embark on the question of evil : we risk defeat, and we risk presumption as well.

It is so easy to mislead those we wish to enlighten. If they want to reflect on evil, we shall necessarily have to draw their attention to several points of metaphysics, because a conception of the relations of creatures and Creator will become of the greatest importance. The doctrine of the permission of evil by an all-powerful and infinitely good God requires delicate presentation, and a readiness to keep all things, the highest and the lowest, constantly in view; it is not unambiguous but relative, and changes its meaning according as its plane is shifted from the evil of guilt to the evil of punishment or the evil in nature. One may well be discouraged by the effort needed; one may even, when coming to grips with evil, have neither strength nor desire left to open one's mind to a discussion. In that case what is said will seem vain and pointless. It is not that the truth is at fault, but rather that the time has come to suffer evil and not just think about it any longer, and for God to speak to one in silence.[4]

Then, too, the forms of evil are unlimited, and it would be impossible to go into them all. Perhaps that particular evil which, for some person willing to listen, has been more significant than all the others, which has appalled his mind and occasioned a crisis in his life might be missed out.

In *The Little Flowers of St Francis*[5] there is the story of a leper who was blaspheming so terribly that the Friars who had been sent to tend him had determined to leave him alone. Then St Francis came along. He warmed some water mixed with sweet-smelling herbs and, having undressed the sick man, started to wash his sores. And as he touched him, the leprosy vanished. Dumbfounded, the leper stopped cursing, then burst into tears, begging forgiveness for his blasphemies. Driving away evil by touching it is a shattering answer to which there is no retort. This was the answer given more than once by Jesus. But it is an answer which is not normal during our period of exile; it belongs to the after-life, the time of the New Jerusalem, when God will dwell with men and 'will wipe away every tear from their eyes, and death shall be no more, neither shall there be mourning, nor crying, nor pain any more, for the former things have passed away' (Apoc. 21, 3-4). The ordinary Christian, the ordinary theologian, when asked about evil, can have recourse only to the answers available to us in our exile.

He will not try to answer an experience by a doctrine, or a doctrine by an experience, but he will counter a wrong and superficial doctrine with a true and thoughtful one, and an experience lived through with little or no Christian love with one in which

---

[4]'I do not say, moreover, that he who is at this moment a prey to evil can find satisfaction in any answer no matter how true it may be. The experience of that which is in itself without any consolation, the experience of death can be surmounted or, rather, absorbed only by another experience, of a divine order,—by the experience of paschal love. Yet it seems to me that we shall not be speaking exactly like the friends of Job if we say this . . .' Maritain, *St Thomas and the Problem of Evil* (Marquette University Press, Milwaukee, 1942), pp. 14-5.
[5]Ch. 25.

Christian love is very intense. This is clear, and yet, if it is right
to counter a doctrine with a doctrine and an experience with an
experience when God and evil are spoken of, the most orthodox
doctrine, if repeated without being plunged back into the flame
where it was wrought or vivified by some secret power of the Gospel
will mislead and may turn to poison. How then are we to avoid
trembling at causing scandal where it was hoped to bring light?
Even when he himself has felt this flame and power, the Christian,
the theologian, would be unable to communicate it : it is the oil
of a lamp which cannot be bartered, which is sold by God alone;
he will at least be able to indicate the path along which it may be
discovered, and know the name of the Source from which there
descends upon our souls the inner light that will banish all their
darkness.

d. *The risk of presumption*

The greatest danger is perhaps that of presumption. 'It is not
good to eat much honey,' says the Book of Proverbs,[6] but to
meditate on evil leads to other dangers; it may be too overwhelming for us. How can we eat without remorse, knowing that two
men out of three suffer from hunger, or go to sleep, thinking about
the affliction of the sick or about the crowds of refugees who lack
the warmth of a home, abandoned by hope and unwanted by those
around them, or breathe freely when each day we hear how
injustice triumphs, how the faith of children is destroyed, nations
led astray by myths and subordinated to tyrannical ends, and
means of torture and destruction brought to perfection? How can
our way of life be bearable any more, how can we help feeling that
the even tenor of our existence rests on ignorance and complicity
and is protected by barriers raised by selfishness, and the only life
free of all falsehood is not ours but the one revealed to the saints,
those who truly love Christ? How can we help falling into discouragement? Our faith also is threatened. Was it essential to
God's plan that evil should deploy so many forces, even after the
redemption of the world? Our certainty of the absolute truth of
what we believe can be wrecked when we come up against the
irreconcilable divergences among minds which are seeking the face
of God with as great a longing as our own, and perhaps a greater.

[6]Prov. 25, 27.

The appalling prospect of even one soul finally rejecting God and securing his own eternal damnation might well be the fatal temptation. How can we dare to set foot in forbidden territory? Qui scrutator est majestatis opprimetur a gloria[7] (Prov. 25, 27).

But Jesus knew the whole of evil. By descending into its depths he has shown us the way and invited us to follow him. All who have loved him have done so without turning away; they have entered into the darkness with the urgency of desire and have opened their minds, in the course of their meditations on evil, to the whole universe. Are we going to hesitate on the threshold and retain at all costs a delicate balance made up of ignorance and the instinct of self-preservation? Would it not be better to founder this ship and capsize in the turmoil lived through by the saints? It would indeed be rashness and even pure folly, ending in certain catastrophe, to attempt such a venture with only our own poor resources. But we have before us the various teachings of the Church, the reasonings of the Doctors and the appeals of the Saints. We should pay attention to these aids and join forces with the friends of God. Much prayer is needed. For it is no mean thing to know evil without losing one's head, and it can only be done to the extent to which we have made contact with God, so as to return afterwards to his creation and see it as he sees it. And God can only be reached by truth and love, not by truth alone, for he is both Truth and Love and 'la vérité hors de la charité n'est pas Dieu'.[8]

2. A CENTRAL VIEW : THE MUTUAL DEPENDENCE OF OUR KNOWLEDGE OF EVIL AND OUR KNOWLEDGE OF GOD

Our progress in the knowledge of evil must be made by progress in the knowledge of God; and likewise our progress in the knowledge of God by progress in the knowledge of evil. Neither knowledge destroys the other, rather each deepens the other and the two are complementary. They are like the two points at opposite ends of the diameter of a wheel : as one goes higher the other goes lower. Paradoxical only in appearance, this view of things which is presented at the outset, and which will remain the central idea of this study, provides the perspective in which,

[7]According to the Vulgate this is the end of Prov. 25, 27. Cf. Eccles., 3, 22.
[8]Pascal, Pensées, ed. Brunschvicg, no. 582.

whether one likes it or not, any attempt to know more about evil
must be placed and finally judged.

a. *The knowledge of one either cancels the other out* ...

An ordinary, superficial knowledge of God will not perhaps be
affected to any startling degree by an ordinary, superficial knowledge of evil. But once evil suddenly reveals the horror of its features, this insufficient knowledge of God will be troubled and
falter; it must either give in to atheism which, having rudely contracted and limited the range of evil to temporal things, will
ultimately leave everything unanswered; or, on the other hand,
it must shake off its torpor, gain more height and grow in awareness of a mystery which it had not before suspected. Neither the
demiurge of Plotinus nor the God of Spinoza is capable of resisting
the true, genuine view of evil.[9] A philosophy which knows nothing
of the absolute purity of divine transcendence and sees God only
as the keystone of the universe will hardly go much further than
the evil of nature, that is, the evil which is the reverse side of some
good necessary to the general order of the world; it will be
tempted to reduce to this the freely chosen evil of sin;[10] and it will
end up by saying that evil is only apparent and does not really
exist, and that what we call evil, or sin, is necessary and
only represents different but equally legitimate forms of being.[11]

[9]Evil 'reveals itself to be necessarily caught in the bonds of beauty, like
a prisoner covered with golden chains; it hides itself beneath them so
that its reality may remain invisible to the gods...' *1st Ennead,* VIII, 15.
[10]'Just as in the pipes of Pan or other instruments there are tubes of different length, souls are placed each in a different position; and each, in
its own place, gives out the sound which accords with its own position
and with the harmony of others. The wickedness of souls has its place
in the beauty of the universe; what is for them contrary to nature is for
the universe conformable to nature.' Plotinus, *3rd Ennead,* 11, 17.
[11]'Perfection and imperfection are in reality only modes of thinking,
by which I mean notions we have been accustomed to form because we
make comparisons between individuals of the same genus or species ...
As to good and evil, neither of them point to anything positive in things
... and are nothing other than modes of thinking or notions which we
form because we compare things ... Although this is true, we still have
to keep these names.' Spinoza, *Ethics,* IV, Preface. 'Why then are the
wicked punished? They act in accordance with their nature and with
God's decree. I answer that it is also by God's decree that they are
punished and if only those whom we imagine to sin in virtue of their own
freedom are to be punished, why do men strive to wipe out poisonous
serpents? For these sin in virtue of their own nature and cannot do
otherwise.' *Metaphysical Reflections,* II, ch. 8. Cf below, p. 94.

b. . . . *or throws more light on it*

The true vision of evil demands an exalted idea of God, and by similar inversion an exalted idea of God offers a deeper understanding of evil. God, in whom are hidden the final reasons for things, invites those who love him to plumb the depths of his providence. One night he revealed to St Catherine of Siena the wickedness of sin, the loss of souls, and the persecution of the Church; next morning at Communion she held herself, because of her lukewarmness, responsible for the evil of the whole world.[12] He gave St Teresa a harrowing awareness of hell and of the devastation caused in Christendom by the Lutheran schism.[13] He made Mary of the Incarnation, enclosed in her convent in Tours, see 'with an interior certainty', over all the inhabitable earth, the pathetic spectacle of rational men as victims of the demons.[14] He let St Margaret Mary experience something of the 'mortal sorrow' of the Garden of Olives.[15] And if it should be asked why God treats his friends in this way, bringing them ever closer to the knowledge which threw Jesus into his agony, the only answer is that by this very action he was to pierce them with the vision of his goodness. 'The Lord,' says St John of the Cross, 'has ever revealed to mortals the treasures of his Wisdom and his Spirit; but now that wickedness is revealing her face more and more clearly, he reveals them in large measure.'[16]

3. A LAW OF THE WORLD'S SPIRITUAL HISTORY

Thus the face of God and the face of evil are together uncovered as time goes on.

The mystery of original sin, that is to say the passing on to all Adam's descendants of a sin which attaches to them and whose consequence is death, although implied in the biblical account of the downfall of the first man, has only been clearly revealed to us

[12]*Dialogue*, ch. 2.
[13]*Autobiography*, ch. 32, *Way of Perfection*, ch. 1.
[14]*Ecrits spirituels et historiques* (Jamet, Paris, 1930), vol. II, p. 310.
[15]*Autobiography* (Paray-le-Monial, 1924), p. 89.
[16]*Spiritual Sentences and Maxims*, I, trans. E. Allison Peers, in *The Complete Works of St John of the Cross*, vol. III (Burns Oates, 1943), p. 241.

in the mystery of our redemption : 'For as by one man's disobedience many were made sinners, so by one man's obedience
many will be made righteous' (Rom. 5, 19).

Only in the revelation of our deliverance can the full revelation
of our disgrace be borne without despair.

Later on it is by asking why the Incarnation and redemption
came about—*Cur Deus Homo*—and investigating the reasons
why a God had to be born and to die for us that theology has been
made so fully aware of the mystery of the infinite offence of mortal
sin.

We touch here on a law of the world's spiritual history, which
advances simultaneously in two directions : on the one hand it
draws nearer to what St Paul calls the apostasy, the supreme
manifestation of the man of sin, Antichrist, and of the forces of
Satan, and on the other to the final victory of the Lord Jesus, who
will annihilate it with the splendour of his coming, of the Parousia
(II Thess. 3, 13).

4. THE ANSWER TO EVIL

At the level of life, only the experience of God can resist the
experience of evil; at the level of intellect, only the progressive
discovery of God can resist the progressive discovery of evil. At
both levels, only the mystery of God allows us to confront the
mystery of evil as a whole. One mystery is opposed to another
mystery, an absolutely infinite mystery to a relatively infinite
one.

a. *One mystery throwing light on another*

Mysteries, in effect, can only be explained by one another : the
higher explains the lower and the lower in its turn throws light
on the higher. Thus, for example, the gift of the Incarnation first
justifies the gift of the Eucharist, but contact with the Eucharist
then allows us to guess at the meaning of the Incarnation. Any
other way of throwing light on mysteries is by its very nature
inadequate.

But can one mystery throw light on another? Can the mystery
of God throw light on that of evil? Surely to make appeal
to mysteries is only to cloud the issue ?

b. *The dilemma: mystery or contradiction*

It is important to be careful here. Whether it is a question of evil or more generally of the relation of the world to God, the moment human reason decides to go right on to the end of the course, it inevitably finishes up in darkness. But there are two sorts of darkness and obscurity, and an early choice must be made between them : one, the darkness of mystery, is above human reason and elevates it; the other, the darkness of incoherence and contradiction, is beneath it and deranges it.

Even at the level of merely natural activities, opposition breaks out between these two sorts of obscurity. Human reason finds itself constrained either to go beyond itself into a mystery or to fall back into contradiction. The mind is not made to adore itself but to give itself; what transports and fascinates the minds of men, in the intuition and the work of genius, in the stars of the heavens, in anything which never wearies them, is the inexhaustible share of mystery they contain, a darkness more excellent and intoxicating than daylight, from which they return strengthened and elated. But to participate in a contradiction disturbs, injures and threatens the mind to its very core. At a superficial glance the two sorts of darkness may seem alike, for both are removed from clear thought : but in opposite directions. It is the same with genius and madness, which both appear equally to flout the normal conventions of men. The darkness of mystery and the darkness of incoherence are the inevitable but opposite poles of thought : the more one of them seems desirable, the more the other seems hateful.

The great discussion of evil on which we are starting goes beyond the limits of rational clarity : we are creatures, posing questions on the condition and the destiny of the world. Darkness will shroud us everywhere. The question is, will it be the darkness of mystery or the darkness of incoherence? The answer is straightforward. By denying God, the reason embraces absurdity; it does the same thing in another way by denying evil. The coexistence of evil and an all-powerful and infinitely good God represents a mystery; but not a contradiction. When confronted finally by the dilemma of mystery or contradiction, we cannot go back on our tracks or have recourse to evasions : what is seen beyond any doubt to be a contradiction should be refused, but what is seen beyond any doubt to be a mystery should be embraced. The question of evil forces the mind to founder in contradiction or to rise to mystery. The contradiction lies in denying God or denying evil; the mystery affirms the coexistence of the two extremes, it does not seek to make either diminish the other, but uses each to produce a deeper knowledge of the other.

5. THE NECESSITY OF CONFRONTING THE QUESTION OF EVIL

Consequently, if there can be no deep knowledge of evil without a deep knowledge of God, and if evil discovers its face to the same extent as God discovers the treasures of his Wisdom and Spirit, have we any right to avert our gaze from the sight of evil? Rather we should ask God, provided our desire is not presumptive and we ourselves are not found too unworthy, to make clear to us the reason for, and the depth and extent of, the presence of evil in his creation.

This holds even for that speculative and communicable knowledge which enables us to grasp, in the light of reason and faith, the nature of evil, its relation to being, the reasons for its being allowed in our universe, and the possibility of its coexisting with an all-powerful and infinitely good God. Of such a speculative knowledge it is true to say that the further it wishes to descend into evil the higher it must rise towards God, and that both extremes throw light on one another and aid a more thorough understanding. The effects it produces are good; it purifies the soul of numberless errors, shatters its pettiness and egoism, humiliates and yet exalts it and opens it to the limitless obedience of divine faith, increases its powers of prayer and suffering and leaves untouched its gratitude for having been created and its joy at having come into the world. This holds even more for that experiential and incommunicable knowledge (gained by experience) which enables us to feel through our tears the coexistence of the twofold mystery of evil and divine Goodness. If God associates certain people, however infrequently and in however small a way, with the infinite sorrow of his Son during the night of Gethsemani, is it not an unmistakable sign that by doing so he is leading them into the intimacy of his love?

CHAPTER TWO

What is Evil?

At the beginning of the eighth treatise of the first Ennead, entitled *The essence and origin of evils,* Plotinus writes: 'Those who wish to know where evils come from and whether they affect beings in general or a particular category of beings, would do well to start their enquiry by asking first what evil is and what is its nature. In this way it can also be learnt where it comes from, what it is founded on and whom it can happen to. And everyone would agree that it is necessary to know whether it is in beings.' In our opinion Plotinus was mistaken about the definition of evil. He identified it, not immediately with the body, but with what he called matter (*hylè*), that which is boundless, formless, deficient, unstable, passive, unfulfilled, in which he saw Evil as such, total evil without any admixture of goodness, which corrupts those who participate in it or even contemplate it. But Plotinus was right to insist that any enquiry into evil should begin with a definition of evil or to form any judgment about solutions put forward without knowing what evil basically is. Only then can anything be said about its origin and the reason why it is permitted.

I. THE DEFINITION OF EVIL

Evil is a privation.[1] But privation can be taken in two senses.[2] Broadly speaking it can designate any lack or absence of good. In

---

[1] 'Malum autem est *privatio* ...' St Thomas, *De malo,* qu. 1, a. 2, ad 3. 'Privatio ... est defectus ejus quod est natum inesse et non inest.' Ibid., qu. 1, a. 3.

[2] 'There is privation when a thing does not have what it ought not to have: thus a stone does not have sight. And there is, in another way, privation when a thing does not have what it ought to have: for example, an animal which cannot see.' St Thomas, *Meta.,* bk. X, no. 2043; bk. V, no. 1070-2. For these two meanings of the word privation (*steresis*), cf. Aristotle, *Meta.,* bk. X, 22; bk. V, 4.

the strict sense privation is opposed to mere negation or absence :[3] it is the *absence of some good which should be present*.[4] This is the definition of evil.

To be unable to see is a mere negation or absence in minerals or plants; in man it is a privation, an evil.

St Thomas, to make quite clear that he understands privation in this strict sense as opposed to mere absence, almost invariably defines evil as *the privation of some good which should be present*.[5]

2. ORIGINS OF THIS DEFINITION

a. *Greek thought: Plotinus*

The work done by Greek thinkers was able to prepare for the elaboration of this definition of evil, but it is not among the Greeks that it is first found. It is not found in Plato. The one who came closest to it and almost formulated it, without seeming to realize it or at least without wanting to make anything of it, was Aristotle, when he listed the various types of privation.[6] It is not found in Plotinus, who defined evil as good which falls short;[7] matter, with which he identified it, was in his eyes deprived of all good.[8] Attempts have been made to show how close these expressions are to those of the Christian doctors, but they reveal a vision of evil which depends largely on Plato and is not far removed from

[3]Malum 'neque est . . . sicut pura *negatio,* sed sicut *privatio.*' I, qu. 48, a. 2, ad 1. 'Remotio igitur boni, *negative* accepta, mali rationem non habet . . . Sed remotio boni, *privative* accepta, malum dicitur.' I, qu. 48, a. 3.
[4]'Relinquitur ergo quod nomine mali significatur *quaedam absentia boni.*' I, qu. 48, a. 5, ad 1. 'Malum est defectus boni quod natum est et debet haberi.' I, qu. 48, a. 5, ad 1. 'Hoc privari dicimus quod natum est habere aliquid et non habet.' *De malo,* qu. 1, a. 2.
[5]'Cum malum nihil aliud sit quam privatio debitae perfectionis.' *De malo,* qu. 1, a. 2. Malum 'est ipsa privatio alicujus particularis boni'. *De malo,* qu. 1, a. 1.
[6]'There is privation (*steresis*) for a being, when the quality which ought by nature to be in it or in its genus, is not possessed: thus it is different for a blind man and a mole to be deprived of sight: for the mole, the privation is contrary to the animal genus, for the man, it is contrary to his own normal nature. And there is again privation when a being, which by nature and at the time in question ought to possess a quality and does not; blindness, indeed, is a privation, but it cannot be said to be so when a being is blind at any and every age, but simply if, at the age when it ought by nature to have sight, it does not possess it . . .' *Meta.,* bk. V, 22.
[7]'to kakon helleipsin tou agathou.' *3rd Ennead,* tr. I, ch. 5.
[8]*1st Ennead,* tr. VIII, ch. 4.

Gnosticism : this leads on to statements which are irreconcilable with Christian teaching.[9]

b. *The Judæo-Christian revelation*

Only the light of the Judæo-Christian revelation enables the definition of evil to be formulated and to display its content. The doctrine of the unmediated creation of the world from nothing by one omnipotent God does, in effect, dispel the illusion of the eternity of matter, the substantiality of evil and the conflict of

[9]Here are some passages from the eighth treatise ('On the Origin of Evils') of the *1st Ennead*: 'Since Good does not exist alone, there is necessarily, in the series of things which come forth from it, or, if preferred, which descend from it and remove themselves further from it, a final term beyond which nothing more can be engendered; this term is evil ... it is matter, which no longer has any part in Good. Such is the necessity of evil' (ch. 7). 'Since evil exists, it remains, therefore, that it exists in what is not; it is in a sense the form of non-being; it is found in things which are tinged with non-being and participate in non-being ... It is to good as measurelessness to measure, limitlessness to limitation, shapelessness to formal cause, eternally deficient being to self-sufficient being; it is always indeterminate and unstable, completely passive, never fulfilled, it is utter poverty; these are not the accidental attributes but, as it were, the very substance of evil ... To what subject do these properties belong? They are not different from their subject; they are the subject itself ... Evil must itself exist first in itself, even if it is not a substance ... There is Good in itself and good as an attribute; likewise there is Evil in itself, and ... evil as an attribute of a being different from itself ... There must, therefore, be something unlimited in itself, something shapeless in itself ... And if, apart from Evil, there are evil things, it is because they are mixed with evil ... The subject in which shapes, forms and limits reside ... the subject, which is to reality as its image, is the one which is the substance of evil, if evil can have a substance; that is the Primary Evil, the Evil in itself which reasoning reveals to us' (ch. 3). 'Corporeal nature is evil in so far as it participates in matter, but it is not the primary evil; for it has a certain form, which nonetheless is not a real one, being deprived of life' (ch. 4). 'Material nature is the principle of becoming and is so evil that it fills with evil any being which is not yet in it and which does no more than look at it. Having no share in goodness, deprived (*steresis*) of it, purely deficient, matter gives its own likeness to anything which comes into the least contact with it' (ch. 4). 'It must be concluded that we are not the principle of our evils and that evil does not come from ourselves, but that evils exist prior to ourselves; evil possesses man, and he possesses it in spite of himself' (ch. 5). 'Matter does not even have the being which would permit it to have some share in goodness; if it is said to be, this is only to equivocate; the truth is that it is a non-being ..., what evil is, is the total defect of good' (ch. 5). In ch. 11 Plotinus maintains that privation can be in itself a reality, as opposed to the Peripatetics, for whom privation (*steresis*) is always in a subject and has in itself no subsistence (*hypostasis*).

two antagonistic first principles, one good, the other evil. This doctrine has its roots in the Old Testament.[10] It is constantly recalled in the New. St John writes of the Word 'He was in the beginning with God; all things were made through him, and without him was not anything made that was made' (John 1, 3). The Acts of the Apostles tells us of the 'Sovereign Lord, who didst make the heaven and the earth and the sea and everything in them' (Acts 4, 24; cf. 14, 14 and 17, 24).

St Paul always comes back to this point : 'There is one God, the Father, from whom are all things and for whom we exist, and one Lord, Jesus Christ, through whom are all things and through whom we exist' (I Cor. 8, 6). 'For from him and through him and to him are all things' (Rom. 11, 36).

Of his Beloved Son it is said : 'He is the image of the invisible God, the first-born of all creation; for in him all things were created, in heaven and on earth, visible and invisible, whether thrones or dominions or principalities or authorities—all things were created through him and for him. He is before all things, and in him all things hold together' (Col. 1, 15-17).[11]

c. *The Greek Fathers: Origen, Methodius, Athanasius, Basil, Gregory of Nyssa.*

The Greek Fathers very soon pointed out the negative character of evil.

[10]The doctrine of creation out of nothing is contained implicitly in Genesis 1, 1: 'In the beginning God created the heavens and the earth,' where God is represented as the Author and only Lord of the whole world. It is formally expressed in II Macch. 7, 28: 'Behold the heavens and the earth, see all that they contain, and know that God did not make them from things which already existed.' Cf. van Imschoot, *Théologie de l'Ancien Testament* (Tournai, 1954), vol. I, p. 98.

Concerning demonology in Jewish literature from the beginning of the Christian era, Joseph Bonsirven writes: 'In all these conceptions there is no appearance of dualism, since the demons are God's creatures, becoming evil through their own will.' *Les idées juives au temps de Notre-Seigneur* (Paris, 1934), p. 54. 'We can find no trace of any tradition which would make the devil a being evil by essence and origin, or which would not place him among God's creatures.' *Le judaïsme palestinien au temps de Jésus-Christ* (Paris, 1935), vol. I, p. 245.

[11]The text of Wisdom 11, 18: 'Thine all-powerful hand has created the universe from formless matter,' corresponds to that of Genesis, 1, 2, where it is said that the earth was 'an empty waste', or according to the Septuagint 'without shape or form', and means that the universe was first of all created in an amorphous state and afterwards organized and brought to completion.

Commenting on Rom. 11, 32 : 'For God has consigned all men to disobedience that he may have mercy upon all', Origen, who elsewhere recognizes that evil is a privation[12] and not a thing,[13] goes on to explain that if God did not from the outset eliminate the evil done by some men, it is because he foresaw that it would result in good for others in the future.[14] Here in germ is the theology of evil.

St Methodius (d. 311), Bishop of Olympus in Lycia, came up against the ever recurring dilemma : either God is the author of all being, and consequently of evil, or it is necessary to say with the Gnostics that evil comes from an eternal matter for which God is not responsible; in the one case God is not good, in the other he is not absolute. He sums up his answer by saying that no evil is a substance (*ousía*).[15]

The problem came up a little later in the *Contra Gentes* of St Athanasius : 'Certain Greeks,[16] straying from the true path and not knowing Christ, have affirmed that evil existed as something subsistent (*hypostasis*) and in its own right. And so they erred in two ways : either they denied that the Demiurge was the Author of all beings—and he could not truly be Lord of all beings if evil, as they assure us, had a subsistence and a substance (*ousía*); or, in order to declare him Author of all things, they had necessarily to concede that he was also the Author of evil.'[17]

St Basil devoted a sermon to establishing that *God is not the author of evil*: 'Do not suppose that God is the cause of the existence of evil, nor imagine that evil has its own subsistence (*hypostasis*). Perversity does not subsist as though it were something living; its substance (*ousía*) can never be put before our eyes as something really existing. *For evil is the privation (steresis) of good.*'[18] There, in clear terminology, is the definition of evil.

In his *Great Catechetical Discourse*, St Gregory of Nyssa likewise teaches that God is not the cause of evils. Wickedness as

---

[12]'Certum namque est malum esse bono carere.' *De Principiis*, bk. II, ch. 9 (*P.G.*, vol. XI, col. 227).
[13]'Ouden esti.' *Comm. in Joan.*, vol. II, no. 7 (P.G., vol. XIV, col. 137).
[14]*Comm. ad Rom.*, bk. VIII, no. 13 (P.G., vol. XIV, col. 1200).
[15]*De libero arbitrio*, (*P.G.*, vol. XVIII, col. 256).
[16]Probably Gnostics or Manichaeans.
[17]*Oratio contra Gentes*, no. 6 (*P.G.*, vol. XXV, col. 12).
[18]'Steresis gar agathou esti to kakon.'

opposed to virtue, blindness as opposed to seeing, are not anything in nature but the privation (*steresis*) of qualities formerly
possessed. There is no need for a demiurge for something which
does not exist; God is not the cause of evils, he is the author of what
is, not of what is not, of seeing, not of blindness.[19]

Henri Marrou, citing these last two passages, follows with this
observation : 'Sermon, Catechesis : note the character of the discourses from which these texts have been drawn. For this *apophatic*
definition of evil was considered, in the Cappadocia of the second
half of the fourth century, as an assured doctrine which the
bishops thought useful to bring to the knowledge of the Christian
people, and which formed part of the official teaching of the
Church.'[20]

d. *The Latin Fathers: Ambrose, Augustine*

1. The same teaching is found in St Ambrose. In *De Isaac et
anima* (ca. 387) he writes : 'What is evil, if not the lack of a good,
boni indigentia? It is from good things that bad ones come :
indeed the only bad things are those deprived of good, *quae
privantur bonis*. And *vice versa* evil things give rise to good ones.
Evil therefore is the lack of a good; it can be grasped by defining
good; it is by the knowledge of good that evil can be recognized.
God is the author of all good things; and everything which is,
comes from him beyond any doubt. In him there is no evil; and
so long as our mind lives in him it does not know evil. But the
soul which does not live in God is the author of its own evil; that
is why it sins. . . .'[21] Opposite the text of *De Isaac* a transcription
has been made[22] of some parallel passages of Plotinus without,
it must be said, managing to show in the latter any equivalent of
the definition of evil as a privation in a subject of a good which it
should have. It is not in fact Plotinus but the Christian thought of
Cappadocia which is continued by Ambrose and later by Augustine. Open the *Hexaemeron* of Ambrose (ca. 389) : 'Why do they
say that God has created evil, when contraries and opposites do
not engender their opposites? Life does not engender death, nor

[19]*Oratio catechetica*, ch. 6 & 7 (*P.G.*, vol. XLV, col. 28 & 32).
[20]'Un ange déchu, un ange pourtant ...' in *Satan, Études Carmélitaines*, (1948), p. 40.
[21]Ch. 7, nos. 60 and 61 (*P.L.*, vol. XIV, col. 525).
[22]Cf. Pierre Courcelle, *Recherches sur les Confessions de saint Augustine*
(Paris, 1950), pp. 107 and 124.

light the darkness. ... If then, on the one hand, evil is not without a cause, as an uncreated thing would be, and if, on the other, God did not make it, where does it get its nature from? For no one in his senses denies that there are evils in this world. It follows from what we have said : that evil is not a living substance but a perversion of mind and soul.'[23] Now this text, which several times contradicts Plotinus[24] is a faithful, but abridged, translation of the *Hexaemeron* of St Basil.[25] Origen, Methodius, Athanasius, Basil, Ambrose and Augustine are links in an unbroken chain.[26]

2. A clear light is thrown upon the definition by St Augustine : 'Removing myself from the truth, I thought to go towards it; for I did not know that evil is only the privation of a good and that it tends to what has no existence in any way.'[27] 'Evil is not a sub-

---

[23]Ch. 8, nos. 30 and 31 (*P.L.*, vol. XIV, col. 139-40).
[24]For Plotinus: 1) Good necessarily causes evil, *1st Ennead*, tr. VIII, ch. 7; 2) an opposite can give rise to its opposite and good can give rise to evil, ch. 6; 3) evil does not come from ourselves, ch. 5. Greek thought, on this point as on so many others, seems to have been transformed by Christianity immediately, and more thoroughly than Pierre Courcelle has here suspected.
[25]Homily 2, no. 4 (*P.G.*, vol. XXIX, col. 338):
'Yet it could not be said without impiety that evil has its origin in God, because contrary does not give rise to contrary. Death, indeed, does not engender life, darkness is not a source of light, and sickness is not a cause of health; but while dispositions change by passing from one state to its opposite, in the matter of generation each being proceeds not from its opposite but from its like. But, it may be objected, evil is not unengendered, and if it does not come from God, where does it get its nature from? That evils really exist will be contradicted by no one who has any part in life. What answer can be given? That evil is not a living, animate being, but a disposition of the soul which is contrary to virtue and comes from a heedless desertion of good. Do not, therefore, look for evil externally or imagine a primitive nature which is perverted; it is for each one to recognize the author of the wickedness which is within himself ...' Basil is here speaking of evil in its pre-eminent form, sin. He adds: 'Sickness, poverty, the loss of position in the world, death, and all afflictions which come upon man must by no means be put among the number of (real) evils, since we do not count their opposites among the greatest goods; certain of these trials have their source in nature; others do not seem to be without advantage for those who undergo them.'
[26]So we must correct a remark made by Henri Marrou concerning the non-substantiality of evil: 'we find it clearly, albeit briefly formulated without any connection with Augustinian thought, in St Basil and St Gregory of Nyssa.' From 'Un ange déchu, un ange pourtant,' in *Satan, Études Carmélitaines*, p. 39.
[27]'Quia non noveram malum non esse nisi privationem boni, usque ad quod omnino non est.' *Confessions*, Bk. III, ch. 7, no. 12.

stance, for if it were a substance it would be good.'[28] 'Evil is nothing but the privation of good.'[29] 'Evil is not anything found in nature, and the name means only the privation of a good.'[30] Throughout his life Augustine incessantly referred to St Ambrose.[31] For all that, it was he who 'in the course of the long dispute which set him against his old fellow-Manichaeans, gave the most thorough and elaborate expression to this classic doctrine of the non-substantiality of evil. This doctrine was not for him an academic problem, set for the sake of speculation : he had lived it and painfully discovered it in the difficult inward struggle which led him, after a long time, but in the full maturity of genius, from the dualism of his youth to the acceptance of the orthodox faith.'[32] His contribution here is of such importance that he could be called the Doctor of the problem of evil.

What does he owe in this to the neo-Platonists? His knowledge of them came through the Christian environment of Milan.[33] He read their books in the translation of Victorinus, guided by the teaching of Simplicianus, the master of Ambrose.[34] What he discovered then was, first, the error of the Manichaean doctrine of two substances;[35] for things which corrupt one another are good : 'If they were sovereignly good, they could not corrupt one another; if they were good in no degree, again they could not do so. . . . A thing is good in so far as it exists. Everything which is, is good'[36] and comes from God. And he also learned that the whole universe

[28]Ibid., bk. VII, ch. 12, no. 18.
[29]*Contra adversarium Legis et Prophetarum,* bk. I, ch. 5, no. 7.
[30]'Cum omnino natura nulla sit malum, nomenque hoc non sit nisi privatio boni.' *De civitate Dei,* bk. XI, ch. 22.
[31]'Ambrose, who is my teacher and whom even your worthless teacher praises, writes in *De Isaac et anima*: "What is evil except the lack of a good?" And again: "It is from good things that evil things come." ' . . . *Contra Julianum Pelagianum,* bk. I, ch. 9, no. 44. 'What Ambrose believed, I believe; what Manes believed, neither he nor I believe ... The Manichaeans say that evil has a substance and its own nature, coeternal with the good substance and the nature of God; for, they say, it is impossible for evil things to take their origin from good things. Ambrose contradicts this and says: "It is from good things that evil things come ..." ' *Opus imperfectum contra Julianum,* bk. IV, ch. 109; cf. Pierre Courcelle, *Recherches sur les Confessions de S Augustin,* op. cit., p. 125, note 4.
[32]Henri Marrou, art. cit., p. 40.
[33]This point is established by Pierre Courcelle, op. cit., pp. 155, 170, etc.
[34]*Confessions,* bk. VIII, ch. 2, no. 3.
[35]Ibid., bk. VII, ch. 14, no. 20.
[36]Ibid., ch. 12, no. 18.

is ordered.[37] It was not the Platonists but the Christians who taught him that the world was created from nothing, that matter is neither eternal nor necessary, that evil is not the same as matter and, from all this, exactly what was meant by the definition of evil as a privation of good.

e. *The definition of evil as privation is a Christian contribution*

The definition of evil as privation was worked out under Christian influence. It has been deepened so as to harmonize with the supreme revelation (in the Scriptures) of God and the act of creation. Historically and philosophically this appears as a Christian contribution. It represents the most delicate and penetrating intellectual handling of evil which the mind can attain to, either on the metaphysical or theological plane. Evil is accorded a great deal of room, so that it can be seen to its full extent, and at the same time the metaphysical poverty of evil is laid bare. But with the affirmation that evil exists, yet lacks any substance, comes the triumph over the dilemma to which those succumb who either deny the reality of evil because of God's goodness and infinite power, or deny God's goodness and infinite power because of the reality of evil.

3. EVIL IS NOT A THING WITH POSITIVE EXISTENCE

a. *It starts with privation*

1. Evil has been defined as a privation, the absence of some good which should be there. But is this correct? Surely evil is a positive thing. Are not Koch's bacilli which devour a lung the most positive and obvious of realities? Certainly they are. But these bacilli, observed sustaining and reproducing themselves in a broth of some suitable culture, are not an evil; on the contrary, their activity is admirable, raising organic matter to the level of life. When they are taken out and introduced into a living lung, their destructive work is carried out, and evil begins, taking the form of a disturbance in the respiratory system, in other words of the privation of an order essential to higher forms of life.

The same applies to the moral sphere. Giving evidence before a court is a positive act. If the evidence conforms to reality and

---

[37] Ibid., ch. 13, no. 19.

presents a truthful account, it constitutes a morally good act. If, however, it is wilfully inaccurate and presents a false account, then inasmuch as it is deprived of rectitude and its normal subordination to the truth, it constitutes a bad act.

In the physical as in the moral world[38] evil always begins with privation or the absence of some good which ought to be present.

2. St Thomas warns us that in this context error can come about by failure to distinguish in beings, organisms and activities affected by evil, between what gives them existence—which is positive—and what alters and deforms them and makes them bad— which is privative.[39]

b. *Pain and suffering*

1. Is not pain, though, the cruellest and most tyrannical of realities? It is the awareness, by means of our ability to feel, of an irregularity or privation; the tactile perception, sometimes useful as a warning, sometimes merely registering it, of any alteration to an organ. It can be broken down into two elements: a positive one, namely knowledge, and a privative one, namely disordered biological activity.[40]

At the level of spiritual existence, suffering as distinct from pain is the spiritual awareness of a separation, a lack, a falling-off, in other words of either a physical or a moral privation. It may be a vision, still positive, of untold privation. Given the presence of some evil, says St Thomas, it is good that sadness or pain should result: their absence would mean that the evil has not been felt or recognized for what it is.[41]

Hence pain and suffering are not ranked in the first place among the forms of evil because they are identical with knowledge

[38]Cf. below, pp. 39-40, 45.
[39]'Malum uno modo potest intelligi id quod est *subjectum mali*; et hoc aliquid est. Alio modo potest intelligi *ipsum malum*; et hoc non est aliquid, sed est ipsa privatio alicujus particularis boni.' *De malo*, qu. 1, a. 1.
[40]Biologists make a finer distinction between motivating aversion, designed to shake off the harmful agent more or less, and awareness of pain, much keener in civilized man than in animals. Cf. Pradines, *L'aventure de l'esprit dans les espèces* (Paris, Flammarion), pp. 129-30. Cf. below, p. 139.
[41]Ia IIae, qu. 39, a. 1.

and awareness, but only because they are knowledge and awareness of a disorder or privation.

2. Pain and sorrow themselves, however, are an evil, but only
inasmuch as they take away the peaceful enjoyment of a good
which ought to be there.[42] All the same the evil of sorrow may,
on a higher plane, turn into good; and sorrow itself may become
good, for example, when it arises from the evil of sin being recognized as such by a righteous mind and detested as such by a
righteous heart.[43] From this can be seen the complicated dialectic
of good and evil, of being and privation, to be found in suffering
and sorrow.[44]

c. *Is evil the opposite of good?*

1. This problem is more directly a matter for philosophy, which
distinguishes four types of opposition : first, the opposition of *contradiction,* which is the most radical, in which one of the terms
automatically excludes the other : not-man as opposed to man;
second, the opposition of *privation,* which allows the common
element of both terms to subsist, but destroys a generic quality
possessed by one of them : in man, blindness destroys sight, and
in an object black destroys white, assuming that black is not taken

[42]Ibid.

[43]Ibid., a. 2.

[44]'We do not mean to say that pain, by itself, is a good. Quite the contrary, it is a good which has been taken away from us: but it is the very
awareness of this deprivation which gnaws within us and which, by strip-
ping us of what we have, makes us concentrate on what we are and, by
revealing to us what we have lost, gives us something immeasurably
greater. Pain enters our consciousness very vividly and harrows it to the
depths, allowing us to judge how seriously we are capable of taking life.'
L. Lavelle, *Le mal et la souffrance* (Paris, 1940), p. 114. Quoted by J.
Ecole, 'Le problème du mal dans la philosophie de L. Lavelle', in
Revue Thomiste, 1953, p. 116. How can Lavelle's philosophy and its solution to the problem of evil be accepted? His fundamental principle is the
axiom of the *univocity of being.* There are no degrees of being, no
things which have more existence than others: one and the same being
is common to God and to the universe. There is no creation of beings by
the supreme Being, but a participation of beings in Being itself, in the
sense that Being itself, as it is essentially a giving of self, 'requires, since
there is nothing outside it, that there should be in it parts to which it
may give itself' (*Présence Totale,* p. 129). Cf. the suggestive study by
Etienne Borne, 'De la métaphysique de l'Être à une morale du consente-
ment, Réflexions sur la pensée de M. Lavelle', in *Vie Intellectuelle,*
25th Dec., 1936, pp. 447-77.

to be a colour, as it is for a painter, but as the privation of all colour, as it is for the physicist; third, the opposition of *contrariety* as between two qualities of the same generic type, such as red and green; and fourth, the opposition of *relation,* the weakest of all, which does not necessarily involve a lack in either of the two terms—e.g. the relations of equality or similarity— and which for this reason can even apply to the Absolute and be a characteristic of the Divine Persons.[45]

2. It is often said that evil is the contrary of good. But is it opposed to good as a thing to its contrary, as one quality to another quality, one type of being to another—for contraries are generically the same—[46] or is this the opposition between privation and possession, blindness and sight, death and life, darkness and light? The importance of the question is obvious.

St Thomas notes that Aristotle's terminology, if not his thought, is somewhat vague about this.[47] Yet properly speaking there is no doubt : evil is the *privation* of good, not the *contrary* of good, 'good and evil are opposed to one another in the same way as *privation* and *possession*'.[48] There will be evil only when there is privation and only in so far as there is privation. This view must be rigorously held to : 'Evil as such, is not a reality in things, *non est aliquid in rebus,* but the privation of a particular good, inherent in a particular good.'[49]

[45]The four types of opposition (*antithesis*), viz: contradiction (*antiphasis*), privation (*steresis*), contrariety (*enantiosis*) and relation (*pros ti*) are indicated by Aristotle, *Meta.,* bk. V, 10, and bk. X, 4; and St Thomas, *Meta.,* bk. V, no. 922.

[46]Contraries—as well as privation—presuppose a subject, a substance. A substance, therefore, has no contrary. Only improperly speaking, and considered as the raw materials which they provide for one another successively, may substantial forms be called contrary to one another: the antelope destroys the grass, the lion the antelope, and microbes the lion.

[47]'Aristoteles frequenter utitur nomine contrarii pro privatione, quia ipse dicit quod privatio quodam modo est contrarium, et quod prima contrarietas est privatio et forma.' *De malo,* qu. 1, a. 1, ad. 5.

[48]'Bonum et malum proprie opponuntur ut *privatio* et *habitus.*' Ibid., ad 2.

[49]St Thomas, *De malo,* qu. 1, a. 1.—Plotinus' thesis, taken from the *Theaetetus,* is: a) that evil is the contrary of being. One is the principle of all good things, the other the principle of all evil things; b) that evil is produced necessarily from good. The universe is only made possible by a mixture of intelligence (all good things come from God) and of necessity (all evils come from primitive nature, *archaia physis,* as Plato calls matter which has not yet been ordered). *1st Ennead,* tr. VIII, nos. 6 and 7.

3. A misunderstanding may arise from the fact that certain evils do not destroy completely, but allow partial subsistence to the good they attack. Illness is not death, ophthalmia is not blindness; they are partial not total evils or privations.

In so far as they respect some good, preserve a positive aspect, and oppose one type of being (a degraded one) to another type of being (a complete one), they appear as opposites.[50] They represent both (a) *contraries and attenuated good* by reason of what they hold back; and (b) *privations and evils, by reason of what they lay waste to*. Evil is to be found in privation.

In the case of two positive opposed forces, equal to one another, two hostile animals, two rivals, two armies, two angels, which struggle together, neither will be an evil for the other until one succeeds in overcoming the other, bringing it down and taking away its well-being, which again is a privation. 'Corporeal creatures', St Thomas notes, 'are good by nature; yet they do not represent universal good, but particular, limited good. Hence there is opposition between them, they enter into conflict with other things which are equally good in themselves.'[51]

4. There is an even more subtle error. Ethical thinkers are wont to describe good and evil as opposites.[52] In this they are right, for moral evil as opposed to moral good is never pure evil or pure privation; it is a partial good which disguises evil, a deceptive good which distracts and diverts from true good. Neither evil nor privation are ever desired as such; it is always something good which is hoped for.[53] But this good is then attached to an evil or privation and can only be obtained by spoiling the life of the man who seeks it, which is too high a price. The desire is made bad only by being turned away from the true good—it is because of this that an action may be called bad.

---

[50]'Hujusmodi *privationes* dicuntur *contrariae,* in quantum adhuc retinent aliquid de eo quod privatur; *et hoc modo malum dicitur contrarium,* quia non privat totum bonum, sed aliquid de bono removet.' St Thomas, *De malo,* qu. 1, a. 1, ad 2.

[51]I, qu. 65, a. 1, ad 2.　　　　　[52]*De malo,* qu. 1, a. 1, ad 4.

[53]Evil can only be desired under the guise of something good, 'non potest esse volitum nisi sub ratione boni'. Ibid., ad 12. 'The aim of the intemperate man is not to lose the good of reason, but to gain a disordered pleasure of the senses. Thus it is not precisely as evil, but by reason of the good which it attaches to itself, that evil takes on a constitutive difference in moral questions.' I, qu. 48, a. 1, ad 2. Cf. below, p. 65.

If good alone can excite desire, and if the free choice of the agent is made not between a good thing and a privation, but between two good things capable of awakening his desire and which for this reason we call *physical good:* one by which he fulfils his life as a rational being, which we call *moral good,* and the other by which he spoils his life, which we call *moral evil,* it is perfectly true to say that in moral matters good and evil, virtue and vice, are opposed to each other as contraries and as positive realities, although terribly unequal, and not at all like pure possession and pure privation. There is a good, though it is illusory, right down in the depths of the worst sin of a rational creature; and this poor, wretched good bears witness that God only made him for Good.[54] But, and this is of capital importance, one of these two opposites is bad only because it contains in itself a privation.[55] Once more the explanation of evil resides in privation.

d. *It is not a substance, a form or a nature*

These detailed considerations have been made in order to stress the purely negative character of evil. The Greek Fathers perceived it from the start. They firmly stated that evil has neither subsistence (*hypostasis*) nor substance (*ousía*).[56] Following in their steps, St Augustine wrote : 'Everything which is, is good; and the evil whose origin I sought is not a substance (*substantia*); for if it were a substance, it would be good.'[57]

Later on this was to be the teaching taken up and deepened by St Thomas. Being, he said, is good; hence, evil, which is opposed to good as darkness is to light, cannot signify any *being,* any *form* or any *nature,* but only some *absence of good.*[58] The subject to

---

[54]'In the sin itself of the creature abides a mystery that is sacred to us; this wound at least belongs to him, it is his miserable good for which he engages his eternal life, and in the folds of which are hidden God's justice and compassion. To heal this wound Christ willed to die.' Maritain, 'Dialogues', in *Art and Poetry* (Editions Poetry, London, 1945), pp. 43-4.

[55]Even those theologians who place the formal constituent of sin in the positive tendency to a false good, are unanimous in proclaiming that there would be no sin were no privation connected with this false good. Cf. John of Saint-Thomas, I-II, qu. 21; disp. 9, a. 2, no. 16, et seq.

[56]'Evil does not exist in itself, it co-exists (paruphistatai) with the privation of good ... Evil is a privation (*steresis*), not a possession (*hyparxis*), of being.' St Gregory of Nyssa, *In Ecclesiasten,* homil. 5 (*P.G.,* vol. XLIV, col. 681).

[57]*Confessions,* bk. VII, ch. 12, no. 18.   [58]I, qu. 48, a. 1.

which evil comes 'is something; yet evil itself is not something, *aliquid*, but the privation of some particular good'.[59] 'Evil is nothing other than the privation of that which someone is fitted to possess and which he ought to have. This is what everyone calls evil. Now privation is not some essence, *essentia*, it is on the contrary a negation within a substance. Evil therefore is not an essence in things.'[60] Evil 'has not the nature either of a substance nor of an accident, but merely of a privation, as Dionysius explains'.[61] Evil has no substance, it is the privation of substance, *privatio substantiae*.[62]

4. EVIL IS A NEGATIVITY OF PRIVATION

a. *The negativity of nothingness and the negativity of privation*

It follows from what has already been said that, if only being is intelligible, evil as such can never be intelligible. It only becomes so by its dependence on, and its activity in, the being which it destroys. Anyone who fails to grasp the nature of being, its demands and its claims, will never grasp the nature of evil. The mystery of evil is the mystery of the destruction of the claims of being, the

---

[59]*De malo*, qu. 1, a. 1.
[60]*III Contra Gent.*, ch. 8.
[61]*I Sent.*, dist. 46, a. 3.—It is clear that, for St Thomas, St Augustine is not the only doctor of evil. He refers to Pseudo-Dionysius, *De divinis nominibus*. Compare the definitions in *De malo*, qu. 1, a. 1: 'Evil is not anything in reality, but the privation of a *particular* good, inherent in a *particular* being,' or in I, qu. 48, a. 5, ad 1: 'Evil is the lack of a good *which something is fitted to possess and ought to have*,' with passages where Dionysius explains that evil, for a *particular* nature, is to be deprived of what is *natural* to it, to be prevented from being joined to *what is proper to this nature*, §26, no. 227; that evil is not a *total* privation of good, otherwise called nothingness, but the *particular* privation of a good, §29, no. 236 (*Commentary* of St Thomas on nos 552 and 569). Dionysius's teaching on evil has much the same inspiration as that of the Neo-Platonist Proclus, (411-85), in his *De malorum subsistentia*, whom we possess only in the translation of William of Moerbeke, dated 1280; it is reproduced at the end of the Pera edition of Dionysius, Turin-Rome, 1950. Proclus, who is very close to Aristotle, does not confuse matter with evil. He defines evil as a privation of a good, just as St Augustine was to do, but there is no trace of the notion of sin, so that his thought develops on very different horizons from those of Christianity.
[62]*De divinis nominibus*, ch. 4, no. 581. This is the text of Dionysius, ch. 4, §31, no. 243: 'What one does is never done in view of evil—evil has no subsistence, *hypostasis*, but a *juxta-* or *para*-subsistence, *parhypostasis*.'

reverse side of the mystery of the positivity of being. In this sense
it can be called a mystery of negativity. This is not, however, the
negativity of nothingness, but the negativity of privation. 'The
negative absence of some good, *remotio boni negative accepta,* is
not an evil; for then it would have to be said that things which
do not exist are evil, or again that everything is bad simply because it does not have the good which another possesses : for
example that a man is bad because he does not have the agility of
a young goat or the strength of a lion. Only the privative absence
of a good, *remotio boni privative accepta,* is an evil.'[63] It is
important not to be mistaken about this.

b. *Leibniz's error: 'metaphysical evil'*

Now it is precisely here that Leibniz went wrong. He adopted
the traditional definition of evil which he took from St Augustine.
He tried to defend it against its critics,[64] but only succeeded in
destroying it.

He called the finiteness essential to creatures 'metaphysical evil'.
'Evil can be taken metaphysically, physically and morally. *Metaphysical evil consists in simple imperfection,* physical evil in suffering, and moral evil in sin.'[65] 'We must consider that there was
an original imperfection in creatures even before sin, because creatures are essentially limited.'[66] The source of such an evil 'must
be looked for in the ideal nature of creatures, inasmuch as this
nature is confined within the eternal truths which are in God's
understanding, independently of his will'.[67] The region of eternal
truths 'is the ideal cause of evil, so to speak, just as much as of
good'.[68] Consequently all creatures, as such, are affected by metaphysical evil; they are bad at least in one sense, and precisely for
being what they are, which is not infinite. Good, in so far as it is
limited, is evil; being, in so far as it is limited, is a state of privation.[69] The traditional definition of evil as a privation was pre-

[63]St Thomas, I, qu. 48, a. 3.
[64]*Essays in Theodicy, on the goodness of God, the liberty of man and the
origin of evil,* no. 29.
[65]Ibid., no. 21.
[66]Ibid., no. 20.
[67]Ibid.
[68]Ibid.
[69]'Just as a lesser evil is a species of good, so *a lesser good is a species of
evil,* if it obstructs a greater good.' *Ibid.,* no. 8. '*Minus bonum habet
rationem mali.*' *Ibid.,* no. 194. Cf. below, pp. 122-3.

served, broadcast and made familiar to the public at large. But it was misrepresented : privation is confused with what is no longer privation, evil with what is no longer evil. The traditional vision of evil and its devastation is obliterated.

2. The notion of metaphysical evil opens up two issues. One is optimistic. On the one hand, if every being is necessarily bad and deficient, then no being is bad or deficient in relation to others; on the other hand, if privation is confused with what is no longer privation, no being is really bad or deficient at all. This leads us to Spinoza.

If, however, we continue to give evil its real meaning, its privative character, it will be said that every creature is right to free itself from its evil, to reject its limits and to cease being a creature. From this stems the blasphemy of Nietzsche : 'Oh my friends : *if* there were Gods, how could I endure it to be no God! *Therefore* there are no Gods.'[70]

c. *Evil is neither non-existent nor powerless*

1. To define evil as a privation is not to declare that it is non-existent and powerless. Privation moves away from nothingness in the same way as in mathematics do negative numbers from zero. It is an inverted positivity, whose ravages can be limitless, and disastrous, in the order both of being and of action.

In the order of being, evil is not non-existent. Let it be said again : it is not mere absence of sight which makes blindness, but absence of sight from where it ought to be, where it is required and assumed to be. Let us therefore not talk of pure non-existence, but of an existence which, like letters hollowed out of stone, can be a terrible reality. The depth of evil will always be measured by the value of the being which it destroys. 'Why should a dog, a horse, a rat, have life, And thou no breath at all?' cries King Lear when he learns that his only true daughter, Cordelia, has been hanged.

In the order of action, evil is not powerless. It can cause catastrophes. It either stifles, by a sin of omission, the salutary, perhaps

---

[70]*Thus Spake Zarathustra*, II, xxiv, trans T. Common, in *The Complete Works of Friedrich Nietzsche*, ed. O. Levy, vol. XI, p. 99 (G. Allen & Unwin, 1923).

even vital act which ought to have been carried out; or, having inwardly corrupted the agent, thwarts the creative process and makes it miscarry, not by acting but by failing to act, *non agendo sed deagendo*,[71] making the causative action to some extent hollow; it is the disparity between what appears—a child still-born or deformed, unlikely to live—and what ought to be produced, which measures the degree of evil. Or again, it may cause an action to go wrong by withdrawing it from the rule which should have governed it; the more powerfully a force can be used, the more ruinous is the deviation : as with the angel who, at the time of his first sin, rushed into action without considering the rule of his action. Or finally, a being, without going against its own nature, only sustains its life at the expense of others : the lion eats the antelope; what is good for the one is bad for the other. So wherever there is activity, evil or privation can attach its hollow, but fatal, stigma.

'Evil is a *privation* : the privation of the good which should be in a thing. That does not mean that evil does not exist, or is merely an illusion ... Evil does exist in things, it is terribly present in them. Evil is real, it actually exists like a wound or mutilation of the being ... Thus evil exists *in good,* that is, the bearer of evil is good in so far as it is being. And evil works *through good,* since evil, being in itself a privation or non-being, has no causality of its own. Evil is therefore efficacious not by itself but through the good it wounds and preys upon as a parasite, efficacious through a good that is wanting or is deflected, and whose action is to that extent vitiated. What is thus the power of evil? It is the very power of the good that evil wounds and preys upon. The more powerful this good is, the more powerful evil will be,—not by virtue of itself, but by virtue of this good. That is why no evil is more powerful than that of the fallen angel. If evil appears so powerful in the world of today, that is because the good it preys upon is the very spirit of man,—science itself and moral ideals corrupted by bad will.'[72]

2. Yet, it is so often said, a privation cannot be said to be active;

---

[71]St Thomas, *De malo,* qu. 1, a. 1, ad 8.
[72]Maritain, *St Thomas and the Problem of Evil,* op. cit., pp. 2-3.

but evil, terribly active, continually corrupts good; therefore it must be a positive reality! St Thomas answers this objection as follows :

First of all, evil itself can corrupt good by being its *formal* cause, that is to say without acting, simply by existing, by establishing itself in what is good, and by taking the place of some form, quality or perfection which it destroys (blindness, dumbness, etc.).[73]

It may very well be retorted that it is obvious that evil also very often acts as an *efficient* cause : beings consume one another, the intemperate man gets drunk, the will to power unleashes appalling wars; in order to act a thing must exist, and in order to act with violence it must have a very forceful nature.

St Thomas answers : In the line of efficient causality it is never evil or the privation which acts; it is a nature, a principle of action, a source of abundance which has become affected by evil and privation.[74] This can happen in two ways :[75] (a) *by default:* once the active principle has been adulterated, its activities and their effects suffer, not by what it does but what it fails to do, *deagendo;*[76] (b) *by concomitance:* the active principle and its activity are good in themselves but pursue vigorously and violently a good which will bring about destruction, that is to say the evil of some other being.[77]

In the sphere of liberty, as in that of nature, evil also comes about in two ways : (a) *by concomitance:* for example in the case of adultery, the will pursues a good which is inseparable from a moral evil; (b) *by default:* because the choice of an irregular good was only possible by deviating in the first place from the moral law.

St Thomas points out in connection with evil that in the sphere of nature, causality by concomitance precedes causality by

[73]'Aliquid agere dicitur *formaliter* ..., et sic malum etiam ratione ipsius privationis dicitur corrumpere bonum, quia est ipsa corruptio vel privatio boni.' I, qu. 48, a. 1, ad 4.
[74]'*Effective* ... malum non agit aliquid per se, id est secundum quod est privatio quaedam, sed secundum quod ei bonum adjungitur; nam omnis actio est ab aliqua forma ...' I, qu. 48, a. 1, ad 4.
[75]'Est duplex modus quo malum causatur ex bono uno modo bonum est causa mali in quantum est deficiens; alio modo in quantum est per accidens.' *De malo,* qu. 1, a. 3. Cf. below, p. 71.
[76]Ibid., qu. 1, a. 1, ad 8.
[77]'Ignis generat ignem in quantum habet talem formam; corrumpit tamen aquam, in quantum huic formae adjungitur talis privatio.' Ibid., ad 9.

default : it is by seeking his own good that an agent subtracts from that of another, as when dampness damages a seed; while in the sphere of sin it is causality by default which comes first : however strong the attraction of a forbidden good it will remain inefficacious so long as the will does not freely turn from its observance of its rule of action.[78]

d. *The paradox of evil: it both 'is' and 'is not'. It exists, not as a positive thing, but as a privation*

1. But it is only too obvious that *evil exists!*—Admittedly, but not in the sense that *a being exists*. A being exists as a *positive* reality, evil exists as a *privation*. When we say that life or sight exists, or that death or blindness exist, the words 'be' and 'exist' do not have the same meaning in both cases. Many minds which may in all other respects have been very penetrating, have been mistaken about this. The word *being*, as St Thomas explains, has two meanings. It can mean the nature, consistence, positivity (*quid est*) of the being which is affirmed and which can be fitted into one of the ten familiar categories : substance, quality, quantity, etc. are truly beings, they are truly something : but neither evil nor privation can be said to 'be' in this sense. And the word *being* can mean simply the truth of a statement as an answer to the question 'is it ?' or 'isn't it ?' 'Is this eye blind, or not ?' (*an est*) : evil, then, and blindness can be said to be without constituting a positive reality. Through failure to make this distinction, continues St Thomas, certain men, when hearing of bad things, or of evil which is in things, have imagined that evil was a thing.[79] 'Evil certainly is in things, but as a *privation*, not as *something real*.'[80]

2. The paradox of evil, as has been said, is that of 'being' and yet 'not being'. It has 'being' in the sense that it is a privation but not in the sense that it is a positive reality.

[78]'In potestate tamen voluntatis est recipere vel non recipere; unde mali quod accidit ex hoc quod recipit, non est causa ipsum delectabile movens sed magis ipsa voluntas ... Inde est quod Augustinus dicit quod voluntas est causa peccati in quantum est deficiens ...' *De malo*, qu. 1, a. 3.
[79]*De malo*, qu. 1, a. 1, ad 19; and I, qu. 48, a. 2, ad 2. Cf. *De malo*, qu. 1, a, 2, ad 1 : 'Dionysius non intendit quod malum non sit in existente, sicut *privatio* in subjecto; sed quod, sicut non est aliquid per se existens, ita non est aliquid *positive* in subjecto existens.'
[80]'Malum quidem est in rebus, sed ut *privatio*, non autem ut *aliquid reale*.' *De malo*, qu. 1, a. 1, ad 20.

It would be wrong to deny that it exists as a privation. Some people, such as the founder of Christian Science, go wildly astray by refusing to admit the reality of sickness, death or sin : all this, they say, has no more substance than a dream. The extreme case of this is to see the whole of creation as maya or illusion : being itself has been denied so as to make sure that evil will be denied too. Others, such as Spinoza, go wrong when they consider that these same processes of sickness, death and sin, which they know to be real, are constructive parts of the universe; they may by general agreement be called evils but they are in truth, in the eyes of a wise man, the best thing that could happen. Likewise Hegelianism does away with evil, since the dialectic works from one good, called inferior, to a different good, called superior. For all of these, evil is merely imaginary, a creation of the mind. Against them all we maintain that evil exists and we proclaim the original, undeniable existentiality of evil. But we add that to exist as evil is not to exist as a thing.

As opposed to those who dispose of evil there are some who make it out to be a reality or a substance, and in order to present a more violent contrast, say that it is by nature totally opposed to good and therefore of the same generic type.[81] Yet precisely the most radical opposition to which being can be subjected is not contrariety but privation. The paradox of evil is the *terrible reality of its privative existence.* On the philosophical and theological plane evil or privation can only be rightly considered if we understand the right of a being to his integrity, the essential law of its existence, the law by which it can become (fully) what it is (inchoatively). But how can we understand this need, this law of superabundance which is at the heart of created being if we do not understand the law of superabundance which is at the heart of the Being who exists in his own right? The watering down of the meaning of being (both created and uncreated) corresponds to a watering down of the meaning of evil; any enrichment of the meaning of being, and particularly of God, corresponds to an enrichment of the meaning of evil. The problem of evil and the problem of God are, on the metaphysical and theological level, the opposite poles of a single intellectual intuition. If this intuition

---

[81]'Utrumque contrariorum est natura quaedam.' St Thomas, I, qu. 48, a. 1, obj. 3. 'Contraria conveniunt in genere uno, et etiam conveniunt in ratione essendi.' I, qu. 49, a. 3, ad 1.

is lacking, then neither of these opposite poles will ever be properly known.

3. The crux of the difficulty is that it is necessary at once to attribute to evil both existentiality and non-subsistence. Only the notion of privation can resolve the difficulty—any other attempt will come to grief. Either the proposed definition will be illusory— and the existentiality of evil as such will be denied, the problem of evil will be classed as a pseudo-problem and the relation of God to evil will disappear. Or the proposed definition will be impure : the originality of evil will be ignored, it will be described as generically opposite to good—the distance between it and God will diminish and it will end up, as in dualism and in certain forms of gnosticism, by being raised to the level of God, who would then be reduced to the status of mere adversary and rival to an absolute Evil. In both cases, although in a different way, the mystery of evil and the mystery of God are simultaneously distorted.

If Christianity had not revealed so forcibly the exalted heights of God, it would never have dared nor have been able to descend so deeply into the analysis of evil and reveal to the world the meaning of the definition of evil as a privation.

5. THE DEFINITION OF EVIL CAN BE APPLIED ANALOGOUSLY

The notion of privation, like the notion of the being it deprives, is analogous, that is to say that it is realized in a transposed and proportional way on the various levels of being.[82]

Privation indeed appears both on the level of material and of spiritual being. It appears in the world of physical or entitative being and in the world of moral or purposive being in which the evil of guilt and the evil of pain come into contact. It appears in the world of nature and civilization, and in the world of grace.

The importance of privation should be judged by the import- ance of what it destroys; its seriousness increases proportionately

---

[82]On a text of Aristotle which required elucidation, St Thomas trans- cribes the commentary of Porphyry: 'Ideo bonum et malum dixit Aris- toteles non esse nec in uno genere nec in pluribus, sed ipsa esse genera, *prout genus dici potest id quod genera transcendit, sicut ens et unum.*' *De malo,* qu. 1, a. 1, ad 11.

as the subject which it erodes is more noble, its needs more sacred and absolute.

And it may happen that what is an evil at the level of physical being, such as sickness or death, can be the occasion of good at the level of moral life; and that sin itself can be redeemed, particularly through that charity which can drown all reproach, shame, sorrow, and make the desert flourish.

CHAPTER THREE

The Forms of Evil

There is a distinction between the evil of nature and the evil of man, which is divided into the evil of sin and the evil of pain, and which is related to the world of the supernatural.

I. THE THREE WORLDS WHERE EVIL APPEARS

The definition of evil as the privation of some good which a being should have, and the realization of its analogical signification, in other words, of its proportional applicability to different levels of reality without losing any of its accuracy, makes possible a *division* of evil, that is to say a general classification of the forms under which it presents itself. If, indeed, privation can only be understood in terms of the needs of the being which it affects, it can be diversified and divided up according to the diversity and divisions of the general forms of being.[1]

A table of reality, drawn up according to its various grades, reveals as it were, three distinct worlds:[2]

1. *The natural or physical world.* This comprises two levels. On the one hand, that of things which are by nature *corporeal and corruptible,* with all their mutually destructive activities; this covers the three kingdoms: animal, vegetable and mineral. Evil appears here under the form of antagonism, destruction, deformation, disease, accident, death, affliction, suffering, etc. On the other hand, that of things which are by nature *spiritual and incorruptible,* with those alone of their activities which result immediately from the indestructible natural impetus which God imparted

---

[1] 'Cum enim malum opponatur bono, necesse est quod secundum divisionem boni dividatur malum.' St Thomas, *De malo,* qu. 1, a. 4.
[2] Only the third corresponds exactly with Pascal's third order. *Pensées,* no. 793.

when he created them.[3] This is the world in which human souls and angels are rooted. In this natural, primordial, fundamental world there is no corruption, no suffering, no death and *no evil*. This is the truth vividly seen by those who, without being able to express it adequately, have sought, at various periods of history, to relegate evil simply to the domain of matter, corporality and corruption.

2. *The world of freedom.* Man, designed in virtue of his spiritual nature to know and desire good in all its fullness, the universal good, could not be determined by the particular good things which surround him, but finds himself governed in regard to them by indifference and it is for him to judge as to their connection with his ultimate end, whether they are chosen or rejected. This is the world of liberty or moral life, the world which is peculiar to man.

It presupposes the world of spiritual beings, but cannot be reduced to this alone; it constitutes its own particular order within the universal scheme. 'St Thomas elucidates the point when he is handling a very special issue. He asks if the natural vision of pure spirits can penetrate the inner secrets of the heart. And his reply is in the negative. Yet he teaches elsewhere that pure spirits have a natural knowledge of the whole order of corporal and spiritual nature, of all the events which happen in this world, which is the work of creative act. And truly it is so; but the moral act taken precisely as such, in the mystery of free choice it makes before the face of God, is not an event in this world; it does not belong to the world of forms and properties of things; or (shall we say) of simple plastic and ontological beauty of creation; it belongs to the world of freedom, which even in the natural moral order (prescinding altogether from the supernatural order of grace), is a world apart, cloistered, sacred, where the vision of God alone has right or power to penetrate. For it is the world of relations between intelligent beings, in particular between the Personality of the Uncreated Spirit and the persons whom he has made in his image.'[4] It is important to remember the singular dignity of the human

[1] Pierre Jean de Menasce, 'Note sur le dualisme mazdéene', in *Satan, Études Carmélitaines* (Paris, Desclée de Brouwer, 1948), pp. 130-3. the torment of the devils. Cf. St Thomas, I, qu. 60, a. 5, ad 5.
[4] Maritain, *Freedom in the Modern World* (Sheed & Ward, London, 1935), p. 25.

person, who is not part of the world of nature, a cog in the universal machine, but something irreducible and immortal, when we have to speak of the physical evil which afflicts man, of his infirmities, sickness and death.

'Certain philosophers, for example Leibniz, try to make the moral order out to be a particular order which is simply instrumental in regard to the universal order. They will say that such and such an evil—be it a question of the pain which in the human order, if one takes account of the existential data provided by religious tradition and theology, is the result of an original fault and consequently depends on another order than simply that of the cosmos—they will say that such an evil committed or suffered by a man is an evil in relation to the individual in question, but that it is a good in relation to the order of the universe. Their concept of moral evil follows the pattern of physical evil. This way of accounting for the existence of evil and of answering the problem of both physical and moral evil, saying that all sufferings endured by free agents are necessary for the good and the glory of the cosmos and to enable the world-machine to work to perfection, is the same as the way Job's friends tried to defend the divine wisdom. The world-machine cannot provide any answer to these things, for the answer is hidden in the glory of him who made the world, and who took upon himself all the evil of the world.'[5]

With the world of liberty there appear two new forms of evil : *guilt* and *punishment*.

Man, as a rational being, should act according to the norms of that reason which is the imprint in him of the eternal law. His free act is morally good if it conforms to the authority of his reason and conduces to his final end ; it is morally evil if it is deprived of this authority and turns him away from his final end. This is the evil of guilt which, being a disorder, finishes by entering into conflict with order, thus provoking the evil of punishment.[6]

[5]Jacques Maritain, *Neuf leçons sur les notions premières de la philosophie morale'* (Paris, Téqui, 1951), p. 71. Cf. below, pp. 191 and 239-41.
[6]'Rational and intellectual nature has a different relation to good and evil from that of other creatures. These are ordered naturally towards a particular good. The intellectual nature alone grasps the common reason of good by the understanding and moves towards the common good through the desire of the will. This is why the evil of the rational creature can be divided into "sin" and "punishment".' St Thomas, *De malo*, qu. 1, a. 4.

The division of moral evil into the evil of guilt and the evil of punishment is based on the fact that guilt is a deviation, a privation of righteousness, freely consented to, which affects the action of the will (*malum actionis, vel operationis*); while punishment is a privation contrary to the will, which affects the being and integrity of the agent (*malum formae, vel agentis*).[7]

St Thomas thus distinguishes on the one side the evil in the domain of nature (*malum naturalis defectus*); and on the other the evil in the domain of the will (*malum in rebus voluntariis*); the latter being again distinguished as the evil of guilt, which deprives man of his ordered progress to his final end (*malum culpae, quod privat ordinem ad bonum divinum*), and the evil of punishment.[8]

The evil of ignorance, which according to St Thomas plays a large part, is connected both with the evil of guilt and the evil of punishment. The words which correspond in St Thomas to the English *ignorance* are first *nescientia*, mere absence of knowledge, which is neither fault nor punishment, and is to be found among the angels in heaven, and second, *ignorantia* or lack of knowledge which one ought to have : either a man is responsible for this privation, which makes it a *sin;* or he is not in a possible position to put it right, which makes it invincible ignorance which can be attributed to the evil of punishment.[9]

3. A third world exists, *the world of grace* which in a real and concrete way invades spiritual beings, and raises their nature and their actions so as to turn them towards the hidden things of God, things which eye has not seen, nor ear heard, nor the heart of man conceived. By refusing to open itself to God's gracious offer and struggling against the invasion of such a life, such a light and such a love, the created will introduces into the universe an evil of *guilt* and an evil of *punishment* whose depth is measured by the exaltedness of God's own bounty, and whose gravity would have remained unknown in a universe where men and angels would have lived in

[7]St Thomas, I, qu. 48, a. 5; *De malo*, qu. 1, a. 4.
[8]I, qu. 19, a. 9; qu. 48, a. 5, et ad 2.—'If good is in itself the object of the will, *evil, as a privation of good, will be encountered in a special way in rational creatures endowed with free will.*' I, qu. 48, a. 5.
[9]'Ignorance and concupiscence constitute the material elements of original sin'; the privation of original justice constitutes its formal element. St Thomas, *De malo*, qu. 3, a. 7. Cf. Ia IIae, qu. 76, a. 2. Cf. below, p. 223.

the state of pure nature. It is in this new order, on the level of the world of grace, that the problem of evil will show its supreme dimensions, but only for those who see by the light of faith. Man's life must be seen in its full perspective, his nature fallen but redeemed, deprived of grace in Adam but restored to it in Christ, if we are to speak either of the evil of guilt, or of the evil of punishment.[10]

2. THE TWO FORMS OF EVIL IN MAN

One point, as has been said, remains to be cleared up. What are we to think of the physical evil which afflicts man, of his weaknesses, old-age, sickness and death? Are they not the inevitable accompaniment of his physical life? They are natural in animals, why not equally so in men?

The mind here comes up against a mystery. It knows that man as a *person*, that is to say as a spiritual centre of liberty and intellectual activity, is greater than the universe of visible things, that he is not a part of it and that he is completely autonomous. Yet at the same time it sees that he is a *human* person, that through his body he is involved in the continuous change of the cosmos, that he is a part of nature and subject to its laws. In so far as a man is a person his hope would be to *elude* suffering and death, but in so far as he is part of the sensible world his condition is evidently to *undergo* what they afflict: from this arises a sort of discordance, which the reason left to its own lights is incapable of harmonizing.

[10]W. Jankelevitch's definition of evil is more summary. He opposes 'the primary or *metempirical* evil, which is the evil of *absurdity,* and the whole gamut of *empirical* evils, wars, sufferings and torments, which are evils of *wrath.* There is constant interchange between *absurdity* and *scandal,* between inherent evil of absurdity and the evils for which our wills have scandalously taken the initiative.' In evil of absurdity he places 'general imperfection ..., general disorder ... There is bad work in this world; that means that Being is scamped, that it could be better than it is, and that it is what it ought not to be'; viz. on the one hand the imperfection of created beings, which Leibniz called a metaphysical evil, but which for us is not an evil; and on the other, what we call the evil of nature, in which he includes our necessity of dying, which according to St Paul is a punishment. W. Jankelevitch, 'Le mal', *Cahiers du College Philosophique* (Paris, Arthaud, 1947), pp. 8, 9.

Man might indeed have been created in the state of pure nature, endowed simply with what the definition of rational animal requires. In that case would philosophy have any explanation for man's trials and sufferings, for the death of young children, other than by recourse to the play of biological laws, or by assimilating them to those particular evils which are the inevitable price of the total good of the universe? The fact that man's desire to escape suffering and death is, like his desire to see God face to face, conditional and inefficacious—is it realizable, is it even possible?—would remain a stumbling-block. (The desire to see God face to face and the desire not to die have just been put side by side to show that both of them are conditional and inefficacious. But there is a gulf, pointed out by St Thomas[11] between these two desires. The desire to see God goes right beyond the hope of *anything created or creatable;* it can be frustrated in young children who have died without baptism without there being in them the slightest shadow of any suffering. The desire not to die goes beyond the hope of the human composite, of human nature *as such;* but it does not exceed the hope of the spiritual soul, which is the form of the body. This is why St Thomas says that the final resurrection of the body, which represents an immense miracle, will be in a certain way natural; no man's desire to regain his own body will be frustrated.[12])

Revelation teaches us that divine love is superabundant and that man was at the beginning clothed with original justice, bearing in himself the privileges of immortality which fulfilled his hopes as a person and were to be handed down to all his descendants. But they did not reach us. Consequently the same bodily miseries and death, which would have been normal, although paradoxical, in the state of pure nature, reveal themselves to us now as the consequence of a catastrophe. From this fact they take on a penal character,[13] and no longer come under the evil of *nature.* As a result the only two forms of evil which affect man to-day come

---

[11]*De malo,* qu. 5, a. 5, ad 5.
[12]*IV Sent.,* dist. 43, qu. 1, a. 1, quest. 3.
[13]'Death and all bodily miseries' resulting from the privation of original righteousness 'are among the pains of original sin'. St Thomas, Iª IIae, qu. 85, a. 5.

under the headings of *guilt* or *punishment*, either submitted to reluctantly or made bearable by Christ.[14]

3. SOVEREIGNTY OF THE SUPERNATURAL WORLD

The notions of good and evil, which are analogous, find such intense realizations in the world of grace that they are capable of polarizing all the lower forms of good and evil, colouring them by their own reflection and in some way changing their meaning.

And so it is that temporal evils turn to good—or rather to occasions for good—for the just who bear them in a spirit of love. So it is also that temporal goods turn to evil—or rather to occasions for evil—for sinners whose passions they feed. Such are the contrary alchemies of grace and sin.

There is fundamentally only one supreme evil, which can vitiate all good things and beside which nothing else need be feared, and that is sin. And there is only one supreme good, which can cast light upon all evils and for which we should give our all, and that is charity.

This is the Christian idea which St Augustine never tired of proclaiming to the Christians whose faith was disturbed by the fall of Rome and the triumph of the barbarians.[15] It is the idea taken up again, after so many others, by Henry Suso, in the chapter of *The Little Book of Eternal Wisdom* where he declares the 'im-

---

[14] 'The suffering of a man is the suffering of a person, of a whole. Here he is considered no longer as part of the universe, but insofar as he is a person he is considered as a whole, a universe to himself; to suffer that pain as part of the universe in the perspective of nature or of the world taken as God's work of art, does not do away with the fact that as far as the person is concerned it is an utter anomaly. The person asks,—from a desire which is "conditional" and "inefficacious", but real and natural— ... that it should not suffer, should not die. In the state of pure nature, these aspirations of the person would have remained forever unsatisfied; ... We see there the most profound reason of suitability for the elevation of the intelligent creature to the supernatural order; I say reason based on fitness! Not on necessity, nor on justice. God could, without the least injustice, have created man in a state of pure nature, man would have been defrauded of nothing which his *nature* as such demands; but in actual fact, God has created man in a state of grace ...' Maritain, *St Thomas and the Problem of Evil*, op. cit., pp. 12-13.

[15] It is taken up again by St Thomas, I^a II^{ae}, qu. 114, a. 10, ad 3 and 4: 'Omnia aeque eveniunt bonis et malis quantum ad ipsam *substantiam* bonorum vel malorum temporalium, sed non quantum ad *finem* ...'

mense nobility' of temporal sufferings : 'Lord when I look upon
you with love, delight of my eyes and heart, it seems to me now
that the great and hard sufferings with which as a good father
you have tested me, and on account of which your loving friends
have feared for me, have only been a gentle shower in May.'[16]
The same idea is already there in the parable of the rich man,
clothed in purple and feasting sumptuously : 'And Abraham said,
"Son, remember that you in your lifetime you received good
things, and Lazarus in like manner evil things; but now he is com-
forted here and you are in anguish" ' (Luke 16, 25).

---

[16]Blessed Henry Suso. English trans. C. H. McKenna, O.P. (New York,
1889).

CHAPTER FOUR

God and Evil

The metaphysical aspect of the problem

Having followed Plotinus' counsel and asked what evil is, we are now in a position to ask where it comes from. The question of the nature of evil allows us to start on the question of its origin.

I. THE NATURE OF THE PROBLEM

If God does not exist, where does good come from? If he does exist, where does evil come from? If God is the source of good, can he also be the source of evil? The question is that of the relation of God to evil, and we shall now try to make our attitude clear.

I. MYSTERY OR ABSURDITY

Evil exists and God exists. Their coexistence is a mystery. But anyone who wishes to avoid this mystery will finish in absurdity and the only choice open to him is to deny either the existence of God or the existence of evil.[1]

As Bossuet said : 'One truth does not destroy another : and although it may happen that we are unable to find a way of reconcil-

---

[1] *Acosmism,* which denies the reality of evil and even of the world in order to glorify the Absolute, is the final outcome of Vedantic thought. When, half-way through the course of its development, it does make room for a personal Lord, Ishvara, it strives to present him as innocent of all evil. Cf. Olivier Lacombe, *L'Absolu selon le Vedânta* (Paris, Guethner, 1937), p. 256. *Atheism,* which denies the Absolute in order to make a god of the world of immanence, of man and the will to power—eventually finishing up in despair and belief in the fundamental absurdity of everything—defies evil without being able to abolish it. Between these two extreme positions, *pantheism* appears as a compromise which is by definition unstable. Cf. below, p. 87.

ing these things, all the same, what we are uncertain about, in so important a matter, ought not to weaken in us what we do know for certain.' We should remember that 'the first rule of our logic is that we must never abandon truths once they are known, whatever difficulties may arise when we wish to reconcile them; but rather we must, as it were, always hold tight to both ends of the chain, although we do not always see where the links between go to'.[2]

Holding on to both ends of the chain, affirming both the reality of God and the reality of evil, stops the human mind gravitating into absurdity either by denying God or denying evil, and saves it from suicide.

But at the same time it compels it to exceed itself and extend its vision beyond the sphere of evidence and clear ideas into the higher world of mystery which remains dark to it down below, just as the midday sun is dark to the owl, not through lack of light but excess of it.

2. THE RELIGIOUS AND METAPHYSICAL LEVELS

Our intention here is not to go into the concrete, existential and specifically religious aspect of the problem of evil, or to listen to the cry of man afflicted by pain, the supplication of a Job or a Jeremiah, overwhelmed by unbearable trials, who call upon God to come out of his silence : 'After this Job opened his mouth and cursed the day of his birth. And he said : "Let the day perish wherein I was born, and the night which said, A man child is conceived ... Why is light given to him that is in misery, and life to the bitter in soul ? ... Why is light given to a man whose way is hid, whom God has hedged in ? ... I will speak in the anguish of my spirit; I will complain in the bitterness of my soul ... How long wilt thou not look away from me, nor let me alone till I swallow my spittle ? ... Why hast thou made me thy mark ? Why have I become a burden to thee ?" ' (Job 3, 1-20, 23; 7, 11, 19-20). To such pleas there is one answer; it is contained in the very question which the distressed soul puts, in a spirit of love, to God; it is heard in the secrecy of the heart : Do you not know that I am your God ? Am I not nearer to you than you are to your-

[2]Bossuet, *Traité du libre arbitre*, ch. 4.

self? Do I not know what you can bear? And for what passes all bearing, will you not go on trusting me, who alone can make you blessed?

There is no way out of the great onslaughts of evil apart from this silent intercourse with the God of love. But below the level of religion and faith, either on the level of spontaneous reasoning and common sense or on that of a more carefully worked out philosophy, there arise serious problems of a more general and impersonal character. The coexistence of God, an all-powerful and infinitely good God, with the evil of the universe, sets a specifically metaphysical difficulty which no one can elude, and which, although it is, as has just been said, not the supreme question, yet is one which urgently requires both investigation and solution; and it is clear that if the answers supplied are wrong, they will be disastrous for the human mind.

What shocks the intelligence and seems to it to be irreconcilable with the holiness of God is evil in the three forms which have been pointed out : *physical* evil, already at work in the world before man, followed by the arrival of man and the still more mysterious evil of the moral order, the evil of *guilt* and the evil of *punishment*. To remove the scandal, a start must be made by establishing that evil could not be created by God, and that it is merely permitted by him, but in very different ways, depending on whether it is a question of physical evil or of moral evil and its two forms, guilt and punishment. So it is necessary, during this first stage, to bear these three forms of evil constantly in mind.

Then there is the second stage : is God forced to permit evil? Then he is not all-powerful. Does he freely permit it? Then he is without goodness. It is the classical dilemma to which so many have fallen victim over the ages.

This explains the two parts of this chapter : God permits evil. Is God without power or without goodness?

II. GOD PERMITS EVIL

1. PURE EVIL, AS A CAUSE OF ALL OTHER EVIL, IS IMPOSSIBLE

One of the first consequences of an exact definition of evil is to show the impossibility of pure evil.

✓ a. *Privation supposes a subject*

There is no privation without a deprived being, a being lacking something it ought to have. There is no evil without something good to support it. Pure evil, evil in its own right, is impossible.

St Augustine, freed at last from Manichaeism, said : 'All things, when they are corrupted, are deprived of good. If they were deprived of all the good which is in them, they would absolutely cease to exist.' The privation of all good is, in effect, equivalent to nothingness. 'Therefore, in so far as they exist, they are good.'[3] In the *Encheiridion* he states : 'No evil could ever exist where no good exists.'[4] The holy doctor goes on to warn us not to allow ourselves to be trapped by the sophists, and to distinguish, in every evil being, that by which it is a being and therefore good, and that by which it is evil.[5] In *De civitate Dei*, it is shown that what the sin of the angels wrecked was by nature good.

The same doctrine is found in St Thomas. We should not say, he reminds us, that the *absence* of a good is an evil. In that case we should have to say that things which do not exist are bad; or again that every being is bad from the fact that it does not have what is possessed by another, that man is bad because he has not the agility of the goat or the strength of the lion. It is the *privation* of the good which should be in the subject which is evil, the privation of sight in higher forms of life which is called blindness. It follows that the subject of evil can only be something good.[6]

Thus the good in the universe is more fundamental than the evil. And from this point of view, it should be said that good is more powerful than evil.

---

[3]'Omnia quae corrumpuntur, privantur bono. Si autem omni bono privabuntur, omnino non erunt.' *Confessions,* bk. VII, ch. 12.
[4]'Nec malum unquam potest esse, ubi bonum est nullum.' *Encheiridion,* n. 13.
[5]'Omnis natura, etiam si vitiosa est, in quantum natura bona est.' Isaias's warning should not go unheeded: 'Woe to those who call evil good, and good evil' (5, 20). If man is a good because he is a being, would an evil man be an evil which is a good? St Augustine replies: 'The evil man is neither an evil because he is a man, nor a good because he is unjust; he is a good because he is a man, an evil because he is unjust.' The prophet's words were addressed to those who say it is an evil to be a man, and a good to be unjust. *Confessions,* bk VII, ch. 12.
[6]I, qu. 48, a. 3 : *Whether evil has good as a subject.*

b. *Evil exists, and therefore God exists*

Those who say : 'Evil exists, and therefore God exists' might receive tit for tat the answer : 'Good exists, and therefore God exists'.[7] But these two affirmations are not of equal value.

The proof of God's existence does not consist in saying that God exists because the world is perfect, or in using the apologetics of Bernardin de Saint-Pierre, marvelling, for instance, that cherries and plums are 'made to fit the human mouth', pears and apples 'for his hand', and melons divided into sections so as to be 'eaten in the family'. Nor do we say that God exists because this world always shows evil ultimately punished and good triumphant. It would be too easy to become confused.

The proof of God's existence consists in saying that *the world,* with the evil in it, *exists* and *therefore God exists.* However wretched and imperfect it may be, the world *exists,* and therefore it is not nothing. However rich and splendid it may be, the world is *complex and changing,* and therefore it is not the Absolute in being, Being in its own right, which can only be one and unchanging. Since the world exists yet is not absolute, it is in fact, at each moment, being which is not there in its own right, which does not contain in itself the reason for its existence; it is lacking something, 'contingent'—to use the philosophical word—and therefore it exists by another's favour. Nothingness has no need of explanation or *'raison d'être';* the Absolute does contain in itself its own *raison d'être;* but the world which is between the two needs a *raison d'être,* a justification; and since it does not possess this in itself, it can only find it in some Other who does exist in his own right : whatever exists, but not in its own right, is dependent on an Other, a self-sufficient being.[8]

The progress, therefore, of the reason which rises to the affirmation of God's existence remains intact, however great the evil in

---

[7]'If God exists, where do evils come from? Boethius puts this into the mouth of some philosopher. To which the answer is the reverse : if evil exists, God exists. There is no evil without good, for evil is the privation of good. Without God this good would not exist.' St Thomas, *III Contra Gent.,* ch. 71.

[8]'It is enough that things exist for God to be unavoidable. Let us but grant to a bit of moss or the smallest ant its due nature as an ontological reality, and we can no longer escape the terrifying hand that made us.' Maritain, *The Degrees of Knowledge* (Geoffrey Bles, London, revised translation by Gerald Phelan, 1959), p. 110.

the world may be. It can be compared with the reasoning of the man who, seeing an effect of light in the midst of shadow, concludes that the sun exists. Better still : while the light and shadow are constantly alternating, it is necessary to remember that evil always needs a subject to find itself in—there would be no blindness without a *being* deprived of sight; beneath the evil, contingent being is always revealing itself. And it might be said, without any paradox in our thought, that *evil proves God's existence.* The paradox lies only in the expression used, and we can make it disappear by saying that evil reveals the existence of a contingent subject, which postulates the existence of the Absolute.

c. *A God of evil would be impossible*

St Thomas says that we must get rid of the notion that there might be 'a first principle of all evils, just as there exists a first principle of all good things. For to start with, the first principle of good things is essentially good : all beings are, from the fact of existing, good; consequently only in something good can evil find a place to establish itself.

'Furthermore, the first principle of good things, which is the supreme and perfect Good, comprises in himself all goodness. But a supreme Evil is inconceivable. For if it is true that evil always diminishes the good in which it appears, it never succeeds in totally destroying it. Therefore if something good always exists beneath evil, nothing can be wholly and perfectly evil. And so Aristotle[9] writes that something wholly evil would destroy itself. Indeed, evil would have to destroy all good in order to preserve its wholeness; but then evil itself would disappear together with the good which is its subject.'[10]

St Augustine had said : 'Where there is a species'—by which he understood a nature, a positive reality—'there is necessarily a mode of being, and a mode of being is something good. Consequently absolute evil has no mode of being, since it is destitute of all goodness. It cannot be included under any species, *therefore it*

[9]'For evil destroys even itself, and if it is complete becomes unbearable.' *Nichomachaean Ethics,* bk IV, 5 (1126a12).
[10]I, qu. 49, a. 3. 'Evil does not remove all good, but only a particular good of which it is a privation. Blindness removes sight, not the animal. It would disappear if the animal disappeared. Total evil cannot therefore exist; by destroying all good it would destroy itself.' St Thomas, *In IV Ethic. Nic.,* bk. IV, lect. 13.

does not exist. The very concept of evil has been formed to designate a privation of species.'[11]

If, metaphysically, evil presupposes something good, it is clear that the notion of evil in itself, or pure evil, is a contradictory notion which is self-destructive.

d. *The dualist illusion*

How is it that all too many thinkers have been able to ignore such evidence? This is a question which preoccupies the religious historian, the philosopher and the theologian.

Being obsessed with the conflict between contrary effects brought about by equally real and consistent causes pulling in opposite directions, the dualist thinkers believed, St Thomas tells us, that if the chain of causes were followed up to its origin the opposition would have to be attributed to the first principles of things, and as a result they imagined a conflict on the highest level between two contrary Causes.

But they forgot that the contraries themselves are beings, and that if they exclude one another and enter into conflict as representatives of opposed *forms of being,* they would resemble one another inasmuch as they have *being* in common. Now in virtue of its contingency every particle of being postulates a first being which *is* Being, the Absolute, and which—in much the same way as whiteness contains all the other colours—gathers together in the pre-eminent richness of its unity all the various realizations of being: 'They could not see how to bring back particular causes, opposed to one another, to a universal common Cause. That is why they considered that the contrariety in causes had to be attributed to the first principles.'[12]

Being is opposed to being to the extent that it degrades, impoverishes, divides, limits and restricts itself. To the extent, however, that the restricted forms of being are traced back to their true Source, it will be seen how being throws off its limitations, becomes more solid and unified, and raises itself above all conflicts.

It is in so far as they are forms of *being* and of *good*— which although opposing one another, all converge upon a universal

[11]'Summum ergo malum nullum modum habet; caret enim omni bono, Non est igitur.' *Eighty-three Questions,* no. 6.
[12]I, qu. 49, a. 3.

order[13]—that opposites, once freed from their limitations as creatures, and *quite secure from the evil, or privation, which affects them,* become reconciled in the primary Source, which is Being and Goodness in its own right.

But what happens with thinkers who define evil as the opposite of good, and not as the privation of good? They confer upon evil a positive reality. Therefore they will have to deny that *all being,* from the very fact of its existence, *is good*; and to divide being into *good in its own right* and *bad in its own right*. Consequently, the principle of causality will have to be applied equally to evil and to good, to blindness and to sight, to death and to life; and just as we conclude the existence of a supreme principle of all good things, we shall have to conclude the existence of a supreme principle of all evils. Two supreme antagonistic principles, then— two gods who share the domain of being: two gods of whom neither exists in his own right, of whom neither is absolute. In its extreme form this is the absurdity of dualism.

Is it not, though, the usual practice to oppose good and evil to one another? Is this not done by ethical thinkers?[14]

Certainly, but their intention is by no means to deny that all beings are good from the fact of their existence; or to divide being into that which is good in its own right and that which is bad in its own right; or to transfer the opposition of good and evil to the very heart of the divinity.

Their intention is simply to bring out that man's free choice is not between a good and a privation; it is between two good things,

---

[13]'The fact that things are in conflict with one another shows that a thing may indeed revolt against the order intended by a particular cause, but not against the order intended by the universal Cause of all being.' St Thomas, I, qu. 103, a. 8, ad 3. *De potentia,* qu. 3, a. 6, develops this view. The ancient philosophers, says St Thomas, who considered only the particular principles of nature and saw them as contrary to one another, came to posit two supreme Principles and were victims of several errors. They paid attention only to the diversity of contrary things, not to the inmost element which is common to them all ... They paid attention only to the mutual relationships of particular things, not to the relationships which they have with the order of the whole universe; consequently they thought that a thing which was hostile to another or less perfect than another, was evil in itself: for Pythagoras, woman was imperfect and therefore evil; the Manichaeans regarded corruptible beings inferior to incorruptible beings, visible ones to invisible ones, the Old Testament to the New, and therefore all of these as evil; and they made them derive not from the good God, but from a contrary Principle.

[14]Cf. above, p. 39.

both positive and capable of waking desire, but for different ends —for example, whether someone else's property is to be respected or appropriated. One of these choices brings man nearer to his final end, and this is morally good; the other turns him away from his final end, deprives him of the means of reaching it, and this is morally evil.

It is solely in the moral, not the metaphysical, sense, that good and evil are in *contrary* opposition as two positive realities. To choose something (metaphysically) good which ennobles me and brings me nearer my end, is morally good. To choose something (metaphysically) good which debases me and turns me away from my end, depriving me of the means of reaching it, is morally evil.[15]

e. *Mazdaism, Manichaeism and Gnosticism*

In the Mazdean phase of Persian religion, evil, instead of being thought of as a privation, the absence of a good which should be present, takes on an embodiment and becomes a positive reality. It requires a cause of the same order as itself. How, then, could one dare to trace evil and good back to a single principle? Such was the difficulty, held to be insurmountable, which the Mazdean dualism opposed to three monotheistic religions at once : Judaism, Christianity and Islam.[16] The cause of evil, the Evil Spirit, Ahriman, appeared as personified, subsistent Evil, as pure evil, from all time opposed to pure good. He was the principle of an anti-creation set up against the creation of Ormuzd.

Dualism was not the earliest religion of Persia : 'In the *Gathas* there was only one supreme God, Ahura Mazda, the Wise Lord,

---

[15]'Bad acts and habits are typified not by privation, in which evil itself consists, but by some object to which this privation is attached, *sed ex aliquo objecto, cui conjungitur talis privatio.*' St Thomas, I^a II^ae, qu. 79, a. 2, ad 3.

[16]'I have investigated all the doctors in the world: the faith they profess can be put under one of these two headings: some say that all good and all evil in the world come from God. Others, that the good which is in the world and the hope the soul has of being saved have God for their cause; that all the miseries of the body and all the perils of the soul have Ahriman for their cause; and that everything proceeds from the dispensation of these two Principles right down to the last atom of every creature.' *Une apologétique mazdéenne du IXe. siècle, Skand-Gumanik Vicar, La solution décisive des doutes,* French text transcribed, translated and annotated by Pierre Jean de Menasce, O.P. (Fribourg, Switzerland, 1945), p. 117.

surrounded by six entities representing aspects of his various powers in the cosmos and in regard to human society : later the *aspects* were to become primordial creatures or archangels. For the moment, they coexisted with two *spirits,* the good and the evil, originally twins, whose fundamental opposition was a basic doctrine of Zoroastrianism. These spirits opted for either good or evil, and we are given no idea about their condition before this choice ... It is very striking that the evil principle was not situated on the same plane as the supreme God : he was on the lower level, opposite to the good spirit whose relations with Ahura Mazda are far from being clear. The same framework was to be found once more in a doctrine, again Persian but of obscure origin, which developed on the fringes of official Mazdaism, contaminating it here and there, and which is generally called Zervanism : the supreme God (Zervan, Chronos) engenders Ormuzd and Ahriman at the same time, the former in virtue of his merits, the latter in consequence of his *doubt.* If Ahriman was here on the same level as Ormuzd, it was because the latter had been reduced to the rank of a sort of demiurge. *Everything happened as though the ambition of evil, its claim to be equal to good, ran up against an impossibility of nature.* Its *secondary,* parasitic, character was never fully wiped out.'[17]

According to the Manichaean concept there first existed, in a 'Time anterior' to the world, 'an absolute and intact duality of two *Natures* or *Substances* or *Roots:* Light and Darkness, Good and Evil, God and Matter. Each was by the same title a principle, being unengendered and thereby eternal; each had equal value and an equivalent power. Neither had anything in common with the other; they were opposite in everything. In this way the problem of evil received from the start its most realistic and extreme solution : Evil cannot be denied, since it exists in itself from eternity, and it cannot be lessened, since it neither derives from nor in any way depends on Good.'[18] These two principles were conceived as forces, extended in infinite space and separated by a frontier. In the 'Time of the Median', when they came into con-

[17]Pierre Jean de Menasce, 'Note sur le dualisme mazdéene', in *Satan, Études Carmélitaines* (Paris, Desclee de Brouwer, 1948), pp. 130-3 (Italics ours.)
[18]Henri-Charles Puech, *Le manichéisme, son fondateur, sa doctrine* (Paris, Civilisations du Sud, 1949), p. 74.

flict, a part of the Light was imprisoned in the Darkness, and this explained the world. In the 'Third Era' the two Substances will finally return to the original separateness.

It has been pointed out that Manichaeism, which made itself out to be a scientific explanation of the universe, appears in reality as a poetic construction, a myth.[19] Mazdaism, which combated it violently, accused it of crudely imagining the primary Substances as extended in space; of explaining the appearance of the world not by a process of creation, but by a process of emanation, the supreme Light itself letting itself be partially imprisoned by the darkness; and of considering matter as existing in its own right and being irremediably evil.[20]

If Manichaeism is essentially a gnosis,[21] it will not be surprising to meet dualism in the very heart of Gnosticism : 'Like all Gnosticisms,' writes H.-C. Puech, 'Manichaeism is born of the fear inherent in the human condition. The situation into which he is thrown is experienced by man as strange, unbearable and radically evil. In it he feels himself enslaved to his body, to time and to the world, mixed up with evil, constantly threatened or actually contaminated by it. From this arises the need for deliverance. But if I am capable of experiencing this need, if I have the desire to discover or (since it is a form of nostalgia) to rediscover a state in which I can possess myself, in complete freedom and purity, it is because, in my inmost being, my true essence, I am really superior to my actual condition and a stranger to this body, this time and this world. Consequently my present situation appears to me as a fallen one. I shall have to explain how and why I came about and how I got where I am. On the other hand, at the same time as I discover or rediscover myself as being essentially a stranger to this world, I discover or rediscover that God himself can only be a stranger to it as well. God, who is nothing but Truth and Goodness, did not will this universe of suffering and falsehood; he is not responsible, or not directly responsible, for the existence of the world and of beings of flesh and blood. Therefore the only thing left is to attribute creation to a principle which is bad in itself, inferior (a demiurge) or even, for the Manichaean, opposed to

[19]H.-C. Puech, op. cit., p. 73.
[20]For the criticism of Manichaeism made by Mazdaism, cf. Pierre Jean de Menasce, *Une apologétique mazdéene* ..., op. cit., pp. 226-61.
[21]H.-C. Puech, op. cit., p. 69.

God. As in all the Gnoses, we finish up in a duality between the good and transcendent God and the God who creates and governs.'[22] The same author, however, brings out a distinction between classical Gnosticism and Manichaeism : in Gnosticism, the world is the work of a demiurge, that is, an inferior God, powerless and evil; in Manichaeism, the physical world is the work of supreme Evil, and the demiurge appears as a beneficent power, emanating from the good principle, so as to work for the deliverance of the particles of light buried in matter.[23]

Metaphysical dualism, having substantialized evil, has to find for it a positive cause distinct from the cause of good and to forbid itself to trace back to one God the production of everything in the world which has being; and although it shocks the intelligence, it can be seen how it has misled whole religious communities and distracted the hopes of men.

f. The nihilistic illusion

Living as we do in a pseudo-Christian society which avails itself of the name of God to justify an iniquitous order of things, we shall always have the task of denouncing hypocrisy and of putting in the place of all the caricatures of him God's real nature and the inflexible demands of Christianity. But the temptation and the illusion will be to fall into the snare and blame God himself for the scandals which offend him and are execrated by him. What began as a holy revolt against injustice turns to blasphemy and ends up by the creature putting on trial the Creator from whom he has received everything, including his sense of justice.

It is not only social injustices and economic and political disorders which may be held as a grievance against God. We may become angry even at the evil in nature, that facet of darkness and misery which remains inherent in every creature from the fact that it has been drawn out of nothingness and cannot but bear the mark of it. We may find unbearable the law according to which the formation of one substance presupposes the corruption of another, according to which the perfection of sensible creatures must be obtained at the cost of vulnerability and suffering, and according to which beings endowed with free will, such as men and angels, could never be by nature impeccable. We may no longer rest content with rebelling against the evil or the powerlessness of

22 Ibid., p. 153.   23 Ibid., p. 69.

creatures, we may rebel against even the being and the good of which this evil or powerlessness are the reverse side, and we may pass from hating created being to hating the uncreated Being from which it has sprung. We may feel angry that God could fashion a universe in which evil has a place, and in which limitations are everywhere to be found; in short, we may be jealous of God for remaining superior to his creatures and for not having made a world equal to himself. Atheism will turn to militant, vindictive, rabid antitheism.

What can underlie such a frenzy? Doubtless the misguided hope of some great happiness. Since German romanticism unleashed in it the forces of desire, humanity has let itself be seduced and driven along by immoderate ambitions. What it wants is to possess the absolute here on earth. And it lays claim to conquer the absolute by its own strength and refuses, as once the rebellious angels did, to implore it as a gift, wishing rather to snatch it as its booty. If happiness is missed and misfortune continues, if reality goes on resisting, then reality must be blasted away, until the day when all the obstacles have been overturned and there must needs arise from the ruins the magic of the Golden Age, the only normal and thinkable state of humanity.[24] The *Revolutionary's Catechism* of Mikhail Bakunin dreams of a sect capable of forcing the world into one pan-destructive force. Section 26 states expressly its end and the means to be employed: 'The Alliance has no other end than the complete emancipation and welfare of the people, that is to say, the working people. Convinced, however, that this emancipation and welfare can only be attained by means of a popular revolution destroying everything, the Alliance will use all its means and resources to guarantee and aggravate wrongs and disasters, which must finally wear out the patience of the people and incite it to mass uprising.'[25]

So long as there are limitations, destruction there will always be. But it is impossible to annihilate created being or to remove its limitations; it will only be possible to change it into another being, still created, and invite it again to destroy itself.

[24]A golden age resulting from atheism: we know what beguiling power Dostoyevsky, in *The Brothers Karamazov*, bk 10, ch. 6, bestowed on this ultimate temptation of atheism.
[25]Quoted by M.-M. Cottier, O.P., 'L'athéisme moderne, Brève esquisse historique,' in *Nova et Vetera*, 1960, no. 1, p. 42.

2. DOES GOD 'CREATE' OR AT LEAST 'CAUSE' EVIL?

If there is a paradox in the definition of evil—it exists, but as a privation—there will be a paradox also in the origin of evil : however terrible its ravages may be, evil is caused as a privation. Let us first look at the relation of evil to created causes.

a. How can evil, being a privation, be 'caused' by creatures?

What *natural agents* tend to introduce into the universe is a new form, some new positivity, which pushes out a previous form : the generation of one being entails the corruption of another, both on the mineral and biological levels. The same agent will produce two concomitant effects : [26] one good, one evil. Good is produced intentionally (an effect *per se*), evil comes about unintentionally and is a sort of reverse side or lining of the intended good (an effect *per accidens*).[27] Good is produced as something positive and is the product of true efficient causality. Evil comes about as a privation; it does not require an explanation *as to its being, its substance or consistence,* for it has none; it is not the product of true efficient causality. What requires a cause is its introduction into the matter of the world, its *existential presence,* its unforeseen arrival as a privation. This can be expressed by saying that the direct efficient cause of the intended good is the indirect or accidental efficient cause of the unintended evil.

That evil only introduces itself into the world hidden beneath something good is true also in the moral order of *voluntary agents.* The sinner does not desire a privation but a particular good, yet he cannot choose it without turning himself away from his final end and laying himself open to disaster. God is desired *per se* and evil *per accidens.*[28]

We have just spoken of evil—physical or moral—as the price paid for a directly intended good, and as something which is part of the *being* or the *effect* produced by the agent. But evil can lodge in the agent himself, and be found in the very principle of his

[26]Cf. above, p. 45.

[27]'Every agent acts for an end, intends a good which is his end: no privation is intended, it comes about as the reverse side of a produced effect.' St Thomas, *II Sent.,* dist. 1, qu. 1, a. 1, ad 2.

[28]'Voluntas est causa mali ... *per accidens* quidem, in quantum voluntas fertur in aliquid quod est bonum secundum quid, sed habet conjunctum quod est simpliciter malum.' St Thomas, *De malo,* qu. 1, a. 3.

action: a weak agent, a defective seed, can only produce faulty action.[29] In this case it may be said that evil is produced not so much by an 'efficient' cause as by a 'deficient' cause,[30] not so much by a cause which 'acts' as by one which, as it were, 'deacts'.[31]

This applies even in the moral order : St Thomas, having said that the will can be the cause of evil by accident, adds that it can be so also by defect.[32]

This raises a problem about the origin of sin. It proceeds from a deficient will. But how can it be deficient, freely deficient, before actually sinning? The answer must be that so long as the will does not act, it is not compelled to be attentive to the rule of its action, that is, to the rule of reason and the divine law. The actual failure to consider the rule is not a privation, for it is a mere absence or silence.[33] But when the will, struggling with the dilemma, good or evil, decides to act without considering the rule, the mere absence at once becomes privation, and irregular action or sin is produced. The workman is not taken to task for not considering the rule, but for acting without doing so.[34]

[29]'Aliter causatur malum in *actione,* et aliter in *effectu.*' St Thomas, I, qu. 49, a. 1.
    'St Thomas distinguishes between the evil that wounds the action or operation of beings—*evil of action*—and evil which wounds the being itself of the agent—*evil of being.* And he teaches in a very general way that evil of action or operation always arises from a certain presupposed defect in the being or the operative powers of the agent.' Maritain, *St Thomas and the Problem of Evil,* op. cit., p. 20.
[30]'Malum, quod in quadam privatione consistit, habet *causam deficientem,* vel agentem per accidens.' St Thomas, Iª IIæ, qu. 75, a. 1.
[31]'Non agendo sed deagendo.' St Thomas, *De malo,* qu. 1, a. 1, ad 8.
[32]'Voluntas . . . est causa mali secundum utrumque praedictorum modorum, scilicet et *per accidens,* et in quantum est *bonum deficiens.*' *De malo,* qu. 1, a. 3.
[33]'Augustine compares this deficiency to silence or darkness; this deficiency, in effect, is mere absence, *defectus ille est negatio sola.*' *De malo,* qu. 1, a. 3. Cf. Iª IIae, qu. 75, a. 1, ad 3. Cf. below, p. 156.
[34]St Thomas, *De malo,* qu. 1, a. 3 and ad 13.—In *De civitate Dei,* bk. XII, ch. 7, discussing the sin of the angels, St Augustine writes: 'Therefore do not seek the efficient cause of evil will: this cause is not efficient but deficient; there is here no production, *effectio,* but defection, *defectio* . . . To try to see in these defections efficient causes, not merely deficient ones, is to try to see darkness or to hear silence.' The question of how moral evil is produced in the will is one of the themes touched upon by Jacques Maritain in his penetrating study. *St Thomas and the Problem of Evil,* op. cit., pp. 20ff.

b. *Does evil come from God?*

Must evil ultimately be traced right back to God, the Maker of creatures?

It is evident first of all that evil, being a privation and having no positive nature, cannot properly speaking be *created,* it is not in itself *creatable:* 'I am not out of my mind, I do not say: God creates evil', cried St Augustine.[35]

When it is said in Isaias 45, 6-7 : 'I am the Lord and there is no other. I form light and create darkness, I make weal and create woe',[36] the prophet's meaning is clear : it is to eliminate absolutely any dualism or polytheism, and to affirm that God is the sole Master of all good and all evil, of life and of death. But to say that God is *just as much* Master of good things as he is of bad does not mean that he is *in the same way* Master of the good which he preserves in beings, and of the evil which comes to destroy them. Therefore, strictly speaking, it is folly to say that God *created* evil, or to ask why he *created* it.

But is it even permissible to ask : 'Why has God *caused* evil?'

We have seen that the 'evil of the action' comes from a physical or deliberate insufficiency on the part of the agent, which de-acts instead of acting (a defective seed, a workman inattentive to the rule). Now it is clear that no insufficiency, physical or moral, could ever be found in God. Consequently, the physical or moral evil of the action, and especially sin, will never in any way have God for their instigator; it would be foolish to transfer to God the cause of evil in action.[37] If God were to any degree whatsoever the cause of such an evil, then and then only would there be any justification in saying that he lacks power and goodness.

But what about the 'evil of the effect', the 'evil in the being', which is not directly intended, *per se,* but which, being the reverse side of, and the price to be paid for, the directly intended good, is thereby willed indirectly *per accidens?*

[35]'Non itaque insanio, nec dico: Malum creat Deus.' *Opus imperfectum contra Julianum,* end of bk. V.

[36]The Vulgate reads: 'creans malum.' St Thomas applies this text to the evil of punishment: God wills, or creates, order, with which the sinner comes into collision. *De malo,* qu. 1, a. 1, ad 1. Cf. below, pp. 80-1.
It should not be imagined that the 'Semites', failing to distinguish expressly between what God *wills* and what he *permits,* could have believed that God considers good and evil, virtue and sin, with indifference.

[37]'Malum ... quod ex defectu agentis causatur, non reducitur in Deum sicut in causam.' St Thomas, I, qu. 49, a. 2.

Its cause, as has been said, can be either a voluntary or a natural agent. In the first case, it can result equally from an honest intention which leads to some evil in nature, such as destroying life to turn it into food; or from a disordered intention, as of the drunkard who directly seeks pleasure and indirectly consents to his own degradation. It is clear that, however much it is produced by a disordered desire, the evil in the effect can only be imputed to creatures.

But the evil in the effect can result from the activity of natural agents : the evolution of the universe does not go on without destruction, new forms of life appear to take the place of the old. Then how is it possible not to trace back to God, the Maker of these things, at the same time but in an entirely different way, both the good which they intend directly and for its own sake, and the evil which they do not intend but which is the indirect and accidental consequence? Thus it can be said that God is directly and essentially the cause of good, and indirectly and accidentally the cause of the evil of the universe.

It can be said without hesitation that God is the cause of good : that means that his action intends good, and tends toward being. But it cannot simply be said that he is the cause of evil : that would mean that his action intended evil, and tended towards destruction, in short that God had created the world with a view to annihilating it.[38] To define very briefly the relation of God to evil it is neces-

---

[38]In *Eighty-three Questions,* qu. 21, St Augustine proves: 'That God is not the Author of evil. How could non-being arise from him who is the Author of all things, from Goodness whence the only thing that springs is the being of all that exists? Everything which falls short moves away from being and tends towards non-being. Not to fall short at all, that is goodness; and evil is to fall short. But he who does not know non-being could never be the cause of falling short, or of the tendency towards non-being. He is the very cause of being. He is the cause only of good, and that is why he is the sovereign Good. He who is the Author of everything which exists is not the Author of evil: for in so far as things exist, they are good.' This passage from St Augustine is indicated by St Thomas, I, qu. 49, a. 2, *sed contra.* And in the *corpus articuli,* St Thomas explains that 'in order to assure the good of the universal order, God, by way of *consequence* and as though *by accident, causes* the corruption of particular beings'; that the 'evil which consists in the corruption of these beings can be traced back to God as its cause, *reducitur in Deum sicut in causam*'. Thus God could never be the cause of physical evil by intending it or seeking it; but God is the cause of physical evil by willing the good of which this evil is the reverse. That is the double aspect signified by the phrase: God *permits* physical evil.

sary to have recourse to a new expression: God *permits* the physical evil in the universe.[39]

It is to the evil in the effect, to the evil of the being that punishment, which deprives man of his wholeness, belongs; while the evil of guilt belongs to the evil of the voluntary action.[40] In absolutely no way at all is God the cause of the evil of guilt, but he is the cause of the evil of punishment in exactly the same way as he is of the evil in the universe.[41] It is the order of the universe that God wills; punishment, which he does not will or intend—and God should not be thought of as a torturer—is the injury self-inflicted by those who rebel against an order which, being divine, could never be upset by a creature. God only 'wills' it in this quite indirect way, reluctantly, *praeter intentionem*. Jesus wept at the tomb of Lazarus and over the coming ruin of Jerusalem. About the evil of punishment as well as physical evil it can be said, to ward off any misunderstanding, not that God 'causes' it or 'wills' it, but that he *permits* it.

c. *Some texts from Plato and the Ancients*

There is a well-known passage in the *Republic* where, protesting against the poets, Socrates permits the tracing back to God only of *apparent* evils which, like the evil of punishment—and he had insisted on this idea in the *Gorgias*—are really benefits:

> *Socrates.* Thus good is, indeed, not the cause of everything; but being responsible for that whose way of being is good, it is innocent of anything evil. *Adimantus.* Completely innocent! *Socrates.* And so it is that the Divinity, being good, must not be responsible for everything, as is generally asserted, but for a very small part of human things; innocent, indeed, of a very great number of them, for among us good things are greatly surpassed by evil ones. And the cause of the good things must be sought in none other than the Divinity; while, as for the evils, I do not know what other causes must be sought for, but it is not the

[39] It is to the notion of permission, *anujna,* as understood in the context of its metaphysic, that Sankhya appeals in order to make Ishvara innocent of evil taken concretely and as a whole. Oliver Lacombe, *L'Absolu selon le Védânta,* op. cit.

[40] I, qu. 48, a. 5.

[41] I, qu. 49, a. 2. The bodily evils of man are primarily meant here. To go further into the mystery of the evil of punishment, it would be necessary to include even the evil of eternal loss, as St Thomas himself warns us, *De malo,* qu. 1, a. 5.

Divinity! . . . And should it happen that a poet sings of the woes of Niobe, of the sons of Pelops, or of Troy, or any other such abomination : either they must not be permitted to be called the works of the Divinity; or, if this is permissible, there must be discovered in these works a justification, roughly the same as we are seeking at present, and it must be said, of the Divinity, that it has therein carried out just and good actions, and of men, that it was to their advantage to have been chastised.[42]

To the young man who was scandalized by the disorders he thought to see in the world—notably the prosperity of the wicked —and who was driven to doubt the knowledge and providence of the gods, the Athenian Stranger of the *Laws* was content to recall the necessity for the subordination of the parts to the whole : 'Even your own being, poor wretch, however prodigiously worthless it may be, is one of those parts whose whole effort is a constant striving after the whole . . . You are not the end in view of which any particular existence is started, but rather the universe is the end in view of which you yourself exist.'[43]

This last idea is common among the Stoics. Marcus Aurelius writes : 'What happens to each one of us in particular, for the sake of the one who governs everything, conditions the even course of his life, his perfection and, by Zeus! even his very existence. The universe is, as it were, mutilated, however little we may take away from the connection and linkage of causes, no less than its parts are. If, then, you break this connection, in so far as in you lies, when you are discontented with what happens, you destroy them.'[44]

Plotinus was later to echo Plato : 'Holiness and piety forbid us to grant that the things objected to (the good being poor and the wicked prosperous) are not what is fitting, or to blame creation, *toip oiemati*. It remains to be discovered in what they are good and how they participate in the world-order; or otherwise, in what they are not an evil.'[45] The actors in a drama or a tragedy may

[42]*Republic,* II, 379,*c*; 380, *a.*
[43]*Laws, X,* 903, *c*—the view of the subordination of the parts to the good of the whole was to become traditional in the *philosophia perennis* to account for *physical* evil. But a new question was to arise: can the *spiritual* personality of man be treated as a part of the material universe? Cf. above, pp. 51-2.
[44]*Meditations,* bk. V, no. 8.
[45]*III 2 On Providence, I,* nos 7, 8.

quarrel among themselves on the stage; but they do not address any insults to the author who composed the drama or the tragedy.[46]

The spontaneous attitude of the ancients confronted by the mystery of the world was humility. There was too much evident splendour for them to dare to blaspheme.[47]

3. GOD 'PERMITS' EVIL

Let us define more exactly the meaning of this statement which Christian teaching has made its own.

a. *Does God 'will' evil?*

God neither *creates* nor *causes* evil. He does not *will* evil. To think that he seeks, desires or intends privation for its own sake would be an absurdity. In *nature* he wills and intends the renovation, not the destruction which goes with it. He wills and intends not the evil of punishment, but the order and good with which disorder and rebellion clash.[48] The evil in nature and evil of punishment, which are not willed for their own sakes or intended, and which are only willed by reason of the good which they include, can be said to be willed *accidentally,* or more simply, *permitted.*

What about the more mysterious evil of *sin* ?

The sinner wills a good, an advantage, and to obtain it he freely

---

[46]Ibid., no. 16.

[47]In our own times, speaking of the 'cosmic religion', which according to him is the 'religion of the scientist', Albert Einstein writes that it consists in wonder at the harmony of the laws of the universe in which so superior a mind is revealed that all the ingenious thoughts and workings of the human mind are, in comparison, no more than a very feeble reflection. This feeling is the guiding principle of his life and work, in so far as he succeeds in keeping himself from the shackles of selfish desire. *The World as I see it* (tr. A. Harris, John Lane, The Bodley Head, London, 1935), pp. 27-8.

Fascinated by the order of the material universe, Einstein inferred a universal determinism which he declared to be incompatible with the existence of a moral religion and a personal God. The principle of causality, limited exclusively to explaining the interconnection of *phenomena,* and void of any *metaphysical* significance, has become incapable of making the mind pass from the world to God. Man's mind, if not his heart, has become godless, and knowledge, or science, has dethroned wisdom.

[48]'Non enim in puniendo intendit malum ejus quod punitur.' *De malo,* qu. 1, a. 3, ad 10. Cf. below, p. 187.

consents to turn away from his final end : this is the evil of sin.
Something good is willed directly, *per se;* something evil is willed
indirectly, *per accidens;* not any evil whatsoever, (for though suffering, for example, is an evil it is good and reasonable to suffer
and die for a just cause) but some evil which makes the created
will swerve from its final end.[49]

Now God can neither turn away from himself, nor make other
beings turn away from him :[50] it is therefore impossible that the
evil of sin should be encountered in the evil which he might will
accidentally. Furthermore, God strives within us to save us from
it. In no way at all does he will it.[51]

It has just been said that God *permits* the evil in nature and
the evil of punishment. But it is already apparent that he must be
said to *permit* the evil of sin in a different, and much more mysterious, way.

b. *Is evil a part of the universe?*

In the universe which God has chosen to create, privation has
not been eliminated and it can find openings, often quite wide
ones, to enter by. It is foreseen, admitted, tolerated, borne with
and suffered. It cannot, however, be said that evil, even the evil
of nature, is a *part* of the universe : this would be once again to
forget the mystery of evil and go back to the position in which
evil is conceived as a lesser good, a contrary, as a good which must
give way to another for the sake of evolution, but not as a privation : '*Evil is not a part of the universe:* it has neither reason nor
substance nor accident, but only *privation.*'[52]

For Plotinus, on the contrary, evil is a part of the universe :
'Universal reason is one; but it is not shared out equally . . . Just
as in the pipes of Pan or other instruments there are tubes of dif-

---

[49]Ia II[æ], qu. 75, a. 1.

[50]'It is impossible that God should be, for himself or for others, the cause
of rebellion against the order which is in himself.' Ia II[æ], qu. 79, a. 1.
Cf. below, p. 161.

[51]'Et sic patet quod Deus nullo modo est causa peccati.' Ibid. Cf. I, qu. 19,
a. 9; qu. 49, a. 2. The sinner is 'like a servant who acts *against* his master's
command'. Ia II[æ], qu. 79, a. 1, ad 3. 'Those who are not with God are,
so far as in them lies, *against* God, from the fact that they go against the
antecedent divine will.' *I Sent.,* dist. 47, qu. 1, a. 2, ad 1.

[52]St Thomas, *I Sent.,* dist. 46, qu. 1, a. 3: 'Malum non est pars universi,
quia neque habet naturam substantiae neque accidentis, sed privationis
tantum.' Cf. below, p. 212, note 69.

ferent length, souls are placed each in a different position; and each, in its own place, gives out the sound which accords with its own position and with the harmony of others. The wickedness of souls has its place in the beauty of the universe; what is for them contrary to nature is for the universe conformable to nature; the sound is feebler but it does not diminish the beauty of the universe.'[53] Souls are wicked when they permit themselves to be dominated by the corporeal substrate, or matter, into which, however, there is still a diminished influx of the universal reason, so that ultimately everything is good.[54] Plotinus appeals to the opposites which clash for the sake of the good of universal order, or to good things for which evil has simply been the occasion. To justify providence such as he conceives it, he finally discovers no other way than to depict evils, not only those in nature but even the wickedness of souls, as lesser goods.

It can only be concluded that he has not grasped the mysterious definition of evil, which, being not a lesser good but a privation, could never be a part of the universe. Only good things, not evil ones, form part of the universe.

In so far as these good things willed by God are liable to corruption they have to give way to others : there is no construction without destruction, no carnivore without some animal's death. Again, there are good things of a very high order, but essentially two-edged, such as free will and free choice, made so that we can rise towards good and fulfil ourselves, but which can also make us sink towards evil and fall short. In all these cases the good comes first, the evil second.

There are occasions, however, when the evil comes first. We have only to think of diseases, infirmities and trials out of which can arise greatness and heroism, or of the evil of sin, which God

---

[53]*III 2 On Providence, I,* no. 17.
[54]*III 3 On Providence, II,* no. 4.—To the objection that 'if men are wicked in spite of themselves and against their will, no one can declare them to be responsible for the wrongs they do, not even the person who is their victim', the answer is that they 'are wicked in spite of themselves, admittedly, because every fault is involuntary; that does not make them any the less beings who act by themselves, and it is in the acts which they perform by themselves that they commit faults; they would not be at fault if it were not they themselves who were acting. The principle of the necessity of their fault is not outside themselves, at least not in every way.' *III 2 On Providence, I,* no. 10. This doctrine will be recognized as one which comes from the Stoics and was to reappear in Spinoza.

can never will and which of itself only tends towards disaster and which God may make the occasion for showing forth either the holiness of the creation against which the sinner freely rebels, or the wonderful ways in which he shows his mercy.[55]

Must it be said that all these evils 'contribute to the perfection of the universe'? This is strongly denied by St Thomas.[56] This would be to make them a part of the universe and to see in them the *causes* of the good things to which they are attached. They are only the reverse side, or the *occasion*.

c. *Evil 'governed' and 'regulated' by God*

Evil, although not intended by God, is nonetheless known to him, governed and controlled by him, and regulated by him towards some purpose; it does not escape his providence. Good and evil, says St Thomas, are subject to the *divine* providence: *evil*, as *known* and *governed*, but not *intended* by God, *malum tanquam praescitum et ordinatum, sed non ut intentum a Deo*.[57]

The *evil in nature*—which as a thing which afflicts man is thereby an evil of punishment—is spoken of in the Book of Wisdom (1, 13): 'God has not made death; he finds no joy in the loss of the living.' Evils are only permitted, but God controls them completely. Everything which appears fortuitous to us, in other words everything which results from causal interferences unforeseen by us, both as to their positive effects and as to the evils brought in their train, is in his hands. This is the meaning of I Samuel 2, 6: 'The Lord kills and brings to life; he brings down to Sheol and raises up.'[58] So too Amos 3, 6: 'Does evil befall a city, unless the Lord has done it?' And Matthew 10, 29: 'Are not two sparrows sold for a penny? And not one of them will fall to the ground without your Father's will.' The tower of Siloe which in its falling crushed eighteen people (Luke 13, 4), the young man who went to sleep by the window and fell from the third floor (Acts 20, 9), the snake which bit Paul (Acts 28, 3), all these chance events came about through a hidden disposition of God's providence by which

[55]For the good which sometimes precedes evil and sometimes follows it, see St Thomas, *I Sent.*, dist. 46, a. 2.
[56]I, qu. 19, a. 9, ad 2.
[57]*I Sent.*, dist. 39, qu. 2, a. 2.
[58]The same affirmations are made in the Koran: 'Everything returns to your Lord ..., it is he who gives both life and death,' LIII, 42-4; 'It is he who will make me die and then raise me up,' LVIII, 81.

they were abandoned to the laws of contingency. God, whose will
is sovereignly efficacious, prepares contingent causes for events
which need to be produced by contingent means.[59] These causes
are regulated with a view to certain good things to which great
evils can by chance be attached. All that happens in the world of
nature is consequently providential—doubly so if they affect man
who is worth more than a multitude of sparrows (Matt. 10, 31)—
and exactly how it works out cannot be known to us; but, the
soul which gives itself unreservedly to God realizes with Léon
Bloy that *tout ce qui arrive est adorable,* which echoes St Paul:
'Give thanks always and for everything' (Eph. 5, 20). Some of these
events, though, seem to answer a secret hope entertained in our
hearts, and we like to call them providential. If divine providence,
says St Thomas, 'never totally abandons the impious, for they
would fall away into nothing if God did not preserve them in
being', the just know that God has for them a special providence
'in the sense that he does not allow anything to happen to them
which would ultimately prove an obstacle to their salvation. As it
is said in Romans 8, 28 : "In everything God works for good with
those who love him".'[60]

Pure *evil of punishment* is not intended by God and results
from a sinful will colliding hopelessly with a good willed by God
and with a universe which God cannot disown without contra-
dicting himself; and it can be seen in what sense it is 'permitted'
and 'governed' by God.

Speaking more expressly of the evil of sin, St Augustine writes
that God is by no means 'a fabricator but a regulator of sins by the
distribution of sanctions, *non operatorem peccatorum, sed ordina-
torem distributione meritorum'.*[61] And by the distribution also of
his forgiveness and mercy. As Jacques Maritain writes: 'Moral
guilt can never under any circumstances become a good in relation
to any higher order whatsoever, but will remain to all eternity an
evil (although it can be fitted in so as to lead to a greater good,
which is another matter); in and by itself, however—and this is
part of the world's tragedy—it will always remain an evil.'[62]

[59]I, qu. 19, a. 8; cf. qu. 22, a. 4.
[60]I, qu. 22, a. 2, ad 4. Cf. below, p. 114.
[61]*De Genesi ad litteram,* bk. I, no. 33.
[62]*Neuf leçons sur les notions premières de la philosophie morale* (Paris,
Téqui, 1951), p. 72.

d. *God wills to permit evil*

In the *Summa,* before even distinguishing between the types of evil, St Thomas teaches in general that God, while not willing evil, permits it.

It is not true to say that *God wills evils to be,* for this would be to make out that he was responsible for them. Nor is it any more true to say that *God wills evils not to be,* for that would be to assert that he lacks the efficacity to carry out what he wills. The only thing left to say is that *God wills to permit evil.*[63] And this, continues St Thomas, is good.[64] Elsewhere he explains[65] : 'If all evils were prevented, many good things would disappear from the universe. The life of the lion would not be preserved by the death of other animals.' So much for the permission of evil in nature. The same answer will apply, but transferred to a much more mysterious plane, to the permission of the evil of sin : 'The suffering of the martyrs presupposes persecution by tyrants.'[66]

In other words, to will evil itself is impossible for God. To will something good, such as the world, without any admixture of evil would be possible for God. To will something good, such as the world, with an admixture of evil for the sake of the good itself and not of the evil which lives on or affects this good, is what God has chosen. And that is good also. It means that God has permitted evil. God, says St Augustine, 'would never permit any evil to exist in his works if he were not powerful enough and good enough to make good come out of the very evil . . .'[67] He has judged it to be better to make good come out of evil than to permit there to be no evil at all.'[68]

---

[63]St Thomas takes up and makes more explicit the doctrine of Peter Lombard. The first two propositions, he says, being affirmative, are not opposed to one another as contradictions, so that the principle of excluded middle is not broken. To the question: is it good that evils should exist? St Thomas replies that it is not, but that what is good is that evils should be occasions for good, 'et ideo hoc bonum est, mala esse occasiones bonorum.' *I Sent.,* dist. 46, qu. 1, a. 4, ad 2; and a. 2.

[64]'Deus igitur neque vult mala *fieri*; neque vult mala *non* fieri; sed vult *permittere* mala fieri. Et hoc est bonum.' I, qu. 19, a. 9, ad 3. Cf. *De malo,* qu. 2, a. 1, ad 4 *sed contra.*

[65]I. qu. 22, a. 2, ad 2. Cf. qu. 48, a. 2, ad 3.

[66]Ibid.

[67]'Neque enim Deus . . . ullo modo *sineret* mali aliquid esse in operibus suis . . .' *Encheiridion,* ch. XI, no. 3.

[68]'Melius enim judicavit de malis bene facere, quam mala nulla esse permittere,' Ibid., ch. XXVII, no. 8.

e. *Where the idea of the permission of evil is misunderstood*

The distinction betwen willing evil and permitting it will be misunderstood by all those who, failing to grasp that evil is a privation, attribute to it a consistence and seek a positive cause for it.

Those for whom evil is the opposite of good will designate as its final cause the will of an evil God (Mazdean or Manichaean dualism). Those for whom evil is merely a lesser good, or for whom good and evil are merely modes of thought in our ignorance,[69] will declare that evil and good are willed equally by the supreme Cause.

We have already seen that, according to St Augustine, God is certainly not the fabricator but the regulator of sins by the distribution of sanctions. Calvin gives another meaning to the word 'regulate'. If sins were positive things, subtracting them from God's influence and hesitating to declare them as willed by him would evidently be to impugn his omnipotence. In effect the distinction between *willing* and *permitting* evil is rejected by Calvin, and in the very same context in which it imposes itself most forcefully, that of sin. In his *Institutes*, Calvin argues thus: 'Some have recourse here to the difference between *willing* and *permitting*, saying that the wicked perish, God permitting but not willing it. But why should we say that he permits it if we do not mean that he wills it? How improbable it is in itself that it is only by the *permission* and not by the *ordinance* of God that man has brought damnation upon himself ... The damned wish to be considered excusable in sinning, being unable to evade the necessity of sinning, especially since this necessity proceeds from the ordinance and will of God: on the contrary, I deny that this excuses them, since this ordinance of God which they complain of is just.'[70] 'God not only foresaw the fall of the first man, and thereby the ruin of all his posterity, but he also willed it.'[71]

4. WHY DOES GOD PERMIT THE EVIL IN THIS WORLD?

God neither 'creates' nor 'causes' nor 'wills' evil, but 'permits' it. The real question is why he wills to permit this evil. see p. 145.

[69]'As to good and evil, they neither of them indicate anything positive in things considered in themselves at least, and are nothing but modes of thinking or notions which we form because we make comparisons between things.' Spinoza, *Ethics*.

[70]*Institutes,* bk. III, ch. 23, nos 8, 9.   [71]Ibid., no. 7. Cf. below, pp. 162-3.

a. *The ultimate answer*

This was given by St Augustine and was to be taken up un-changed by St Thomas. It is formulated as follows in the *Encheiridion* (421):

'Almighty God, to whom, as even unbelievers recognize, be-longs the sovereign dominion over all things,[72] being sovereignly good, would never allow any evil to exist in his works unless his omnipotence and goodness were such that he could make good come out of evil itself.'[73]

And further on : 'God has judged it better to draw good out of evil than not to permit the existence of any evil at all.'[74] Yet again further on : God, knowing that Adam would sin, made his plans 'with a view to using for the sake of good that very thing which would bring evil about, in such a way that the sinful will of man would not bring it to nothing but, on the contrary, carry out the will of the Almighty'.[75]

St Augustine's view is taken up again by St Thomas at the be-ginning of the *Summa*. To the objection that an infinitely good God, if he existed, would not leave any room for evil, he answers with the first quotation from the *Encheiridion,* underlining the paradox : 'It belongs therefore to the infinite goodness of God to permit evil to exist and to make good come out of it.'[76] He is con-sistent in thinking that particular deficiencies are permitted with a view to the good of the whole universe and hence with a view to a greater good : 'As God is the universal moderator of all being, *universalis provisor totius entis,* it belongs to his providence to permit certain faults in particular beings rather than set limits on the complete good of the universe. If, indeed, all evils were to

---

[72]Cf. Virgil, *Aeneid,* X, 100: 'Tum Pater omnipotens, rerum cui prima potestas.'

[73]'Neque enim Deus omnipotens, quod etiam infideles fatentur, rerum cui summa potestas, cum summe bonus sit, ullo modo sineret mali aliquid esse in operibus suis, *nisi usque adeo esset omnipotens et bonus, ut bene faceret et de malo.' Encheiridion,* ch. XI.

[74]'Melius enim judicavit *de malis bene facere,* quam mala nulla esse permittere,' ibid., ch. XXVII.

[75]Ibid. Ch. CIV.

[76]'Hoc ergo ad infinitam Dei bonitatem pertinet, ut esse permittat mala, et ex eis eliciat bona.' I, qu. 2, a. 3, ad 1.

disappear, many good things would be lacking in the universe.'[77]

b. *The universal and analogical validity of this answer*

Just as the definition of evil is truly applicable, though in an analogical and transposed sense, to all the forms of evil, so the answer given by St Augustine and St Thomas, according to which evil is permitted by God for some greater good, is truly valid, though in an analogical and transposed sense, to all the forms of evil : the evil in nature, the evil of punishment and even the evil of sin.

If God did not order evil to a greater good, if he let the forms of evil triumph on the whole and in the end in the world, he would either keep control over the world and be a perverse God, aiming to destroy what he created, or lose control over the world and not be all-powerful. It is important to realize the metaphysical character of the Augustinian answer.

c. *Its mysterious character*

For what *good* is evil permitted ? Sometimes we can indicate it—it may become evident with time that a particular illness, misfortune or sorrow has brought about the renewal of a life; some wrong may call for forgiveness and magnanimity, some sin for God's mercy. But more often than not we shall be left without clear answers and be faced only by the darkness of mystery. St Thomas puts it very succinctly : generation presupposes corruption, the lion's life the death of the hind, and martyrdom persecution.

No inductive process is used; we are compelled *a priori* by a metaphysical necessity independent of any inquiry or verification to say of all evil that it is permitted with a view to some great good. We are confronted with three terms, all three mysterious : an infinitely good and powerful God, a world in which evil rages, and an inevitable triumph of good over evil. Two of these mysteries, however unfathomable they may appear to us, are only

[77]I, qu. 22, a. 2; cf. qu. 48, a. 2, ad 3.—Even when an inferior being destroys a superior being, as when a lion devours a man, bacilli eat away a lung, a plant eats a fly, or even any being dissolves back into its chemical constituents, it is the good of the universal order which is preferred to the good of particular beings, and the recurrence of chemical substances and living species which is to be looked for in any of these types of destruction.

relatively infinite, they are absolutely speaking *finite:* the evil in the world and its superabundant compensation by good. The third mystery is 'infinitely more infinite', it is absolutely speaking *infinite.* This is to say that there are in God infinitely more resources than are needed to make good come out of the evil in the world, and to make a better world. We are always faced by mysteries, but never by contradiction.

Evil is permitted for a *greater* good. But what greater good? Primarily, and as regards the evil in nature, for that universal good which is more precious than that of which particular creatures are deprived by evil. It is better for the world to move on and species to reproduce themselves than for individuals to go on for ever. Philosophy on its own can go no further.

Ought we to go further and think that evil, in the unpredictable dispositions of God's mercy, can condition the appearance of a universe which is by and large better than the one which preceded it and on which it wrought its havoc? This is where theology starts from, and Christian philosophy can go with it.

Commenting on the *Felix culpa* in the *Exsultet,* St Thomas writes that, in Christ, human nature was raised to a state which it would not have dreamed of at the time of the original universe.[78]

III. IF GOD PERMITS EVIL, IS IT FOR LACK OF POWER OR LACK OF GOODNESS?

I. THE CLASSICAL DILEMMA

a. *Its formulation*

The ultimate answer given by St Augustine and St Thomas is that God can only permit evil so as to order it to some mysterious good, and that this permission is precisely an effect of his infinite power and goodness.

But not all the questions have been resolved. Why did he choose a world with an admixture of evil? Surely an all-powerful and good God should have, and could have, chosen to create a world free from evil, a better world, in fact the best of all possible worlds?

[78] III, qu. 1, a. 3, ad 3.

If not, it was for lack of power that he did not, and if so, it was for lack of goodness.

We have been appealing all along to the *mystery* of the coexistence of God and evil : now this is the *contradiction* to which we are supposed to be reduced. This is the classical dilemma, and it drags its weary course everywhere from the *Avesta* to Voltaire's *Dictionnaire philosophique*. But it is a fragile thing and shatters against the mystery of God.

b. *Its meaning*

Let us put the meaning of the dilemma more clearly; the mystery of the coexistence of evil and an infinitely powerful and good God is rejected because a contradiction is seen in it. One of the two terms must be suppressed.

There are two very radical ways of doing this, but they will not be dealt with here. They demand a sort of heroism, that of pushing error to the point of absurdity.

One of them is to suppress the world, and at the same time all the evil in it, as being sheer magic, an illusion which keeps us in error but from which we can be delivered by our awareness of the total identity of our inner being with the Absolute. This is the Sankhya perception of *acosmism*. The Absolute is resplendent in its purity and infinitude. Pantheism has been completely thrown off and left behind.

The other is to suppress God. This is *absolute atheism*,[79] which utterly denies 'the existence of the very God in whom the believers believe—God the Creator, Saviour and Father, whose name is infinitely over and above any other name we can utter . . . A man does not become an absolute atheist as a result of some inquiry into the problem of God carried on by speculative reason . . . The starting point of absolute atheism is . . . a basic act of moral choice, a crucial free determination. If at the moment when he takes stock of himself and decides upon the whole direction of his life, a man confuses the transition from youth to manhood with the refusal not only of childhood's subordinations but of any subordination whatsoever; if he thus considers the rejection of any transcendent law as an act of moral maturity and emancipation; and if he decides to confront good and evil in a totally and abso-

[79]e.g., Freidrich Nietzsche, Karl Marx, Auguste Comte.

lutely free experience, in which any ultimate end and any rule coming from above are cast aside forever—such a free moral determination, dealing with the primary values of existence, will mean that this man has entirely excluded God from his own universe of life and thought. Here is, in my opinion, the point at which absolute atheism begins in the depths of a man's spiritual activity. But what is this I have just been describing if not a kind of act of faith, an act of faith in reverse gear, whose content is not an adherence to the transcendent God, but, on the contrary, a rejection of him? . . . Now what does all this mean? Absolute atheism starts in an act of faith in reverse gear, and is a full-blown religious commitment. Here we have the first internal inconsistency of contemporary atheism: it proclaims that all religion must necessarily vanish away, and it is itself a religious phenomenon.'[80]

From the point of view which we are interested in it must be added that acosmism might have been the truth: it is only made absurd by the fact that the world exists; while atheism is intrinsically and metaphysically absurd. Furthermore, in the framework of acosmism evil is impossible and the answer to the problem of evil is peremptory; while in the intrinsically absurd framework of atheism, the evil in this world, pain, death, injustice and crime are without answer; the world itself, with all the acts of heroism in it, is without any reason; a suffering generation is asked to sacrifice itself for another suffering generation, until finally everything falls back into nothing.

The absurdity of acosmism is evident to our senses. The metaphysical absurdity of atheism is not less so, for if it is difficult for the reason unaided by grace to attain without error to a developed knowledge of God,[81] it is nonetheless immediately obvious to it that the contingent being of the universe depends on a self-sufficient Being. St Paul takes the Gentiles to task not for failing to know God through their reason, but for not having worshipped him as such (Rom. 1, 19-21).

It is not at this deep level—absolute acosmism or absolute atheism—that the dilemma presents itself to us at the moment. We are not being driven—at least not directly—into acosmism or atheism. The world being what it is, we are being driven into

---

[80]Jacques Maritain, 'The Meaning of Contemporary Atheism', in *The Range of Reason* (Geoffrey Bles, London, 1953).
[81]St Thomas, I, qu. 1, a. 1.

sacrificing either the true idea of the Creator's omnipotence or that of his goodness, and it is easier to sacrifice the former than the latter. Either God can only do what he actually does and only be powerful in this diminished sense, in which case let us not accuse him of lacking goodness: this is the broad way. Or God is truly omnipotent, but then how is his goodness to be saved? There is only one outcome, which is to say that he has created the best of all possible worlds: this is the narrow way. The first way, says St Thomas,[82] is that of certain ancient philosophers; it is also that of Spinoza. The second is that of theologians like Abelard; and it is the one taken by Leibniz. Both are blind alleys.

2. DOES GOD LACK POWER?

a. *How is God's omnipotence to be defined?*

How is God's omipotence to be defined? What do we mean by saying God can do all things?

Power, replies St Thomas,[83] must be seen in relation to what is possible. That God can do all things means that he can bring about everything which is possible, and hence he is called all-powerful. He is all-powerful not because he can do everything he has actually done—this would be going round in circles—nor because he can do everything which is possible for such and such a creature; but because he can do everything which is, *in itself and absolutely speaking,* possible, that is to say, *everything which does not imply a contradiction.*

Must it be said that his omnipotence comes to a halt at these contradictions? He cannot make a square circle, a valley without mountains, nor wish to be finite, nor wish to have sin in himself, nor will that it should be good to hate him and evil to love him. But if there is any impotence in all this, it is clear that it is not on God's part but on that of the things proposed, which are self-destructive. We should say, rather, not that God is unable to do them but that they are not susceptible of realization.[84]

It would be impossible to define correctly the all-*powerfulness*

[82]*De potentia,* qu. I, a. 5.
[83]I, qu. 25, a. 3; *De potentia,* qu. I, a. 7.
[84]'Unde convenientius dicitur quod ea non possunt *fieri,* quam quod Deus ea non possit *facere.*' St Thomas, I, qu. 25, a. 3.

of God without bringing in the idea of what is intrinsically and absolutely speaking *possible*.

b. *The universe of possibles*

The uncreated essence of God is pure Being, Being in itself. By reason of the limitless wealth of its utter simplicity it admits of being imitated and shared in various modes which, while transferring it in some sense from the absolute plane so as to translate and shape it in terms of the relative, nonetheless essentially remain infinitely inadequate expressions of it, and consequently the number of forms they can take is literally infinite. Just as Plato said that time is a sort of changing image of a changeless eternity,[85] so possible things are a sort of complex image of God's sovereign oneness. Before *existing,* writes St Thomas, the world was *possible*. This can be understood in two ways: the obvious one, that the world was possible in relation to the *active power* of God, or capable of realization; and the more radical one, that the world was *absolutely speaking* possible, in the sense that the possible is opposed to the impossible from the sole fact that it represents a collection of ideas which are neither inconceivable nor incapable of co-existing, *ex sola habitudine terminorum qui sibi non repugnant*.[86]

The Divine intellect, from the fact that it knows the supreme wealth of that divine Being which can be shared and imitated in an infinite number of ways, is the source of all the divine ideas. In God's speculative knowledge, these ideas express the 'reasons' or essences of all possible things and all their possible combinations; in his practical knowledge, if he freely decides to give them reality, they will constitute the 'exemplars' or types of the universe to be brought into existence, and of the elements which it will include.[87]

---

[85]*Timaeus,* 37, d.

[86]I, qu. 46, a. 1, ad 1.—This *possible* belongs to *reality*: the principle of non-contradiction is a *yardstick* for our minds and is *imposed* on them. Being is divided into *ens rationis* and *ens reale,* the latter being subdivided into *possible* and *existent*. On the distinction between, on the one hand, the *universe of existence* and the *universe of intelligibility*; and, on the other, the *ens rationis,* see, e.g., Jacques Maritain, 'Critical Realism', in *The Degrees of Knowledge,* op. cit. Cf. below, p. 96, note 101, p. 97, note 102.

[87]St Thomas distinguishes the divine ideas, following Plato, as to whether they are: either a) merely *principium cognoscitivum* and 'reasons' for speculative things; or b) also *principium factionis,* and 'exemplars' of created things. I, qu. 15, a. 3. Cf. below, p. 180.

It is not God who depends on possible things but the possible things and the whole order of necessary truths which depend on the necessity that is in God, just as the image which is obtained in a mirror depends on the object. Possible things, being participations in, and imitations of, God, are what they are because God, whom they reflect in a finite way, is what he is. Necessary truths depend on the divine essence to such an extent that for them to be abolished the divine essence would have to be abolished also. Certainly we are not saying that the divine intellect depends on eternal truths, or that it is determined by them or subject to them. Its only specifying object is the divine essence, which is identical with the divine intellect. What we are saying is that, seeing in this essence all the admissible modes of participation, the divine intellect thereby knows and determines all possible creatures and the truths which concern them, and which depend to such an extent on God that to change them it would be necessary first to change God's essence itself.[88]

The universe of possible things and eternal truths is what it is because it reflects the unchangeable essence of God. To change them it would first be necessary for God's essence itself to change.

But God possesses in himself the fullness of being and could never produce any action outside himself by an inner necessity or by constraint; consequently, out of the limitless number of possible things, the choice of those which he wished to bring into existence was a free one : such and such a universe in which evil would have no place, or such and such a universe in which good would triumph over evil.

Just as the absolute infinity of possible things, whose possibility is necessary, will always exceed the relative infinity of existing ones, whose existence is only contingent, so the absolute infinity of what can be created will always exceed the relative infinity of what actually has been created.

---

[88]Maritain, *The Dream of Descartes,* (Editions Poetry, London, 1946), pp. 114-5. Cf. p. 117: 'In order to abolish the principle of identity, as to abolish the possibility of an ant, one would first be obliged to abolish the divine essence. The eternal truth of this principle does not depend upon the divine will and creative freedom, it depends upon divine necessity, I mean upon the knowledge that God necessarily has of his infinitely necessary essence, knowledge which bears for that very reason upon all that is possible and creatable, not, of course, as upon a specifying object, but as upon an object specified and materially attained.'

'God's power,' says St Thomas, 'is infinite in a double sense. Quantitatively, it can never make so many things that it could not go on making yet more. Qualitatively, it never acts with such intensity that it could not act with greater intensity still, since its degree of intensity is measured by the action, not by the fact that it proceeds from God, in whom it is always infinite, being identical with the divine essence, but by the more or less perfect way in which it attains its effect.'[89]

To ignore in any way at all the margin which separates the creatable from the created would be to impugn God's transcendence.[90]

c. *To do away with the margin between the necessity of possible things and the contingency of existent ones would be to impugn God's transcendence: Descartes and Spinoza.*

This margin can be destroyed in two entirely different ways. In the hope of giving a better definition of God's omnipotence, one could impugn his transcendence either by denying the *wisdom* of his omnipotence, or by denying its *liberty*.

Under the pretext of exalting the divine omnipotence, Descartes destroyed it when he undertook to separate it from the divine wisdom. Fearing that if one spoke of the absolute character of possible things and their laws, and of necessary truths, such as mathematical and metaphysical truths, one would subject the divinity to them, he preferred to give up this notion of intrinsically necessary truths and reduce everything to contingency. God, he said, 'was as free to make it untrue that all lines drawn from the centre to the circumference are equal, as he was not to create the world. And it is certain that these truths are no more necessarily conjoined to his essence than are other creatures'.[91]

---

[89]*De potentia,* qu. 1, a. 2.
[90]That there is a margin between what God could make and what he has made, and between his absolute power and his subordinated power, is the constant teaching of the Church. Cf. the seventh proposition of Abelard, condemned at the Council of Sens, in 1140: 'God can only do or not do what he has actually done, in the way he has done it, and at the time he has done it.' *Denz.,* no. 374. And the twenty-seventh proposition of Wycliffe, condemned at the Council of Constance, in 1418: 'All things come about by an absolute necessity.' *Denz.,* no. 607. Cf. below, pp. 111-2.
[91]Adam-Tannery, vol. I, p. 152. Quoted by Maritain, *The Dream of Descartes,* op. cit., pp. 115-6.

Descartes's mistake was to confuse 'the creatable and possible with the actually created. Everything—and by this I mean all the laws of essences, the distinction between being and non-being, between the intelligible and the absurd, between good and evil—would then simply come under the will and freedom of a supreme arbitrary being. Descartes does injury to God's wisdom and intellect. St Thomas, laying aside his usual serenity, considers it blasphemy to make good and evil depend simply on the will of God.'[92] Thus God would not forbid us certain things like falsehood, hatred or crime because they are evil; but these things would only be evil because God forbids them to us. Hell would not be the free rebellion of the will against an order chosen by God in his unerring wisdom; it would be rebellion against an order which God could have declared perverse, a rebellion God could have declared holy. That is the confusing answer which would have to be given to the problem of evil: in fact, it is sheer blasphemy.

The second way of destroying God's transcendence lies in denying the contingency of existing things, and is the way followed by Spinoza. It takes up an old error. 'Certain philosophers,' says St Thomas,[93] 'have thought that God acted outside himself as though compelled by his nature. Now, the action of natural things cannot result in anything other than what they in fact produce: the nature of man engenders man, that of the olive-tree engenders the olive. Thus God's working could result neither in other things nor in another order of things than that which in fact exists.' But, St Thomas continues, 'God expressly does not create by internal

---

[92]Maritain, op. cit., p. 118. (The quotation from St Thomas is taken from *De veritate*, qu. 23, a. 6.) Leibniz likewise was to say that this would be to 'dishonour' God: 'Why should he not be the evil principle of the Manichaeans as well as the good principle of the orthodox?' *Theodicy*, nos 176, 177. Cf. below, p. 120, note 149.

[93]I, qu. 25, a. 5. One has only to think of Plotinus, or of Avicenna himself, who 'posits the existentialization of possibles as an eternal, absolute necessity of the full burgeoning of the divine essence into act (...) Ibn Sina would certainly make on his own account the great Muslim affirmation that *God is the creator of evil as well as of good,* but here again giving it a meaning which is no longer the traditional one. God, the necessary Being, is the creator of evil to the extent that evil cannot but be inserted in the necessary emanation of every existing thing from the primary Being downwards. And so the problem of moral evil as such cannot be posed ... In the thought of Ibn Sina, the problem of evil remains very nearly the same as in Plotinus.' Louis Gardet, *La pensée religieuse d'Avicenne (Ibn Sina)* (Paris, Vrin, 1951), pp. 68, 135.

necessity; it is his will which is the cause of all things. And his will is by no means determined by nature or by necessity to produce this thing or that. In creating the present course of things, God has not acted by necessity at all : other things could have been produced.'[94]

What is Spinoza's idea? We read in the *Short Treatise:* 'We say, then, that whatever comes about, since it is made by God, must therefore be necessarily predetermined by him, because otherwise he would be changing, which in him would be a great imperfection; and that this predetermination must be in him from all eternity, in which eternity there is neither before nor after; from which it surely follows that God could not originally predetermine things in any other way than they are now determined for all eternity, and that, prior to this determination or without it, God could not have existed . . . We therefore deny that God can omit to do what he actually does.'[95] And in the *Metaphysical Reflections:* 'If men knew clearly the whole order of nature, they would find everything as necessary as all those which are treated of in mathematics; but since that is so far above human understanding, certain things are judged by us to be possible and not necessary.'[96] And finally in the *Ethics:* 'From the sovereign power of God, or from his infinite nature, an infinity of things in an infinity of modes, in other words everything, has necessarily flowed from it or follows it, always with the same necessity; just as from all eternity and for all eternity it follows from the nature of a triangle that its three angles are equal to two right angles. That is why the omnipotence of God was active from all eternity and will remain in the same actuality for all eternity. And in this way, the omnipotence which we admitted to be in God is much more perfect, at least in my opinion.' 'Everything has been predetermined by God, not indeed by the freedom of his will, otherwise called his absolute good pleasure, but by his absolute nature or infinite power.'

The omnipotence defined by Spinoza is that of a God who could

---

[94]Ibid.
[95]*Short Treatise,* Part I, ch. 5. It seems evident that Spinoza here intends to refute Descartes. But he throws the baby out with the bath-water, the Judæo-Christian doctrine of omnipotence together with that of Descartes.
[96]*Metaphysical reflections,* Part II, ch. 9.

not have failed to create without being imperfect, who cannot exist without the world, who under pain of being changeable had to create from all time, and whose activity is not free but is deployed with mathematical necessity. All possible things and their necessity are consequently brought into existence so as to make them necessary. 'Spinoza's essential error is to confuse with the pure possible or the creatable, which is nothing outside of God, the created and the existent, which as such is willed, loved, chosen. Thus he wrongs the divine freedom.'[97]

What, according to this view, becomes of evil? It disappears. The same ignorance which makes us call certain things necessary and others contingent makes us judge certain things good and others evil, whereas all of them are necessarily produced by God: '*Good* and *evil* (or *sin*) are nothing but modes of thinking, not things, and do not in any sense possess existence . . . For all beings and all works found in nature are perfect.'[98] There must now be asked the question: are good and evil *figments of the mind* or *real things*? But, considering that good and evil are only purely relative things, it is beyond doubt that they must be ranked among the figments of the mind; for it is never said that a thing is good except in relation to some other which is not so good or so useful to us . . . Good and evil, as for example the flight of Peter and the wickedness of Judas, cannot be defined outside the essence of Judas or Peter, for this essence is the only thing to be found in nature; so they cannot be defined independently of the essence of Peter or Judas. It follows from this that good and evil are neither things nor effects that many be found in nature.'[99] 'It may be asked, why then are the wicked punished? They act in accordance with their nature and God's decree. I answer that it is also by God's decree that they are punished and if only those whom we imagine to sin in virtue of their own freedom are to be punished, why do men strive to wipe out poisonous serpents? For these sin in virtue of their own nature and cannot do otherwise.'[100] He set out in the *Ethics* to dissipate 'the prejudices relating to good and evil, merit and sin, praise and blame, order and confusion, beauty and ugli-

---

[97]Jacques Maritain, *The Dream of Descartes,* op. cit., p. 118.
[98]*Short treatise,* Part I, ch. 6.
[99]*Short treatise,* Part I, ch. 10.
[100]*Metaphysical reflections,* Part II, ch. 8.

ness.' He restates his idea : 'As to good and evil, neither of them point to anything positive in things, considered, that is, as things, and they are nothing but modes of thinking or notions which we form because we compare things to one another . . . Although this is true, we still have to keep these names.'[101]

Let us note in passing that there are several errors in these opinions of Spinoza. Certainly the *idea* of good and *idea* of evil are, as such, mere figments of the mind. But good and evil do not merely exist in the mind; *they both exist in reality:* good as something *positive,* and evil as a *privation;* sight exists, blindness exists, quite apart from whether our mind is thinking about them. As for relativity, there are real relations which exist in things independently of our minds, such as those of equality or similarity;

---

[101]*Ethics.* This idea, that good and evil are products of the mind, which is much too convenient a way of resolving the problem of evil, is surely to be found also in Henri Bergson. To the objection: could not God, in virtue of his omnipotence, create a better world, Bergson answers that he could not: 'What exactly does "omnipotence" mean? We have shown (in *Creative Evolution*) that the idea of "nothing" is tantamount to the idea of a square circle, that it vanished under analysis, only leaving an empty word behind it, in fine that it is a pseudo-idea. May not the same apply to the idea of "everything", if this name is given not only to the sum-total of the real, but also to the totality of the possible? I can, at a stretch, represent something in my mind when I hear of the sum-total of existing things, but in the sum-total of the non-existent I can see nothing but a string of words. So that here again the objection is based on a pseudo-idea, a verbal entity.' *The Two Sources of Morality and Religion* (Macmillan, London, 1935), pp. 224-5. To this we reply that the pseudo-idea would be to want to make one *whole* out of creator and created, out of the possible and the existing; these two totalities would not add up. Again, the pseudo-idea would be to imagine a God constrained to create, and to create a certain world; in other words, to imagine an Absolute which, in order to be such, must attach himself to his creation. Maritain, in 'The Metaphysics of Bergson', in *Redeeming the Time* (Geoffrey Bles, London, 1943), discusses Bergson's analysis of *nothingness* (pp. 61-3), and his idea of the *possible* (pp. 68-72).

Bergson opts for an empirical optimism which is imposed 'without philosophy having to plead God's cause. Shall it be said that if life is good as a whole, it would nonetheless have been better without suffering, and that suffering could not have been willed by a God of love? But nothing proves that suffering was willed. We have shown that what, on the one side, looks like an immense multiplicity of things, among which indeed suffering can be found, can be presented on the other as an indivisible act, so that to eliminate a part would be to suppress the whole.' *The Two Sources . . .,* op. cit., p. 245. We can see in this, although it is suggested with the author's natural delicacy of thought, the argument for the sacrifice of the part—even of the human person—to the good of the whole.

we do not create them, we verify and declare them.[102]

Thus in Spinoza's outlook, what we call *evil* and *sin* are things which are equally willed by God; sinners necessarily sin and are necessarily punished; the flight of Peter and wickedness of Judas proceed from their respective essences, and ultimately from the omnipotence of God, just as the properties of a triangle proceed from its definition. This new notion of God's omnipotence, which reduces evil to a creature of the mind, annihilates man's free will and does not hesitate to attribute to God's omnipotence what we call sin, ends up finally, in its turn, as another blasphemy.

It can be seen that it is by entirely different ways that Descartes and Spinoza, while trying to define God's omnipotence and mistaking the relation of the possible to the existent, finish by forgetting the mystery of God, on the one hand, and the mystery of evil itself on the other.

d. *Irrationalism: Nicholas Berdyaev*

In order to heighten the importance of God's omnipotence, Descartes, detaching it from the tutelage of wisdom, and Spinoza, refusing it any freedom, ignored in different ways both the mystery of divine transcendence and the mystery of evil.

If reason, the reason of Descartes and Spinoza—and even that of St Thomas, whom we certainly do not have time to investigate —is wrong about the mystery of evil, let us then renounce reason and also the doctrinal validity of its pronouncements, both those which are on the plane of metaphysics and those which claim to be the orthodox dogmatic expression of the Judæo-Christian revelation. The reason which uses concepts, judgments and arguments, or cataphatic reason—Nicholas Berdyaev, a scorner of

---

[102]There are some types of *ens rationis* which cannot exist because they are *intrinsically contradictory* (the square circle, the best of all possible worlds). And there are others which cannot exist only because their being brought into existence is incompatible with one of their objective characteristics: 'Since these beings of reason imply in their very notion a relation to something real which is attained by the mind, they are said to be *founded on reality* . . . To say that Neptune is observed by an astronomer is to put a relation of reason in Neptune, but it is a *real* fact that the astronomer does observe Neptune. Evil is a being of reason in the sense that to think of the lack of a good that should be in a subject I am compelled to conceive that lack as if it were something. But evil does exist in a very real and very positive way, in the sense that the subject in question is indeed deprived or despoiled of a good that should exist in it.' Maritain, *The Degrees of Knowledge*, op. cit., p. 135.

metaphysics, would call it Euclidean reason—is incapable of giving any true answer about God and evil and can only end up in discrepancy and in awakening the objections of atheism.

There will remain for us the 'mystic', whose sole secret for avoiding contradictions is silence; and when it is necessary to speak, there will remain the Christian religion and its mythology. Myth is more efficacious than theology; it is capable of charming our exile, sustaining our hope and encouraging our action. This is irrationalism such as is met with, for example, in the Gnosticism of Berdyaev.

Let us try to sum up the answer to the problem of evil given by Nicholas Berdyaev. He comes back to it in every one of his works. His masters are Jacob Boehme—his 'tutelary spirit'—Schelling and Dostoyevsky.

This is how he presents the question in *Freedom and the Spirit* : 'The rationalist consciousness of contemporary man considers the existence of evil and suffering as the main obstacle to belief in God and the most important argument in favour of atheism. It seems very difficult to reconcile the existence of God, the all-powerful Bestower of mercy, with the existence of evil, which is so terrible and powerful in our world. This argument, the only serious one, has become classical. Men lose faith in God and the divine meaning of the world because they come across evil triumphant and experience sufferings devoid of all meaning, brought about by this evil.

'But in the historical development of the human consciousness faith in the divine arose just because men experienced great sufferings and felt the need of freeing themselves from the power of evil. If this evil which confounds our world had not existed man would have been content with this world here below, and the latter, free of all evil and pain, would have become his only god. Deliverance would not have been indispensable. The sufferings of life which attest the existence of evil are a great school of religion through which mankind has to pass. A life knowing nothing of evil in any shape or form would in this world have meant a self-satisfied existence. The existence of evil is not the only obstacle to our faith in God, for it is equally a proof of the existence of God, and the proof that this world is not the only nor the ultimate one. The experience of evil directs man's attention towards another world by arousing in him a discontent with this. It is pessimism and not optimism which lies at the bottom of religious experience and the religious consciousness. All religions of deliverance are pessimistic with regard to life generally and the natural world, and here Orphism and Buddhism are one with Christianity. The positive meaning of being belongs to another order and to the spiritual world. Our natural world is apparently in the victorious grip of the inane for it is dominated by corruptibility and death, animosity and hatred, egoism and discord. Man is overwhelmed by the meaningless evil of the whole of life. In religion and in faith he turns towards the world of meaning and receives strength from that world where love triumphs over hatred, union over division, and eternal life over death.'[103]

In short, evil compels men, in their minds and in the expectation of another life, to surpass their present condition. Evil, suffered in humility, is the price humanity has to pay for greatness. Dostoyevsky wished to lead his readers to this conclusion in the legend of *The Grand Inquisitor*.[104] This is certainly most valu-

---

[103]Berdyaev, *Freedom and the Spirit* (Geoffrey Bles, London, 1944), pp. 158-9.
[104]*The Brothers Karamazov*, bk. 5, ch. 5. Cf. Dostoyevsky's letter to V. A. Alexeyev, dated St Petersburg, 7th June, 1876: 'In the temptation of the Devil are summed up three colossal world ideas; eighteen centuries have gone by since then, and still there exist no problems more difficult, that is to say, more involved, and attempts to resolve them are not always successful. *The stones and the bread*—that means the actual social problem, the environment. It is not a prophecy, this sort of thing has always existed ... *You are the Son of God, and so you can do all things ... Command the earth henceforward to bring forth without labour; teach men knowledge and an order which will make their lives from now on secure. Do you not see that the principal vices and evils of men are born of hunger, cold, misery and the impossible struggle for existence?* Such is the first problem that the Spirit of Evil put to Christ. You will have to admit that it is difficult to give the right answer. *Socialism* nowadays in Europe, and even here with us, does away with Christ in everything, is primarily concerned with *bread,* makes appeal to science and affirms that all the evils of humanity have only one cause: *misery,* the struggle for existence, *people being caught up in their environment.* To this Christ replied: *Man does not live by bread alone;* in other words, he replied with the axiom of the spiritual origins of man. What the devil asked for could only suit an animal-man. Christ himself knew that man cannot be revived by bread alone. If there is no longer any spiritual life, no ideal of Beauty, man will fall into melancholy, die, lose his reason, kill himself or throw himself into pagan fantasies. And since Christ bore in himself and in his word the ideal of Beauty, he decided that it would be better to implant in people's souls the ideal of Beauty; men, carrying it in their souls, would all become brothers to one another, and would become rich. While if they

able and touches on a profound truth of the ethical order.
It even connects up with the evangelical precept of carrying the
cross.[105]

But let us see in what mythical context it will be swallowed up
by the gnosis which in Berdyaev takes the place of metaphysics
and dogma.

The fundamental error, as Berdyaev never wearies of repeating,
is to regard God as the Creator of liberty. If he has all power over
freedom, he is then responsible for its deviations and is himself
the author of sin : 'In expecting an answer to his call from man
whom he endowed with freedom, God is expecting an answer
from himself. He knows the answer beforehand, and is only playing with himself. When in difficulties, positive theology falls back
upon mystery and finds refuge in negative theology.'[106]

But the main answer given by Berdyaev to atheism is precisely
that God did not create freedom. The God of the Bible, the Holy
Trinity, the God who created the world and redeemed mankind,
the God of Christianity, is not all-powerful. From all eternity he
has always been confronted by a freedom which, originating from
the same source as God himself, is responsible for evil and beyond
all control. Thus the problem of the coexistence of a good God
with evil is resolved. The price is obvious.

At this point reference can be made to Jacob Boehme and his
gnosis. Above and beyond everything which can be expressed and
conceived in terms of being and non-being, good and evil, there
should be imagined an original Mystery like a bottomless abyss,
the *Ungrund* : this is the divine Nothing, the Absolute of apophatic

are given bread, they run the risk of becoming enemies from sheer bore-
dom.—But supposing bread and Beauty were given at the same time?—
In that case man would have taken away from him his work and
his personality, and the sacrifice of his own good for others; in short, he
would have taken away from him the whole of life, the ideal of life. For
this reason it is better to proclaim only a spiritual ideal.' This unpub-
lished letter, in the French translation of M. Wilczkowski, of which this
is a rendering, is reproduced in the first and only number of the review
Les mains libres (Paris, Desclée de Brouwer, 1955, pp. 97-9).
[105]'More than that, we rejoice in our sufferings, knowing that suffering
produces endurance, and endurance produces character, and character
produces hope, and hope does not disappoint us, because God's love has
been poured into our hearts through the Holy Spirit which has been given
to us' (Rom. 5, 3-5).
[106]Berdyaev, *The Destiny of Man* (Geoffrey Bles, London, 1937), p. 32.

theology. It is too exalted to be concerned with the world.[107]

This divine Nothing or Ungrund, in which everything is undifferentiated and unintelligible, gives birth eternally, though without ever being exhausted, to the Trinity, that is to say, the God who in relation to the world, in virtue of the drama unfolding within the divine life, is successively creator, saviour and sanctifier. No *rational* concept of the world's creation could ever be formulated : here again the *myth* alone is possible.

Born at the same time as God from the divine Nothing or Ungrund is a Freedom which is always on the move, meonic (from the Latin *meo*, to pass). This is the second manifestation of the Ungrund.

God the creator, who is declared to have all power over the world, has none over Freedom. 'Consequently God the Creator is absolved from all responsibility as regards the freedom which has engendered evil. Man is at once the child of God and the child of freedom, nothing, non-being and the meon.'[108]

And so we are presented with two forces : a finite God, driven by his inner dynamism to create the world (the word 'create' being allowed, as we have said, only a mythical meaning); and freedom, uncreated non-being (again a myth) which can answer God's appeal either positively or negatively. It first answered positively, then rebelled, whereupon evil and suffering made their appearance. How is this tragedy to be understood ?

---

[107] For the *Ungrund* in Boehme, see Alexandre Koyré, *La philosophie de Jacob Boehme* (Paris, Vrin, 1929), p. 323. 'The *Ungrund* is the eternal element of mystery in the Absolute, unrevealed and unexpressed: it is its "innermost heart"; it is what it is "before" it manifests and expresses itself; "before" it posits itself and bestows on itself its own absoluteness of being. This does not mean that the Absolute could really have being without manifesting and expressing itself, or without positing and engendering itself eternally, but simply that although it eternally illumines and fathoms its own mystery, it remains eternally "in itself" a mystery to be illumined and fathomed ... The *Ungrund* is the eternally fertile substratum of the life of the Absolute, the absolute germ which, as a germ, no longer has being, and is still nothing, but which contains in itself all that it will be ... The *Ungrund* is this absolute germ ... in so far as we consider it in its eternal remnant of non-being which never attains realization.'

[108] Berdyaev, *Freedom and the Spirit*, op. cit. Cf. Berdyaev, *Dream and Reality, An Essay in Autobiography* (Geoffrey Bles, London, 1950), p. 99 : 'I identified *Ungrund* with primordial freedom ... According to Boehme this freedom is in God ... whereas I conceived it to be outside God.'

It is primarily God's tragedy.[109] In the first act, 'God the Creator has done everything to bring light into that freedom (i.e. man's freedom) in harmony with his great conception of creation . . . he sacrifices himself for this world and for man whom he loves and yearns for.'[110] The response was first an assenting to creation, then a rebellion against God and a hatred towards him, in other words a return to the original non-being. At this moment Nothing, which is not an evil in itself, effectively becomes one.

But a second act follows: 'God appears not in the aspect of Creator but of Redeemer and Saviour, in the aspect of the suffering God who takes upon himself the sins of the world. God in the aspect of God-the-Son descends into the abyss, into the *Ungrund,* into the depths of freedom out of which springs evil as well as every kind of good . . . He descends into non-being, into the abyss of freedom that has degenerated into evil; he manifests himself not in power but in sacrifice. The Divine Sacrifice, the Divine self-crucifixion, must conquer evil, meonic freedom by enlightening it from within, without forcing it, without depriving the created world of freedom.'[111]

It can be seen where the torrent of irrationalism leads to. It turns upside down the idea of an all-powerful God, Creator of all things visible and invisible and of the whole universe of free angels and man. It substitutes the feeble image of a finite God, who is powerless in the face of a freedom as eternal as himself, and whose creative process is reduced to a myth. It submerges in myth the dogmas of the Trinity, the creation of man in a state of innocence, the fall,[112] and that of the redemptive Incarnation which is the supreme hope of Christianity.

It is indeed true that God has need of our love. But it is the absolutely transcendent God, in whom there is no shadow of potentiality and who has need, if you like, a foolish need, of our love, but only because *he has freely willed this to be so.* It is not a mythical God, a finite God, an idol who seeks our love so as to add something to himself and *in the hope of self-fulfilment.*

[109]Berdyaev, *The Destiny of Man,* op. cit., p. 37: 'The God of the Bible, the God of revelation, is by no means *actus purus:* in him are manifested an affective and emotional life, a drama inherent in all life, an inward movement, although these appear in an exoteric form.'
[110]Ibid., pp. 39-40.
[111]Ibid., pp. 34-5.
[112]It distorts the dogma of hell. Cf. below, p. 188.

3. DOES GOD LACK GOODNESS?

All the attempts to explain the coexistence of God and evil which invite us either to modify the idea of God's omnipotence by depriving it of wisdom (Descartes) or, with an irrationalism like that of Berdyaev, deliberately to substitute the mythical idea of a finite and powerless God confronted by freedom for that of an infinitely powerful God, all finally abandon us to absurdity.

But if God is all-powerful and infinitely good, how, with his infinite goodness, could he fail to create the best of all possible worlds? This is where Leibniz comes on the scene.

a. *What is God bound to do in his infinite goodness?*

What can and cannot be expected of God in his infinite goodness? Which idea of creation is compatible, and which not, with the idea of infinite goodness?

By reason of his infinite goodness, *it is impossible that God could ever will any world to be radically evil,* a self-destroying world,[113] a world in which the absurd triumphs everywhere and where evil ultimately gets the upper hand over good, and non-being over being; a world in which evil, however horrible it may be, is not simply the reverse side or the occasion[114] of the triumph of good. Let us say, to go on to the worst evils—those committed by men—that the act of the atheist is the reverse side of the act of free adoration; that it would be necessary to suppress all adoration in order to make all atheism disappear; that it is better to let the tares and the wheat grow together than to burn the field. Let us also say that the rebellion of the atheist will be vanquished if God puts pressure on his rebellious will by a ray of mercy that melts his obstinacy; but, if God respects his rebellious will and the obstinacy persists, then in order to prevent it from shattering against the divine order of things, God would have to renounce his own nature.

If evil was not permitted for the sake of a good, the action by

---

[113]Like that of Arthur Schopenhauer or Edward von Hartmann.
[114]'Bonum quod *occasionatur* ex malo, quod est ... aliqua perfectio ad quam materialiter malum se habet, sicut persecutio ad patientiam, vel aliis infinitis modis.' St Thomas, *I Sent.*, dist. 46, qu. 1, a. 3.

which God permits it, so far from being good,[115] would be perverse. Instead of following up the creative action towards more being, it would revert towards less being. It would mean that even in the eyes of God evil finds within itself its own justification, and that being can be created simply in order to be destroyed, the beloved to be hated, and minds and wills given help to be as suddenly abandoned again. God's heart would be obsessed by the negation of existence.

This is perhaps one of the most baneful ideas which can poison man's literature and imagination. But at the same time it is metaphysically the most contemptible.

The mere statement of the thesis of an infinitely good God letting evil come into what he has made is enough to make our hearts contract and prepare to make a cry of protest. So long as it remains confused this protest is ambiguous. It can be either holy or presumptuous, and tend either towards adoration or towards blasphemy. It must first be shown what makes it holy before showing what makes it hasty, illusory and anthropomorphic. It is *holy and legitimate* when it rises up against the idea that God in his infinite goodness could give licence to evil to ravage his creation and let it have the last word. It would be *foolish and presumptuous* if it wished to go beyond this and, for instance, to forbid God in the name of his infinite goodness to create a world where there appeared those forms of good which are a triumph over evil.

Let us say then that, by reason of his infinite goodness, God, if he created, is certainly bound to create a world of which the sum total will be good.

b. *What is God not bound to do in his infinite goodness?*

The mistake is to think that by reason of his infinite goodness God is bound to create rather than not to create; or to create such and such a better world, rather than some other one which is simply good; or to create such and such a world from which evil and sin would be banished rather than that other one in which, with a view to some great good, evil and sin would be admitted; or to create the 'best of all possible worlds'. True, God *could* create a world with neither evil nor sin in it. If, then, we argue that because

---

[115]'Deus ... vult permittere mala fieri. *Et hoc est bonum.*' St Thomas, I, qu. 19, a. 9, ad 3.

of his infinite goodness, he *ought* to have created such a world, we shall inevitably be led to say that he is, at least indirectly, responsible for evil, and especially for sin. But to say this, to argue in that way, is simply to make God an idol. One of the 'uses' of the mystery of evil—and they are truly countless—is simply to make us worship no idols, nothing less than God.

c. *Was God bound to create?*

An instinct, which seems genuine but is only anthropomorphic, urges us to answer that he was. God, who is all-powerful, was able to create. Anyone who can bring about something good and does not do so is blameworthy.[116]

Therefore God, to avoid being blameworthy and to remain infinite goodness, had to create.

But this reasoning, which seems exemplary, is worthless. The minor proposition is true of all created wills, which are ordered to good as potency to act, as emptiness to fullness, and which consequently, in virtue of their very nature, are bound to tend towards an increasing participation in the sovereign good, to become better and from this fact constantly to raise the level of being of the universe. We are only bound to do good because we are bound to become better and to tend towards the sovereign good.[117] It is impossible for us to tend towards God, the common good outside the universe, without becoming better and thereby raising the level of the common good inside the universe. The obligation to become better ourselves coincides ontologically with that of doing good to others.

Where the obligation to become better ceases, and with it that of raising the good in the universe, *the obligation of doing good ceases likewise.* And to become better is an impossibility for God.

Briefly, the minor proposition: 'anyone who can bring about something good and does not do so is blameworthy', is true of all created wills, because the law of their created being is to tend towards the Absolute. But if this minor is transferred anthropomorphically to the Absolute, it becomes absurd. An infinite Good-

---

[116]'To do less good than one might have done is to offend against either wisdom or goodness.' Leibniz, *Theodicy,* no. 201.
[117]'Ex hoc volumus benefici esse, non principaliter ut aliis bona velimus; sed, quia volumus quod nos decet, sequitur aliorum bonum.' Cajetan, I, qu. 19, a. 2, no. 5.

ness bound to create is, on any hypothesis, an infinite Goodness which would not be such if it did not create and which would therefore be infinite only in dependence on its own creation. And, in the perspective of a world which was not created from all eternity but which had its beginning in time, it is an infinite Goodness which would not have been infinite prior to creation and which would have become infinite at the moment of creation.[118]

Now, a God bound to exercize his creative power in order to add to his own perfection, that is, to his own Being, is properly speaking a fabrication, an idol. Metaphysically it is contradictory and unthinkable that the production of participated, created and dependent being can add anything to Being in itself, uncreated and independent, so as to raise its level. If God creates, there will not be, after creation, any more perfection, any more being, any more existence (*plus esse*); there will simply be more existing beings (*plura entia*). In the quantitative order, a foot plus an inch certainly makes more than a foot; but in the qualitative order, it is obvious that the degree of knowledge possessed by the teacher is not raised by adding the knowledge possessed by his pupils. With even more reason, God by himself does not represent less perfection, less being or less existence, than God plus the world. When we say that God created all things *for himself*, it means *in order to turn them towards him*, to turn them immediately towards their own perfection, which is a likeness of, and a participation in, his infinite Goodness.[119] It can in no way mean *in order to acquire anything by creating*. While all other beings, consciously or not, act for their own enrichment,[120] being magnanimous if they tend towards a good which debases them—God alone acts in a purely gratuitous way, without receiving anything, but simply for

---

[118]The supposition of a world created from all eternity which, viewed from the standpoint of metaphysics, quite apart from what is learnt from revelation, appears merely *possible* to those who hold an undiluted conception of divine transcendence, appeared *necessary* to the pagan philosophers, for whom the notion of divine transcendence was debased.

[119]The *divine actions*, be they necessary or free, are God himself, they do not have to be ordered to any end. But the *divine works* have an end in view. God, says St Thomas, wills them for their end, 'vult ea quae sunt ad finem, ordinari in finem,' I, qu. 19, a. 5. 'Each of them tends towards its own perfection, which is a likeness to the divine perfection and goodness,' I, qu. 44, a. 4.

[120]'Etiam in agendo intendunt aliquid acquirere.' Ibid.

the sake of giving.[121] And this is doubtless why our Lord said that 'it is more blessed to give than to receive' (Acts 20, 35).

Insofar as he is infinite Goodness, God is *able* to pour himself out in a limitless number of ways, admittedly. But does he *have* to? This is impossible and unthinkable, precisely because he is infinite Goodness. What is possible for any finite goodness is impossible for infinite goodness, that is to say, to become better and, in order to do so, to be subject to the need of pouring itself out, as potency is ordered towards act. Infinite goodness is so transcendent and free in relation to finite things that it can let them sleep out their eternal nothingness or awaken them to existence, without displacing the slightest atom of its being. If, however, God creates, and evil appears in his work, this will not be so that evil may prevail. Any concept of God's goodness which does not get as high as that is unconsciously a sacrilege. It does violence to the mystery of God, and substitutes a feeble image. *Dixi Domino: Deus meus es tu, quoniam bonorum meorum non eges.*

So much for the thesis of the necessity of creation. Let us go on to the closely related thesis of the necessary eternity of the world.

d. *If God wanted to create, did he not have to create from all eternity?*

When the philosophers of the pagan reaction, Plotinus, Porphyry and Proclus, opposed the Judæo-Christian revelation of a world having a beginning with their idea of the necessary eternity of the world, they doubtless thought to exalt the mystery of God, but their labours were all on behalf of a mere image. 'To what intent,' Proclus asked the Christians, 'did God, after an idleness of infinite duration, come to create? Because he thought it was better? But either he knew this beforehand, or he did not. To say that he did not is absurd. And if he did, why did he not set about it earlier?'[122]

The sophism about God's being able to create from all eternity

---

[121]'Sed primo Agenti, qui est agens tantum, non convenit agere propter acquisitionem alicujus finis; sed intendit solum communicare suam perfectionem, quae est ejus bonitas.' Ibid.

[122]*Commentaire sur le Timée* quoted by Pierre de Labriolle, *La réaction païenne* (Paris, L'artisan du livre, 1934), p. 484.

which we have just encountered can be recognized here.[123] Anyone who can bring about something good immediately and does not do so, is blameworthy. Therefore God, to avoid being blameworthy, must have created immediately, that is to say, from all eternity, and the world is necessarily eternal. To say that God was able to exist on his own without coexisting with the world would be to say that God has been imperfect, being able to create yet not creating.[124]

[123]According to St Thomas, I, qu. 46, a. 1 and 2, who is here in opposition both to the Averroists and the Augustinians, reason cannot *demonstrate* either that the world is eternal or that it is not. It could have been dependent from all eternity on God. It would then be eternal, not, certainly, with the eternity of God, which is absence of succession, but with the eternity of which a creature is capable, viz., an eternity of succession, an eternity of indigence. Following Plato, Boethius, *Philos. consol.*, bk. V, pr. 6, no. 14, in this context opposes God, who is *eternal,* to the world which is *perpetual.* Revelation alone can settle the question definitively and show us how the world started. For the Old Testament, Genesis, 1, 1; and II Macch. 7, 28. For the New, John, 17, 5, 24; Eph. 1, 3; I Peter 1, 20. Cf. below, p. 128, note 8.

[124]The resemblance between Eckhart and these philosophers is only apparent. To declare, as he does, that 'God, ever since he has existed, has created the world', and that 'it can be conceded that the world has been created *ab aeterno*', is, to keep to the usual meaning of these propositions, to declare that the world had no beginning in time, which is an error in a matter of faith; this is why these propositions were condemned by John XXII, *Denz.*, nos 501 and 502. That is what Eckhart *actually said*.

But what did he *mean*? He comments on the biblical text: 'In principio Deus creavit ...' This beginning, from the very depths of which God created, and out of which the creative act came, is the divine essence, the '*nunc aeternitatis*', the single moment of changeless eternity. 'It must not be imagined,' he says, 'that God waited for the moment to come when he would create the world.' This is the error he wishes to dispel from the minds of his hearers. He tried to do this by saying that God created *ab aeterno*; which, in his mind, does not mean that the world *appeared ab aeterno*. This is better understood if we say that, for him, the world is *ab aeterno Dei,* but not *ab aeterno sui.* Cf. G. Thery, 'Le procès d'Eckhart,' *Vie Spirituelle,* May 1925, p. 178. St Thomas, I, qu. 46, a 1, ad 6, had written: 'Although God has had the *eternal will* to produce an effect, it does not follow that he has produced an *eternal effect* ... God produces both the substance of the world and time. And so it should not be imagined that he acts after having not acted, as if everything was happening for him in time. But it should be thought that he has given time to the world, as and when he wanted.' The same thought is developed by St Augustine, *Confessions,* bk. XI, ch. XIII & XIV, nos 15-17: 'And so there has not been a time when You have done nothing, since You have made time itself.'

It is easy to see how these philosophers who treated Christianity with disdain could not get away from anthropomorphism. The idea they formed of God was too low. They did not understand the exaltedness of God's liberty which resides in an absolute and dominating indifference [125] in regard to the universe, so that he can either create or not create, create this thing or that, create a world with no beginning in time or one with a beginning in time, exist on his own or coexist with the unfolding of time—without being increased or diminished or in any way affected. This is the whole mystery of the transcendence of God's freedom in regard to the world, perhaps even more than the fact of creation in time, which was revealed to us in the great prayer of Christ: 'And now, Father, glorify thou me in thy own presence with the glory which I had with thee before the world was made . . . Father, I desire that they also, whom thou hast given me, may be with me where I am, to behold my glory which thou hast given me in thy love for me before the foundation of the world' (John 17, 5, 24). Or in the words of St Paul about God: 'He chose us in him before the foundation of the world, that we should be holy and blameless before him' (Eph. 1, 4).

It is one and the same illusion to believe that because of his infinite goodness God is bound either to create, and create from all eternity, or to create the best of all possible worlds.

e. God was able to create worlds better than ours

Once again it is the same inevitable syllogism: you grant, they say, that God was able to create a better world than ours; therefore, in virtue of his infinite goodness, he should have done so. It may even be added: an infinitely good God must only create the best of all possible worlds.

[125]It is necessary to make with St Thomas, *I Contra Gent.*, ch. 82, a distinction between two sorts of indifference or indetermination. On the one hand, the *indifference of poverty and imperfection*; for example, that of a mind which has not yet emerged from hesitation. On the other, the *indifference of plenitude and perfection*: that of a strength so perfect and sure of itself that it can make use of any instrument whatever to attain its end. The divine will necessarily desires infinite Goodness, and necessarily attains it. Because of this it is necessarily fulfilled and gratified: 'finis ejus a nullo aliorum dependet, quum tamen ipsa fini suo perfectissime sit unita.' Whether or not it wills the world does not bring the divine will either nearer to or further from its end, and thus it is absolutely indifferent towards all created things.

To this line of reasoning Leibniz sees only one answer, which is to deny the major proposition[126] : he will not agree that God was able to make a better world. Yet he knows well enough that evil, and a great deal of it, exists in our world. He learnt from St Augustine[127] that evil is only permitted for some good, that the world in which it appears draws certain advantages from it and becomes thereby better than it would otherwise have been. All this is quite correct; and consequently it is correct to say that this present world is good. Would a better world be possible? Leibniz says no, and St Thomas says yes. Which of these two answers opens, and which closes, the door to the mystery of God's transcendence?

St Thomas's view is simple and profound. On the one hand, he says, it is impossible that God should not love himself. The divine will is necessarily directed towards the divine being and goodness.

On the other hand it is evident that if God creates, it is in order to manifest and give outward expression to the infinite and uncreated good that he is in himself.

Let us suppose the impossibility that some universe is capable of manifesting and adequately expressing the infinite, uncreated good. God, having decided to create, could in his wisdom will only this world, he would necessarily will it and could will no other. But the point is that the hypothesis is absurd : a world adequately expressing the infinite, uncreated good is not creatable. There is a contradiction in terms.

An unbridgeable gap separates the infinite, uncreated good from the whole universe of created and creatable things. He is completely disproportionate to them, *improportionabiliter excedens*

---

[126]He does so by figuring it as the minor, for example in the *Summary:* 'Whoever does not take the best course lacks either power or knowledge or goodness. God has not taken the best course by creating this world, therefore God has lacked power or knowledge or goodness.' Leibniz will deny the minor of this objection.

It is the universal principle that Leibniz, as a philosopher, sets down as the major. But in the theological syllogism it is always the revealed proposition—in this case the divine omnipotence and goodness—which figures as the major. The minor is only an instrument of investigation into the content of the revealed major. Cf. St Thomas, I, qu. 1, a. 4, ad 2. And F. Marin-Sola, *L'evolution homogène du dogme catholique* (St Paul, Fribourg, 1924), vol. 1.

[127]He quotes St Thomas with deference, but obviously without having read him.

res creatas. The final good to which the whole movement and
progress of our universe is directed—and by this is understood its
intrinsic, immanent common good, its supreme level of existence
—is a finite, created good essentially incapable of equalling the
infinite uncreated good. Even for God it will never be possible to
pour out the fullness of uncreated being into the vessels of created
beings, or to enclose the infinite within the finite. Whatever world
he decides to make, what will be manifested of his infinite fullness
will never be equivalent to what remains to be manifested. There
will always be an infinite margin in which other worlds could
occur.

It was more or less at the same point that St Thomas, in both
the *De potentia*[128] and the *Summa*,[129] asked the question :
Could God make the things which he does not make? He meets
with two types of error. First, that of ancient philosophers who
thought God had made the world not by free will but by natural
necessity. And secondly, that of theologians such as Abelard[130]—
and later of Leibniz—who thought God's power was limited by his
wisdom and justice to choosing the present course of things. But
'the order imprinted in things by the divine wisdom, in which the
rationale of justice consists, could never be equal to the divine
wisdom or enclose it within its limitations, *non adaequat divinam
sapientiam, ut sic divina sapientia limitetur ad hunc ordinem'.*
When the work is proportionate to the end, the wisdom of the
craftsman is limited to a given order. 'But the divine goodness is
an end which goes disproportionately beyond created things.
Whence it results that the divine wisdom is not determined to a
given order of things to the extent that no other course of things
could have been put into being. Consequently it must be said
absolutely that God can do other things than those which he actually does';[131] and that 'whatever he has made, he could make
something better still'.[132]

The same ideas are expressed in the *De potentia.* The natural
end of the divine will is the divine goodness, which it is impossible
for it not to desire. What God demands of creatures is to manifest

---

[128]Qu. I, a. 5.
[129]I, qu. 25, a. 5.
[130]For the condemnation of Abelard, cf. above, p. 92.
[131]I, qu. 25, a. 5.
[132]I, qu. 25, a. 6.

this goodness. But they are incapable of doing it adequately, and
so the divine will, without prejudice to its wisdom, can always go
beyond its own realizations. The error of Abelard—and others
after him—was to imagine that the creation of anything at all can
be *commensuratum,* an adequate means of expressing the infinite
goodness of God, and consequently impose itself as necessary.[133]
For the rest, if it is supposed that God chose to create this present
world, it necessarily follows that this present world should exist :
this necessity follows logically from the supposition.

f. *The distinction between a) absolute divine power, and b)
subordinated divine powers, subdivided into ordinary and extraordinary*

The margin separating the unlimited amplitude of the divine
power and what it actually chooses to do is denoted by the distinction between the *absolute divine power* and the *subordinated
divine power.* It is important to have a clear idea of this distinction.
'Among ourselves . . . that which is in our power need not proceed
from a just will and a wise intelligence. But in God, power and
essence, will and intelligence, wisdom and justice, all are one and
the same thing. Therefore there can be nothing in his power which
is not at the same time in his just will and wise intelligence.[134] But
since the divine will is not determined necessarily to any particular
choice, nothing prevents there being in the sphere of the divine
power something which God does not want to realize and which is
not included in the order which he has imposed upon things . . .
As to what is produced by the divine power considered in itself,
it can be said that God can do it according to his *absolute power*;
and that comprises everything by which the reason for a thing's
existence can be preserved. As to what is produced by the divine
power in so far as it carries out the decision of his just will, it can be
said that God can do it according to his *subordinated power.'*[135]

Use, therefore, may be made of the opposition of absolute
power to subordinated power to keep in mind the infinite distance

---

[133]*De potentia,* loc. cit., qu. 1, a. 5.
[134]By this St Thomas does away with an anthropomorphic way of
opposing the *absolute power* (or all that God can do *without* taking his
wisdom and justice into account) to the *subordinated power* (or all that
God does *while* taking into account his wisdom and justice).
[135]I, qu. 25, a. 5, ad 1.

which exists between the worlds which God might have made in his wisdom and goodness, and the world which he freely decreed to make, still in his wisdom and goodness. And in this world of his *subordinated power,* it can be added that God can act either in accordance with the rules of his *ordinary* power or, in a miraculous way, according to his *extraordinary* power.

It is clear that these distinctions between absolute power on the one hand, and subordinated power, with its subdivision into ordinary and extraordinary, on the other, qualify the divine power not according to what it is *in itself,* but in relation to its *different effects.*[136]

g. *Could God make this present world better?*

God could, according to his absolute power, make better worlds than ours. But could he, and might he now still, make this present world, created according to his subordinated power, better than it is?

The question is not whether God could add to it any new parts or nobler and more numerous types of being, or include it in some vaster and richer set of relationships. This would be to produce another world.[137]

The question is really whether the things in this world, being what they essentially are, could be better in their arrangement or in their qualities. The question is asked specially in connection with free beings: could men be wiser and more virtuous?[138] Could the level of the world's internal order be raised, thereby reflecting better the goodness of its supreme End?[139]

To this question there must be no hesitation about answering that all this would indeed be possible. God could, and still may, make this present world better. This does not make the answer to the problem of evil any easier. We are not looking for an easy answer but for a true one : and our minds are once again obliged to lose themselves in the transcendence of the mystery of God.

---

[136]The distinction between *absolute* and *subordinated* divine power, and the subdivision of the latter into ordinary and extraordinary power, is found again, though in a misleading sense, in Spinoza, *Metaphysical Reflections,* Part II, ch. 9.

[137]*I Sent.,* dist. 44, qu. 1, a. 2; I, qu. 25, a. 6, ad 3.

[138]I, qu. 25, a. 6.

[139]*I Sent.,* loc. cit.

The whole course of *events in nature* is governed by the divine omnipotence, which does not violate the natures of things, but prepares necessary causes for necessary effects, contingent causes for contingent effects, and chance causes for chance effects.[140] And we know that the evolution of the universe is not a mechanical activity but the unfolding of a story.[141] But then, instead of letting his *ordinary* power act, could not God intervene, not necessarily all the time—for then we would have had another world and it would be more expedient to change the natures of things— but at least more often, according to his *extraordinary* power, to modify the course of events, to avert certain combinations of circumstances which are a scandal for us, as for example when a church collapses on the assembled faithful at prayer, or to forestall numberless misfortunes which fall no less upon the good than the evil? Indeed, God could.

And even on the *plane of freedom*, in this world of fallen and redeemed humanity which is ours, could not God put a brake on the progress of evil? We know that he does not will sin in any way. But why allow sin to triumph so much? Why give evil so many entries through which it can rush into what he has created? Why leave the field open and assure it such terrible fair play, and let it display its frightening conflict of opposites? Could not God, who has 'laid the foundations of the earth . . . and shut in the sea behind bars' (Job 38, 4, 8), come out of his silence and shatter the im-

---

[140]St Thomas, I, qu. 19, a. 8. What is *by chance* or *fortuitous* in respect of particular causes, is ordered, *provisum,* in respect of the universal Cause of all being, I, qu. 22, a. 2, ad 1.

[141]'The solar system is no more a machine than the universe itself. It has resulted from the long historical evolution of a multitude of inter-acting factors not in advance unified within the causality of any natural agent which was the proper cause of the unity of the whole. Undoubt-edly the intelligent first Cause has directed this historical evolution according to his creative design, but God is not a mere maker of clocks and watches but a maker of beings with their own inbuilt principle of action, The world is a republic of such beings, not a clock; and God's infallible causality, by the very fact that it is transcendent, makes events happen in accordance with their natural condition, causing necessary events to happen by necessity, contingent events contingently, and fortuit-ous events by chance.' Jacques Maritain, 'Réflexions sur la nécessité et la contingence,' in *Raison et raisons* (Paris, Luf, 1947), p. 62. This essay does not appear in the English version of this book: *Translator's note.*

petus of evil more often and prevent certain excessive horrors?[142]
He could. Yet at the same time there would also disappear from
the earth a certain cry to him from out of our anguish, a certain
limitlessness of our self-surrender, and that quality which St Paul
loved so much in Abraham, our father in faith : He 'believed, hoping against hope' (Rom. 4, 18).

Would the world as a whole be better? Perhaps it would. But
if God creates, what is he bound to do in virtue of his justice, wisdom and infinite goodness? He is bound to make a good world in
which evil cannot ultimately prevail over good. Is there a level
or degree of goodness in the world that is not infinitely insufficient
to express infinite Goodness? Is there a world, better than such and
such another one, that God would have to choose if he did not
want to be blameworthy? Here again is the illusion which makes
us think that God's justice and wisdom, and especially his goodness, would be better to the extent that the world he created was
better—in which case he would have to create an infinitely good
world—and that, if he decides to create, he is constrained to make
the best of all possible worlds.

h. *Could God who could make our world 'better', improve on
its making?*

St Thomas carefully distinguishes two propositions which have
become confused in Leibniz : 1. God could make things *better*;
2. God could not improve on the making of the things he has
made.[143]

In other words, God could put more justice, wisdom and love
into our world; but he could not put more justice, wisdom or love
into his making of the world. Once given the level of existence
and goodness, the quality and intensity of the ultimate common
good to which God—taking into account from all eternity the
free acts of assent he makes us give to his love and of the free refusals with which we oppose his grace—decides to raise the

[142]I am thinking particularly of the harrowing story of the raft of the
Medusa. Or of the page where Fr Lenz tells of the arrival at Dachau, in
November, 1942, of six or seven hundred prisoners, mostly Russians, sealed
up in railway trucks in which scenes of cannibalism took place. *Christus
in Dachau oder Christus der Sieger* (Vienna, 1957), p. 355, English trans.
It is the evil contrived by man's free will, not the evil of nature, which is
the more frightful.
[143]I, qu. 25, a. 6, ad 1.

universe, it is absolutely certain that it is with truly infinite justice, wisdom and love that God orders everything to this ultimate common good, both necessary and contingent things, free and fortuitous things, the progress of good and the ravages of evil.

i. *The creative act, fundamentally identical with God, is completely free in regard to what it produces*

Let us turn our attention once more towards the divine mystery. Whether he creates or not, whether he creates one particular world or other better ones, God, since he is the absolute Being, will be neither diminished nor increased. Cajetan expressed this great mystery by saying that the act of willing the world, the creative act, is a 'completely free voluntary perfection', that is to say, able to exist or not exist, without adding to or taking away from God. Fundamentally identical with the divine essence, the creative act is, as regards what it produces, completely free at its point of application, and without being in any way modified intrinsically it can, if it is exercized, make the world appear out of nothing.[144] The world, or any possible world one might think of, would never be anything but a mixture of potency and act, of being and non-being. It will always represent sufficient reality for God to be able to say 'Let it be!' and sufficient nothingness not to be adequate or, consequently, necessary to God's glory. God's indifference is absolute and dominating, and he is utterly and completely free in regard to all possible universes. If he creates, then being infinite wisdom he will only be bound to regulate the universe, together with the evil which ravages it, so that there is some ultimate triumph of good.

If it is asked for what reason God, who in his infinite wisdom could equally well create or not create, in fact decides to create, the only answer which can be given, and it is quite sufficient, is: in order to communicate a finite participation in his infinite splendour. And if it is asked for what reason he decides to create one world rather than another one, less good or more so, the

---

[144]'If God willed nothing other than himself, he would be as perfect as he is now; to will other things adds no perfection to him ... It must be acknowledged, without any objection, that for God to will other things is a voluntary and absolutely free perfection.' Cajetan, I, qu. 19, a. 2, nos II and III. This perfection is free inasmuch as it extends freely to exterior things which can either exist or not exist. John of Saint-Thomas, I, qu. 19; disp. 4, a. 4, no. 16.

answer is much the same : in order to communicate one sort of finite participation in his infinite splendour rather than another, less good or more so.

j. A comparison

If a comparison is needed to help sustain the imagination, there is one suggested by St Paul. Think of a sculptor whose inspiration had become so full that he lost all hope of expressing it sufficiently in stone. This happened with Michelangelo. who at the end of his life said that the whole of painting and sculpture were too poor to attract the soul finally turned towards the Love which died on the cross. The sculptor, who had such mastery over the ends and means of his art, could, with complete indifference, give up or go on with his sculpturing—and if he went on with it, he could choose any subject whatsoever : a vase, a bust, a statue or a group, all things being absolutely unequal to his idea. Yet the works which came from his hand would all bear witness, according to their resources and in different degrees, to his supreme mastery.

k. The notion of the best of all possible worlds is contradictory

The notion of the best of all possible worlds is by definition un-realizable—like that of the fastest possible speed—for 'whatever thing he has made, God could make a better one',[145] and so on

[145]'However exalted the external glory of God as shown forth by creatures may be, one can always conceive a further glory which would be more excellent, and there would never be any necessity to stop doing this. Consequently God himself would never be able to choose to realize the best. He will always choose something lesser, *nunquam Deus potest eligere id quod praestantissimum est, sed semper eligit aliquid minus*; for creation will always offer the possibility of better realizations to give a greater glory to God. *Thus God could never be bound to choose the best.*' John of Saint-Thomas, I, qu. 19; disp. 4, a. 7, no. 16.

Cajetan, I, qu. 25, a. 6, nos III-VII, points out the error of those who deny that there is an infinity of possible worlds of which each is better than the one before. Basically, they imagine that by rising indefinitely from one created world to a better one it should be possible to close the gap between the created and the uncreated, thereby arriving at a parti-cular created world to which not the slightest addition could be made without it forthwith becoming uncreated.

Malebranche, in his *De la nature et de la grâce,* maintains in his turn that if God does create he can only create a perfect world, and adds that therefore the Incarnation of the World was required, for without it the world would have been unworthy of God. On Fénelon's 'Réfutation du système du P. Malebranche', cf. H. Leclère, in *Revue Thomiste,* 1953, pp. 347 et seq.

indefinitely. To demand that God, to be above reproach, must make the best of all possible worlds is to demand him to make what is not feasible, and to give existence to something absurd.

Yet the thesis according to which there is, among the infinite multitude of possible worlds, one which is the best, and in consideration of which God was morally bound to come out of himself to create, is the keystone of the *Theodicy* and the whole argument with which Leibniz opposed Bayle. Why did this thesis necessarily include in itself a double incoherence : that of the Absolute morally bound to create, and that of the best of all possible worlds?

Leibniz admitted that there is an infinite number of possible worlds, starting with our world and descending towards nothingness; but there is no possible world going up from ours towards God. Now the gap in the first case, though infinitely divisible, is finite; while that in the second is strictly infinite. How could this inconsistency not have struck him? It is because, for want of a sufficiently strong metaphysical view—or a theological view aided by faith—to raise him up to the mystery of the Creator's sovereign dominating indifference, he was forced to maintain that our world is the best of worlds, and that if any better world was possible and God had not given it reality, God would not be above reproach, and would not be God.[146]

[146]Leibniz does not doubt that the multitude of possible worlds is infinite. To the objection that 'each possible universe can be better than the last *ad infinitum*', he can really give only one reply: that in this case it would be necessary to stop believing in God: 'If this opinion were true it would follow that God had produced none of them; for he is incapable of acting without reason, and this would be to act against reason.'

And so he has to resort to subterfuges, imagining that the infinite multitude of possible worlds is arranged like a pyramid, whose apex is taken by our world, and which has no base.

He considers that even were it possible to go on indefinitely from one particular creature to another, this ought not to be applied to the universe, which, 'extended throughout all eternity to come, is infinite.' Cajetan replied that the universe, even if infinite, would only be so as part of a genus: on top of a universe composed of an infinity of minerals and endowed with everlastingness, it is possible to suppose another universe of plants, then another of animals, then of men, and then of angels, of which each is more resplendent than the last.

Leibniz compares God, had he decreed a world which was not the most perfect, to a workman who sets out to make a sphere without deciding its diameter. But though it may be absurd to make a sphere without first deciding its diameter, it is not absurd to choose out of an infinity of possible spheres, one particular sphere with one particular diameter. Cf. *Theodicy*, nos 195-6, and 416.

4. THE 'LEIBNIZIAN THEODICY'

So, at the threshold of the eighteenth century, it was a pale image of the true God that the *Theodicy*, with a manifestly theistic intention, raised against the attacks of the *Dictionnaire historique et critique* of Bayle.[147]

a. *The guiding thread of the 'Theodicy'*

The depths of the twofold mystery of God and evil hid themselves from Leibniz's mind. The *Theodicy* is admittedly a work written for the glory of God, the God of the philosophy of the Enlightenment and the impetus which runs right through it has as such the value of a testimony.[148]

But the mystery of God, even as it has revealed itself to the mind,

---

[147]The *Theodicy* came out in 1710. Pierre Bayle, born in 1647 of Protestant parents, was converted to Catholicism after a month's stay in Toulouse, on 19 March, 1669. The following year, when he had been studying only four or five months in the Jesuit college, 'the excessive worship which he saw given to creatures having seemed very suspect to him, and philosophy having made him more aware of the impossibility of transubstantiation' (these are his own words) he reverted to Protestantism. He died in 1706 in Rotterdam, where he had come into conflict with the Protestant ministers. The *Dictionnaire* appeared for the first time in 1697. Its intentions are similar to those of the *Encyclopédie*, and also to Voltaire's *Dictionnaire philosophique,* in which we read, in the article on *Bien*: 'The question of good and evil remains an inextricable chaos for those who seek in good faith; it is an intellectual game for those who make disputations: they are convicts playing with their chains ... Let us write at the end of almost every chapter of metaphysics what the Roman judges wrote when they did not understand a lawsuit: N.L., *non liquet,* it is not clear.' This is what Voltaire elsewhere likes euphemistically to describe as 'wanting to be not a philosopher but a man'.

'Convicts playing with their chains'? Yet it is by no means a game, this torturing question which the depths of the human mind throw up time and again, 'cet ardent sanglot qui roule d'âge en âge'. Not to seek deliverance from it would be to give up being a man.

[148]The Christianity professed by Leibniz in the *Preface to the Theodicy* is really only a natural religion. *It is completely emptied of all its mystery*: 'Jesus Christ succeeded in making natural religion pass into law, and in giving it the authority of a public dogma. He did on his own what so many philosophers had tried in vain to do: and since the Christians at last had the upper hand over the Roman Empire and domination over the greater part of the known world, the religion of the wise men became that of the people. Mahomet, at a later date, did not stray from these great dogmas of natural theology ...'

since the creation of the world, through its workings (Rom. 1, 20) has become debased in it, and notably in connection with this question of evil. The guiding thread of the whole work, which maintains the argument from start to finish, is that, if God is infinitely good, he could only make the best things. Not for a moment does Leibniz dream of disputing this principle of his opponent. No statement seemed to him more certain.

Leibniz, therefore, presupposes in God an inclination which necessarily carries him to create, and to create the best world. Doubtless it is not comparable with the essential inclination which leads him to love himself. It is an inclination which requires that God, by reason of his infinite goodness and wisdom, should necessarily will to choose the best among several intrinsically possible alternatives. According to Leibniz it represents neither a constraint nor a servitude nor a need nor a metaphysical necessity, which would have to be extended indefinitely to everything which does not imply a contradiction. It represents a moral necessity, a happy necessity which is entirely a reason for praising God.[149]

149Leibniz writes: 'The love which God bears for himself is essential to him, but this is by no means true of the love of his (external) glory or the will to procure it: the love which he has for himself has by no means driven him of necessity to external actions; these were free.' *Theodicy*, no. 233. Very true. But less true is the following: 'God's creating decree is free: God is inclined to everything good; the good, and even the best, disposes him to act; but it does not necessitate him: for his choice does not render impossible that which is distinct from the better, nor does it make what he omits imply any contradiction. Therefore there is in God a liberty exempt not only from *constraint,* but also from *necessity.* By this I mean *metaphysical necessity*; for it is by *moral necessity* that the all-knowing is bound to choose the best.' Ibid., no. 230. 'God has chosen from among different alternatives, all of them possible: thus, *metaphysically* speaking, he could have chosen or done what was not the best; but he could not have done so *morally* speaking.' Ibid., no. 234. 'The *metaphysical necessity,* in respect of God's actions *ad extra,* is as absurd as the *moral necessity* is worthy of him.' Ibid., no. 175.
We impugn the transcendence of God and ignore his absolute indifference in regard to all created things, when we assume in him a moral necessity to create. He is able to create or not create: if he creates, the only thing to which he is bound, under pain of destroying his own nature, is to create a good world in which evil does not ultimately prevail over good.
But to proclaim the sovereign indifference with which the creative act can realize this or that possible world is a completely different thing from saying with Descartes that God can make metaphysically possible what is metaphysically impossible, that he can make a square circle or a valley without mountains. Leibniz is right to oppose Descartes in this. He is

But precisely here is concealed the sophism, the anthropomorphism, of which Leibniz is victim. If there is an obligation or moral necessity for a being to choose what is good and better, it is because there is an obligation or moral necessity for this being, by doing what is good and better, to become better and tend towards the sovereign Good, to which it is subordinated as potency to act, the lower to the higher, or the imperfect to the perfect.

Where the obligation or moral necessity to become better is removed, the *moral necessity*, though certainly not the *possibility*, of doing good is removed with it.

b. *To pass from the 'fittingness' of the creative act to its 'moral necessity' is to cover an infinite distance*

The *fittingness* of doing good is not removed either. Where there is supreme abundance and supreme actualization, there is also, from that very fact, supreme fitness in giving oneself and pouring oneself out on others,[150] but not the slightest suggestion of any obligation. If a world is created, it will be by an act of sovereign liberty. But there will be a metaphysical necessity that this world should be turned towards God according to the way in which the divine perfection can be participated in by each of its creatures; and there will be a metaphysical necessity that this world should

again right to protest against the aberration which bestows on God the *freedom of indifference to good and evil*, so that nothing would be unjust or morally evil in God's view, or before he prohibited it, and that, without this prohibition, it would be a matter of indifference whether we loved God or hated him. Ibid., nos. 175, 176. St Thomas writes: 'To say that what is just depends only on the will of God (not on his understanding), is to say that the divine will does not proceed according to the order of his wisdom; which is a blasphemy.' *De ver.*, qu. 23, a. 6. Cf. above, p. 93.

[150]'If even the things of nature, to the extent that they become more perfect, communicate their own good to all around them, this can be said with greater truth of the divine will to make others share in its own goodness, so far as this is possible. God, therefore, desires himself as his own end; and he wills that creatures be directed to this end, inasmuch as it befits the divine Goodness to pour itself out in them.' St Thomas, I, qu. 1, a. 2: *Utrum Deus velit alia a se?*

Fr Garrigou-Lagrange, *Dieu, son existence et sa nature* (Paris, Beauchesne, 1919), vol. II, p. 661, writes: 'The creative act is free . . . Does this mean that it is without motive or sufficient reason? Not at all. It is highly fitting that God should create. But is it fitting to such an extent that this constitutes a *moral necessity*, as Leibniz insists? Does it follow that he would be neither good nor wise if he did not create and that a necessary perfection would be lacking in him? By no means.'

be good, that it should not be evil, and that evil, however vast, far-reaching and terrible it may be, should not prevail.

Between the view of those who acknowledge in God a supreme *fittingness* in communicating himself externally, and the view of those who posit in God a *moral necessity* to communicate himself thus, there is an infinite gap. Leibniz leapt across, not realizing that by doing so he destroyed the mystery of divine transcendence and changed the true God to an idol.[151]

Such are the wonderful depths of the unfathomable mystery of God's good pleasure and of what St Paul calls 'the designs of his will' (Eph. 1, 11).

c. *The origins of the Leibnizian notion of 'metaphysical evil'*

Failing to rise to the mystery of the freedom of the creative act, Leibniz was forced to answer those who took evil as a pretext for disputing either the divine omnipotence or goodness by stating that God had created the best of all possible worlds.

What is the value of the axiom which Leibniz loved to quote, according to which 'a lesser good is an evil if it prevents a greater good, *minus bonum habet rationem mali*'.[152] It cannot mean that a lesser good would be *in itself* an evil. It means quite simply that a lesser good can be *accidentally* an evil, that is, exactly to the extent to which it is accompanied, *hic et nunc,* by a privation, or absence of some due good, in the being to which it happens.

But Leibniz' God is bound to create the best of worlds. Any creation of lesser worlds, however good they might be, would for him be evil, because it would prevent him from doing what he is bound to do. Always for Leibniz' God the claims to existence of the best of worlds represent something good and legitimate; the claims to existence of all the other worlds only represent an attempt at usurpation, something evil and illegitimate. Only the best world is a good, and any lesser world an evil *in relation to the choice of the creative act*. But even admitting this, what is to stop anyone

---

[151]According to the First Vatican Council, God created 'by an utterly free design', *Denz.*, no. 1783; 'by a will exempt from all necessity,' *Denz.*, no. 1805. The following proposition of Rosmini was condemned by Leo XIII: 'The love by which God loves himself even in his creatures, and which is the reason why he determined to create, constitutes a *moral necessity*, which in the sovereignly perfect Being is always followed by its effect', *Denz.*, no. 1908.

[152]*Theodicy*, nos 8, 195; and end of the *Summary*.

saying that only the best world is a good and that any lesser world is, *metaphysically and in itself*, an evil?

It would appear that it was by following this path that Leibniz ended up with his strange notion of 'metaphysical evil', which, he says, 'consists merely in imperfection',[153] and which made him consider as an evil something which is not a privation but a mere limitation, essential to every creature as such. 'There was,' he writes, 'an original (*sic*) imperfection in creatures before sin, because creatures are essentially limited, from which it follows that they could never know everything and can deceive themselves and make other mistakes'; with the result that 'the source of evil must be sought in the very idea of a creature's nature' and 'in the region of eternal truths'.[154]

This is a strange turning upside down of optimism : in this best of worlds, any creature, from the fact that it is a creature, is evil; God alone is good. How, then, can Genesis (1, 31) say : 'God saw everything that he had made, and behold, it was very good'?

5. A WORLD WITH EVIL MAY BE INCOMPARABLY BETTER THAN OTHER WORLDS WITHOUT EVIL

Leibniz knew this.[155] He even quoted the *felix culpa*, which is sung 'on the eve of Easter Sunday in the churches of the Roman rite'.[156] But, it could be asked, to what are reduced the limitless perspectives opened up by the *Exsultet* for eyes which can only see in Christ the founder of natural religion. Neither the mystery of the depths of the redemptive Incarnation, nor the correlative mystery of the depths of sin can assume their true dimensions in the mind of Leibniz.

The *felix culpa* introduces us directly to the world of faith in the Judæo-Christian revelation. God is infinitely good and powerful, he could not create a world which was evil in itself, nor create the best of all possible worlds, he would not allow evil to come into his work if he was not sufficiently good and powerful to order it to some mysterious good—these metaphysical certainties,

[153]*Theodicy*, no. 21.
[154]*Theodicy*, no. 20.
[155]'The best alternative is not always that which tends to avoid evil, since it can happen that evil may be accompanied by a greater good.' *Summary.*
[156]*Theodicy*, nos. 9 and 10.

which are immovable, and so apparent to us, remain definitively settled; but touched by the light of divine revelation they require to be transferred from the level of the reason to that of faith, from the level of the natural world to that of the world of grace. The divine power and goodness of which revelation speaks to us are situated, in effect, at a point to which reason cannot attain. They are the power and goodness of the one God in three Persons who at a first moment of time freely made the world emerge from out of nothing; who, in creating the first man, clothed him with the gifts of original righteousness, bestowed on him his friendship and exempted him from suffering and death; of a God who only allowed the irruption of the evil of sin into this first universe of creation because he foresaw the setting up of a universe of redemption which as a whole would be better, in which the head of humanity would no longer be Adam, a mere man, but the second Adam, or the Word made flesh. It is in relation to these revealed truths that the mystery of evil in man, the evil of guilt and the evil of punishment will require from now on to be explored. And it is right up on this highest level that these metaphysical certainties which we have recalled to mind and which we cannot deny must be found again.

But before we do this, we must linger for a moment over the consideration of the evil in nature. To say that a world with evil may be better than a world without evil is to pose some very pressing questions, even at the level of the evil in nature, and even if the mind is metaphysically compelled to give its assent. It will wish to know as nearly as possible how what is apparently so paradoxical an axiom can be verified, and to be inwardly convinced about the way in which the suppression of evils might bring about the suppression likewise of great good. The early doctors recalled in this connection certain considerations of a very general sort : no new generation without destruction of plants, no sensitivity without vulnerability, etc. Modern views on the formation of the world and the evolution of life would seem able to expand these facts and dispel petty objections, and bring some light to bear on the subject.

So there will be a short chapter devoted to the evil in nature before we go on to discuss, in relation to man, the evil of sin and the evil of punishment.

CHAPTER FIVE

The Evil in Nature

Earlier teachers like St Thomas are very restrained on the question of evil in nature. They content themselves with pointing out that 'natural agents intend not a *privation* or corruption, but a *form,* an advantage, which does, it is true, involve the destruction of another form; so that the generation of one thing does involve the corruption of another : the lion killing the hind seeks its own preservation and this cannot be obtained without the slaughter of other animals'; destruction is tolerated for the sake of universal order.[1] 'He who is responsible (*provisor*) for the universal good permits that there should be some deficiency in particular cases in order that the good of the whole shall not be thwarted. Hence the corruptions and deficiencies in natural things go against a particular nature, *but are within the design of nature as a whole,* inasmuch as the deficiency which affects one thing serves the good of another or even of the whole universe. *For the corruption of one thing is the generation of another, and this accounts for the recurrence of species.* And since it is God who is universally responsible for all being, it is part of his providence to permit that there should be certain deficiencies in particular things in order that the perfect good of the universe shall not be thwarted. *For if all evils were suppressed, many good things would be missing from the universe.* The life of the lion is not possible without the slaughter of animals . . .'[2] *'Many good things would be suppressed if God did not per-*

---

[1] St Thomas, I, qu. 19, a. 9—From the fact that 'the destruction of one thing is the generation of another', Aristotle thought he could deduce the perpetuity of the world. *De generatione et corruptione,* bk. I, ch. 3, 318, 25. See St Thomas's *Commentarium,* less. 7, text 17.
[2] I, qu. 22, a. 2, ad 2. St Thomas does not want it to be thought that lions ate grass in the earthly paradise: 'There are those who say that the animals which are now savage and kill others were gentle not only towards man but even to other animals. But this is completely unreasonable. The sin of man has not changed the nature of animals, has not meant that those which are by nature carnivorous, like lions and vultures, would otherwise have been grazing animals.' I, qu. 96, a. 1, ad 2.

mit any evil to exist. Fire cannot be engendered without the air becoming fouled, the life of the lion cannot be preserved without the ass being slaughtered.'[3]

Let us follow this line of reasoning to its conclusion. Physical evil is a reality. 'But this real evil is finally absorbed into the good which explains it, it has to do with a particular order which is instrumental to and explicable in terms of the universal order. We should consider the case of good or evil in animals, not as regards man who uses them, but as regards their own particular order : for an animal, to be lame is contrary to the law of its particular order; this is true, too, of hens which kill their chicks, which is not in accord with the particular order of that type of being; or of ants, drugged and perverse, which, in order to enjoy the sweet secretion they get from them, maintain domesticated insects that destroy the ants' eggs or suck their blood. In these cases, the particular order disturbed is instrumental in regard to the universal order. *In regard to the universal order* it is not evil but good that this animal should be lame, or that hen devour her chicks, or those ants be intoxicated by the drug.'[4] When a dog, for instance, is deficient as regards the particular law of canine nature, it is only obeying the universal law of nature, in virtue of which it was born with such a deficiency. It is involved only in the ontological, not the moral order.[5] The error would lie in explaining the evil in man which, as we know from revelation, springs from the moral evils of sin or punishment, in the same way as we would explain the physical evil in animals, and to say 'that any evil committed or suffered by a man is an evil in relation to the individual in question, but in relation to the order of the universe, it is a good'.[6]

The earlier thinkers knew that beings devour one another, that the bigger eat the smaller and so on, in order themselves to be consumed in the end by micro-organisms, and that

'La faim sacrée est un long meurtre légitime
Des profondeurs de l'ombre aux cieux resplendissants'.

[3]I, qu. 48, a. 2.
[4]Maritain, *Neuf leçons sur les notions premières de la philosophie morale,* op. cit., p. 71. These anomalies with regard to one particular order result from the very interplay of forces which goes to make up the universal order.
[5]Maritain, *Neuf leçons* ... op. cit., p. 34.
[6]Maritain, *Neuf leçons* ... op. cit., p. 71.

The picture they formed of nature may have been of universal and perpetual struggle, a struggle *for* life, of an order that was hard, pitiless and bloody, but it was an order nonetheless unimpeachable and impressive.

2. MODERN RESEARCH : HOW IS THE NATURAL ORDER TO BE CONCEIVED?

a. *It is the order of a universe which is called upon to perfect itself*

Modern knowledge enables us to make more precise statements about this overall view on several points, by allowing us, as it were, to be present at the formation of our universe and by describing the important stages of its evolution. The order which earlier thinkers marvelled at was not created in its present shape ready-made. It has a history. It is the outcome of an extraordinary adventure in which we see the particles of matter reassembled in increasingly complex structures, giving birth to ever richer and more differentiated beings. Then for the first time life is able to appear in micro-organisms; it propagates and differentiates itself, and bursts forth in the rich harvest of the great species of plant and animal life. Creation is not a limited, economical process in which each element or particular thing has a definite use, an irreplaceable rôle, and in which every event can be satisfactorily explained in terms of the present state of the world. It is a process of unbelievable profusion, the expression of an upward thrust endowed with countless potentialities; it is like an ever-growing mass in which order arises by a sort of miracle in the midst of many endeavours and setbacks and any number of frustrated attempts.[7] Obviously the fruit of modern research, which so remarkably widens our outlook on the necessary entanglement of good and evil in the world of nature, can save us from much naïvety and a great deal of presumption.

---

[7] The views of Pierre Teilhard de Chardin in *The Phenomenon of Man* and *Le groupe zoologique humain* would be very valuable here, were they stripped both of the animistic philosophy in which they are wrapped and of their whimsical extrapolations in the fields of sociology, philosophy and religion.

b. *The hypothesis of the original atom*

Study of the actual structure of the universe leads most astro-physicists to suppose a moment, about five thousand million years ago, when there were neither earth, nor planets, nor stars, nor interstellar nebulae, nor galaxies, nor molecules, nor atoms. Matter existed in a pre-atomic form: 'We picture it as a gaseous sub-stance composed of particles (protons, electrons and neutrons) from which atoms were formed, or simply of neutrons, or even more simply as a pre-atom. The events which were to transform it into elements (hydrogen, iron, carbon etc.) had not yet begun; the universe was still awaiting them.'[8]

We should, then, imagine the universe as something like a dense and unstable primitive atom with at least the dimensions of our solar system, in which an explosion unleashed a process of expan-sion in the course of which were formed, by the concerted action of the forces of attraction and repulsion, at dates much closer to one another than had at first been thought, our chemical ele-ments, the galaxies, the stars, the sun and the earth. Two thousand million years after that explosion, the universe had attained its present structure; but, with the never-ceasing pressure of the forces of expansion, the distance between the galaxies has already in-creased tenfold since then. This is the meaning of the 'hypothesis of the original atom' or of the universe growing like an 'expanding sphere'; it enables us to collect and co-ordinate the present data of

---

[8]V. Mersch, S.J., 'L'origine de l'univers selon la science', *Nouvelle Revue Théologique*, March 1953, pp. 225-51. Cf. Louis de Broglie, *Physics and Microphysics* (Hutchinson's Scientific and Technical Publications, Lon-don, 1955), p. 69: 'Giving free scope to our imagination, we could suppose that at the beginning of time, on the morrow of some divine "Fiat Lux", light, at first alone in the universe, has little by little produced by pro-gressive condensation the material universe such as, thanks to light itself, we can contemplate it today.'

In a Discourse to the Pontifical Academy of Sciences, given in Italian on 22 October, 1951, Pius XII recalled that by arguing from the law of entropy, which finds its equivalent in the microcosm, we are led to the vision of a material universe which progressively exhausts its original reserves of energy, and whose beginning and end can thus be dated: 'It would indeed seem that present-day science, going back in an instant over millions of years, has managed to witness this original *Fiat lux,* this moment when out of nothing there arose, with matter, an ocean of light and radiations, while the particles of the chemical elements separated and reformed in millions of galaxies.' (*Documentation Catholique,* 16 Dec., 1951, col. 1547).

astrophysics.[9] The passage from the pre-atomic state of matter to its differentiated condition, the construction of increasingly complex atoms and molecules, represents the first great step in the transformation of the universe; it comes about in the domain of physico-chemical activities and leads on to the threshold of the domain of biological activities.

What fascinates the scientists is the order that has arisen from a beginning like that. 'What a deep conviction of the rationality of the universe, and what a yearning to understand, were it but a feeble reflection of the mind revealed in this world, Kepler and Newton must have had to enable them to spend years of solitary labour in disentangling the principles of celestial mechanics! ... The scientist is possessed by the sense of universal causation ... His religious feeling takes the form of a rapturous amazement at the harmony of natural law, which reveals an intelligence of such superiority that, compared with it, all the systematic thinking and acting of human beings is an utterly insignificant reflection. This feeling is the guiding principle of his life and work, in so far as he succeeds in keeping himself from the shackles of selfish desire.'[10]

c. *The astronomical order is not mechanical but historical*

Struck by the regularity they saw in the revolutions of the stars, 'the ancients attributed to the celestial spheres a *divine and eternal structure*'. For the same reason there is sometimes a temptation

---

[9]The Pope has extolled the recent triumphs of astrophysics which graphically reveal both man's weakness and the greatness of his mind: 'In its boldness and intrepidity, the human mind ... goes in pursuit of galaxies receding in space, tracing back the course they have followed for millions of years past, and thus, as it were, becomes the spectator of cosmic processes which started to unfold on the morn of creation. What, then, is the mind of this tiny being called man, lost in the ocean of the material universe, that he should have dared to ask his senses, so infinitesimally small, to uncover the features and the history of this vast universe, and that he should have been able to unveil them one after the other? Only one answer is possible, so obvious as to be dazzling: man's mind belongs to a category of being essentially different from matter and superior to it, however limitless the dimensions of matter may be ... May the modern conception of astronomical science, which was the ideal of so many great men in the past, of Copernicus, Galileo, Kepler, Newton, continue to be rich in marvellous progress for modern astrophysics and enable the astronomical picture of the universe to acquire ever greater perfection.' Pius XII, *Allocution,* given in French to those taking part in the eighth general assembly of the International Astronomic Union, received in audience on 7 September, 1952.
[10]Albert Einstein, *The World as I see it,* op. cit., pp. 27-8.

'to regard the universe as a *machine* whose blueprint reflects its essential structure and imposes on everything that happens in it the same necessity as a geometrical form imposes on its properties (Spinoza's concept of nature). But in reality things are quite different : the world of the stars and the solar system is the result of a long evolution governed both by the demands of the nature of matter and by an immense series of actual circumstances.'[11]

If astronomical events 'always in fact come about without ever being prevented, it still remains that, *de facto,* they could have been, and *de jure* might still be, prevented from coming about. If the sun rises tomorrow, and if Neptune completes its revolution round it in 165 years, these are events which do not result simply from the nature of matter, but from an immense multitude of actual circumstances which have taken place in the past in the course of the genesis of the astral world, and which a perturbing cause arising unexpectedly in the solar system (which astronomers tell us is at the moment a most unlikely thing) *might* prevent from happening. Once constituted in the system by which they are conditioned, such events depend on a *de jure* or hypothetical necessity which is *de facto sufficient,* because in fact the causes which would prevent them do not exist, although even this non-existence itself is a *de facto* circumstance; they belong to a type of contingent events which *always* happen in fact ... and which assume the guise of events which are necessary *de jure*. These contingent events are quasi-necessary *de jure*.'[12]

An eclipse, since it results from an encounter of two independent series of causes, is a *chance* event; nonetheless it is absolutely *calculable and predictable,* since the orbit of the earth round the sun and of the moon round the earth are both completely regular and represent contingent events which are quasi-necessary *de jure*. And so it can be said that an eclipse is a *chance event in disguise*. 'If the solar system were a machine, an eclipse would not be a chance event in disguise but one quasi-necessary *de jure*, because the many elements active in the machine would depend on the unity of the essential structure of this machine as conceived by the engineer who put it together. But the solar system is no more a machine

[11]Maritain, 'Reflexions sur la necessité et la contingence', in *Raison et raisons,* op. cit., p. 53.
[12]Ibid.

than the universe itself . . . It has resulted from the long historical
evolution of a multitude of interacting factors not unified beforehand within the causality of any natural agent which might have
been the proper cause of the unity of the whole. Undoubtedly the
intelligent first Cause has directed this historical evolution according to his creative design, but God is not a mere maker of clocks
and watches but a maker of beings with their own inbuilt principle
of action. The world is a republic of such beings, not a clock; and
God's infallible causality, by the very fact that it is transcendent,
makes events happen in accordance with their natural condition,
causing necessary events to happen by necessity, contingent events
contingently, and fortuitous events by chance.'[13]

It is these astronomical events, seemingly necessary, but in fact
resulting from a multitude of actual circumstances and therefore
contingent, which in the course of several hundred thousand years
have enabled the Earth to realize, in some way unknown to us,
the elements of an extraordinarily delicate balance which conditions the maintenance and development of life within it.[14]

[13]Ibid., p. 62.
[14]From the *scientific* point of view we must give credit to Teilhard for
having formulated and made explicit 'the law of universal promotion . . .
Throughout the duration of real time . . . the sum total of reality (the
given set of circumstances at the very beginning of a universe) goes on
unceasingly reinforcing its unity, because, proceeding from partial unifications to unifications more complete and extensive, *everything becomes
more and more One* . . . Can this be put more precisely? Thanks to hyper-
physics it can: what has been called "Teilhard's Law" gives a more
detailed account of two points. First, *unification comes about by com-
plexification,* which means that the element is by no means lost, but saved
and exalted in the whole where it is reunited to the rest. And secondly,
unification comes about by auto-complexification: the element or part
does not have to undergo any constraining violence from outside in order
to pass over into the whole which is so much greater than itself; it is from
its inmost being that this striving starts towards the whole in which it will
find itself more and more fully. In short the law of universal Promotion
is a law of auto-complexification.' Paul-Bernard Grenet, *Pierre Teilhard
de Chardin ou le Philosophe malgré lui* (Beauchesne, Paris, 1960), p. 214.
Let us make quite clear that it is Teilhard's *philosophy* which is unacceptable: creation conceived as completion, conclusion, pleromization,
'for the Absolute Being himself', the effect no longer of creative causality
but of creative union'—unity of the material of the universe—actual pre-
existence, although imperceptible, of the higher in the lower—psychism
of molecules and extension of consciousness to all levels of being—'mind
emerging by the pan-cosmic operation of matter' (cf. the Catholic doctrine
of the immediate creation of the human soul)—extrapolation of the laws
of biology into the social and historical spheres, etc.

d. *The contingency of the biological order: tentative gropings and the unexpected*

The universe is not a machine; it is the outcome of a long development. God is not a maker of clocks but a maker of autonomous beings, directing their activities without infringing on them, causing necessary events to happen by necessity, contingent events contingently, and fortuitous events by chance. What is true of the inanimate world is incomparably more so of the world of living things. [15] The forms of life cannot be entirely explained by reference to the present structure of the world; they have a history and result from the incalculable interplay of causes set in motion by God's omnipotence which, having created the universe, uses the energies of that universe to make it gradually improve upon itself, lower orders being raised right up to where the higher order starts, so that the mineral opens the way to the plant, the plant to the animal, and the animal, perhaps, finally to man.

Such a view is illuminating, and explains life's experiments, its gropings, its monstrosities, its freaks[16] and its setbacks. It prevents the scandal which could be caused to an over-simplifying mind by the preservation of rudimentary organs, the appearance of recessive characteristics, degenerations and the phenomena of dysteleology, ateleiosis and hyperteleiosis.[17] It will no longer be fancied, for example, that parasites were created expressly to torment animals; they have come from the upspringing flow of life under some still undifferentiated form rich in adaptive possibilities; and by fortuitously succeeding in attaching themselves to other living creatures they have become what they are.[18]

---

[15]While the perfection of a machine results from the utilitarian character of each of its elements, what constitutes the organic world, as F. J. J. Buytendijk explains, as well as its ontological value and its degrees of perfection, is its wealth, proliferation and superfluity. *Traité de psychologie animale* (P.U.F., Paris, 1952), pp. 6 and 86.

[16]Counting *all* freaks, even trifling ones, their number is estimated 'at several hundred for every hundred thousand births'. René Royer, 'Sens et non-sens de la vie', in *Qu'est-ce que la vie? Semaine des intellectuels catholiques 1957* (Pierre Horay, Paris, 1958), p. 184.

[17]For these phenomena, see L. Cuénot, *Invention et finalité en biologie* (Flammarion, Paris, 1941), pp. 64ff.

[18]St Augustine contented himself with the reply that gnats and fleas were created to humiliate our pride. *In Joa. Evangelium*, tr. I, no. 14 and 15. Pascal speaks of the buzzing of gnats which 'murders' us. The Curé d'Ars when dying did not want anyone to chase 'the poor flies' from his face.

To illustrate the formation of life by a sort of parable, let us quote from the *Légende de Prâkriti* a passage in which Claudel, through his own creative experience, tries to rediscover in what ways God, in his magnanimity and condescendence, as it were brings to his aid the life forces, the spontaneity and resources of his own creatures, in order over the course of thousands of years to construct his universe :

'Everything that has received a name from God is capable of answering to this name; it is responsible for producing a required effect, and is endowed with its own peculiar power to fulfil this demand which seems beyond it, and to carry out this task which has been allotted to it . . .

'During the time we were the guests of Prâkriti and sharing her revels, we had time to study and understand her ways of working. Let us take advantage of this moment when she is pretending to be asleep to read up our notes. What contradictions, and at the same time what stubbornness in her ideas! what routine and fancy! what naïvety and cunning! what a conservative instinct and a revolutionary frenzy! what slyness and uproars! what patience and rousings! After hundreds and thousands of years, during which she has set a whole greenhouse, a whole menagerie going, she suddenly seems disgusted with it all and, sick at heart, sweeps the board clean with the back of her hand and starts all over again from the beginning. She flings down the drain whole orders of being, genus, sub-genus and species alike, and keeps only a louse or a cricket. At the same time she carefully keeps in reserve certain principles deeply rooted in herself, symmetry, for example, and ideas whose possibilities she has not yet exhausted, such as the little glimmer of light which is found everywhere from the primitive cell to those skilful, toiling hands that man wields over the whole of Creation and that he raises up to God. She can be relied upon to exploit to the smallest detail all the possibilities of a given shape or situation. When, for instance, the theme of a palm or a fern or a mushroom is set for the competition, she submits variations by the tens of thousands. She goes to enormous trouble to paint on the breasts of her birds or fishes the correct armorial bearings. There is a whole side of nature which is decorative and sartorial, a dresser's technique . . . She conceals 'surprises', little riddles right down in some of her creations, like the pastry-cook who puts a jelly-baby into the Epiphany cake. At other times she gets bored, plays the fool, becomes wilful and devotes herself to all the abuses of industrial production, multiplying the meanest articles at the expense of superb models, so that it would almost seem that she could not stop. Or she has obviously received a command and stopped in the middle of carrying it out, and it would seem that she has found it too difficult or that she has suddenly started to think about something else. She dreams, yawns, says yes, says no, deliberately misunderstands, or gives herself over to punning, if not to sheer farce. For example, if you say to her, "horse", she comes up immediately with that ridiculous little chess-man known as a sea-horse, which she slips into her aquarium . . . Or she is torn with a misplaced enthusiasm : you said to her, "lizard", and she makes an ichthyosaurus; you said, "horse's tail", and she proudly introduced equisetums as tall as fir-trees and utterly useless. We shall never be through with visiting the storehouses, the shelves full of back-numbers and white elephants, missing bits, and trials and errors. Curators of museums rummage round in it lovingly, like a ladies' tailor among his grandmother's dresses. But the profoundest thing in nature is humour, waggishness; it could be said that Prâkriti well knows that the Creator only made her for his amusement, although she pretends not to notice. She does not act her part badly, and she is very co-operative. When scolded she closes her eyes, and with a bewitching smile, pure and rose-like as the breath of a girl, she breathes forth a butterfly.'[19]

To this flight of fancy let us add a few lines in which Teilhard de Chardin sums up his vision as a biologist :

'Life advances by mass effects, by dint of multitudes flung into action without apparent plan. Milliards of germs and millions of adult growths jostling, shoving and devouring one another, fight for elbow-room and for the best and largest living-space. Despite all the waste and ferocity, all the mystery and scandal it involves, there is, as we must be fair and admit, a great deal of biological efficiency in the *struggle for life*. In the course

[19]Paul Claudel, 'La légende de Prâkriti', in *Figures et Paraboles* (Gallimard, Paris, 1936, pp. 109 and 144-8.

of this implacable contest between masses of living substance in irresistible expansion, the individual unit is undeniably tried to the limit of its strength and resources. "Survival of the fittest by natural selection" is not a meaningless expression, provided it is not taken to imply either a final ideal or a final explanation.

'But it is not the individual unit that seems to count for most in the phenomenon. What we find within the struggle to live is something deeper than a series of duels; it is a conflict of chances. By reckless self-reproduction life takes its precautions against mishap. It increases its chances of survival and at the same time multiplies its chances of progress.

'Once more, this time on the plane of animate particles, we find the fundamental technique of *groping*, the specific and invincible weapon of all expanding multitudes. This groping strangely combines the blind fantasy of large number with the precise orientation of a specific target. It would be a mistake to see it as mere chance. Groping is *directed chance*. It means pervading everything so as to try everything, and trying everything so as to find everything. Surely in the last resort it is precisely to develop this procedure (always increasing in size and cost in proportion as it spreads) that nature has had recourse to profusion.'[20]

It will now perhaps be easier to understand our previous assertion that God is not a maker of clocks but of independent beings, and that the universe is not a machine but a republic of such beings; and to understand also the profundity of St Thomas's reflection that 'since the will of God is sovereignly efficacious, it follows not only that the things he wishes to make are made, but also that they are made in the way he wants them made, some by necessity, some contingently.[21]

e. *The ascent of the Tree of Life*

At the very heart of these teeming and conflicting activities the 'Tree of Life' rises progressively from marine forms to amphibians, to reptiles, mammals and primates. The Ariadne's thread which

---

[20]*The Phenomenon of Man* (Collins, London, 1959), p. 109-110.
[21]I, qu. 19, a. 8.

makes it possible to measure the progress of this ascent is what Teilhard de Chardin calls the appearance and development of *cephalization* or *cerebration*.[22] 'From the moment that the measure (or parameter) of the evolving phenomenon is sought in the elaboration of the nervous systems, not only do the countless genera and species fall naturally into place, but the entire network of their verticils, their layers, their branches, rises up like a quivering spray of foliage. Not only does the arrangement of animal forms according to their degree of cerebralization correspond exactly to the classification of systematic biology, but it also confers on the tree of life a sharpness of feature, an impetus, which is incontestably the hall-mark of truth.'[23]

The development of the nervous system and of cerebration, which in the animal is the physiological condition of the development of its psychic system, becomes exceptional in the primates : 'What makes the primates so interesting and important to biology is, in the first place, that they represent a *phylum of pure and direct cerebralization*. In the other mammals too, no doubt, the nervous system and instinct gradually develop. But in them the internal travail was distracted, limited and finally arrested by accessory differentiations. *Pari passu* with their psychic development, the horse, stag and tiger became, like the insect, to some extent prisoners of the instruments of their swift-moving or predatory ways . . . In the case of the primates, on the other hand, evolution went straight to work on the brain, neglecting everything else, which accordingly remained malleable. That is why they are at the head of the upward and onward march towards greater consciousness. *In this singular and privileged case, the particular orthogenesis of the phylum happened to coincide exactly with the principal orthogenesis of life itself* . . . it is "aristogenesis" '.[24]

---

[22] *L'apparition de l'homme* (Seuil, Paris, 1956), p. 309, in which Teilhard replies to Jean Rostand, who regards a spider as as perfect in the animal world as a mammal.

[23] *The Phenomenon of Man*, op. cit., p. 145. In his *Traité de psychologie animale*, Buytendijk, who contrasts the exoskeleton of arthropods with the esoskeleton of vertebrates, and the ganglionic nervous system of the former with the central nervous system of the latter, sees, with Cuvier and Bergson, in the nervous system the organ which, more than any other, 'makes' the perfection of the animal species (p. 76).

[24] *The Phenomenon of Man*, op. cit., p. 159 (italics in the original).

f. *Modern knowledge concerning the order of the universe widens the vision of the ancients and makes it more exact*

We can see how modern research gives both breadth and precision to the vision which the ancients formed of the conflict of forces, both on the plane of matter and even more mysteriously on the plane of life, out of which our universe appeared; and also to their view of this mixture of destruction and construction, of evil and good, to which the appearance of biologically and psychically more perfect beings gives supreme significance.

It remains true that, as the ancients were able to establish, the universe of nature taken as a whole does represent an order, but an order hard and implacable. This is not, and cannot as yet be, the Christian order. It would be naïve to express surprise at this or to claim that the 'countless phenomena discovered through the telescope or microscope have a *Christian look* about them', or to be shocked at not encountering Christianity while observing the Great Bear. Pierre Termier,[25] taking up this objection of Sully-Prudhomme, has no difficulty in answering that it is necessary to cross a threshold and to attain the realities of the spiritual soul touched by grace before the Christian order can appear.

3. THE SUFFERING OF ANIMALS

We have now reached the point where we can properly discuss the suffering of animals.

This problem is side-stepped both by those, like the Cartesians, who deny animals any psychic activity and make them a sort of machine, and by those who, on the contrary, claim for animals a sensibility which is proper to human beings. One thing at least is certain, which is that animals are neither machines nor men. 'It is absolutely impossible for a man to imagine how a dog *thinks*; nonetheless there is a canine knowledge which really does exist and is the object of animal psychology.'[26]

a. *Our obligations towards animals*

This is perhaps the place to stop for a moment and try to define

[25]*La joie de connaître* (Nouvelle Librairie Nationale, Paris, 1926), pp. 322-3.
[26]Maritain, *On the Philosophy of History* (Bles, London, 1959), p. 78.

our moral attitude towards animals. In order to explain that duties and rights are not always correlative and that there can be obligations without corresponding rights, Jacques Maritain puts the question of our duties to animals in these terms: 'Have we duties *towards* animals, or duties *concerning* animals? In the second case, it would really be a question of duties *towards* human beings or society or myself, in the sense that cruelty towards animals develops feelings and habits of insensitivity or sadism which vitiate one's personality and menace others. Thus I have duties *concerning* the tidiness of my room, for instance, but I have no duties *towards* my room. Only towards myself; and also, most certainly, towards my visitors. I think that something more than this is involved in the case of animals. And indeed, more is involved in the case of anything existing in nature, and bearing in itself the imprint of creation.[27] We really do have duties *towards* them. And yet they themselves have no corresponding rights. This is by no means because they are deprived of the power to vindicate such rights—children and idiots possess rights without having the capacity of claiming their enforcement—but because animals are not moral agents or persons. The theory of the absolute correlation of rights and duties comes to a dead end here. If animals had rights, it would be necessary to say also that they had duties, and no one would support this contention. In short, in this instance we have duties towards certain beings without these beings themselves having any corresponding duties towards us. By this I mean we have duties towards this or that particular individual animal, this horse, that dog: for they are living individuals, foreshadowings of human persons; I have the duty of feeding them, and of not killing them without necessity. And indeed it can be said that since they are foreshadowings of human persons, and since the internal senses in the highest animals are a glimmering of intelligence, there is in them likewise a foreshadowing of those rights,

[27]Cf. Maritain, *The Degrees of Knowledge,* op. cit., p. 110: 'Round about us is a vast multitude of transobjective subjects, and they are designated by the second person, the "one to whom we speak" and who speaks to us, each a centre of mystery. The second person is also rich in a certain ontological or metalogical depth and is one who, in the relation of *I* to *Thou,* wants to be treated respectfully and lovingly. Thou spring, thou fish, thou sparrow; but let charity intervene supernaturally to complete our weak philosophical perception between things, and St Francis will speak to his sister water, his brothers bird and fish . . .'

properly so-called, which will be vested in free agents. But these rights are only a foreshadowing : while the duties which we have towards them are real duties. The basis of these duties must lie in respect for life and for existence and in natural piety, and in the sense of cosmic solidarity, which is so highly developed in India.'[28] Now that this has been said we can go back to our main theme.

b. *The reason for the suffering of animals*

Fundamentally, what accounts for the presence of suffering in animals is precisely the perfection and delicacy of their organic constitution. Suffering is the price they have to pay for their sensitivity. A camera does not suffer, but then it cannot see.

To do away with the vulnerability of an animal's organs would be to do away with the animal itself; and that would be to deprive the universe of this immense reach of life, incomparably rich and variegated, which stretches from the lower world of minerals and plants to that of man.

Doubtless all this will be granted without any difficulty—as, also, that to ask God constantly to intervene with miracles to remove the suffering of animals would be to reject the world of independent beings that he has made and to require him to create some other universe.

But, it may be said, granted the existence of our animal world, and hence of suffering, could not the sum of suffering be less? The only answer, of course, is that it could be less. And also it could be greater. Here again we must avoid the perpetual trap, in which Leibniz was caught, of a God bound by his infinite goodness to create one particular better world rather than any other one, and bound ultimately to create the best of all possible worlds. In virtue of his infinite goodness God is bound, not to create an infinitely good world, which would be a pure contradiction, but to create a world which is by and large good.

Suffering, in an animal, is the perception of a disorder coming about in its organism or in its usual environment. It may, therefore, in certain cases—and this is one of its secondary aspects— play the beneficial rôle of a warning, and cause the animal to regulate its behaviour accordingly.

But here again it seems that nature has proceeded by groping

[28]Maritain, *Neuf leçons* . . . , p. 150.

and approximation rather than by aiming at anything absolute or rigorous. Biologists affirm that 'the pain which after being felt makes us avoid traumatisms is ill-regulated; exaggerated in certain cases (toothache, neuralgia), it does not appear at all in some other dangerous ones (nephritis, pulmonary tuberculosis, incipient cancer)'.[29] From the philosophical point of view, it is not a question of knowing whether better adjustments might be possible—this will be agreed without difficulty—but of knowing whether this world of nature, put together by God himself, but with a free rein given to his creatures' activities, is by and large a good world, in which life prevails over death, good over evil, and existence over nothingness.

c. *Human and animal suffering*

Human suffering is the suffering of a person endowed with an immortal soul, which can bear the permanent mark of having experienced temporal suffering. To this can be applied the words of Léon Bloy: 'Suffering passes, having suffered does not.'

Animal suffering is a suffering in which there is no thought of the future, because it is the suffering of beings whose souls entertain no thought of the future. It is the matter and form of the mineral, the body and soul of the plant, which is the subsistent being, and not just the form of the mineral or the soul of the plant. Likewise it is the whole animal, body and soul, which is the subsistent being, not just the soul. It is metaphysically impossible for the form of a mineral,—hydrogen, chlorine or iron—to subsist without the matter which it informs; or for the plant or animal soul to subsist without the body which it animates.[30] The forms of perishable beings disappear to make room for other forms which will also disappear; the destruction of one being ensures the generation of another; in this way is explained the recurrence of species. Only the human soul, being spiritual, can subsist on its own and survive the dissolution of the body.

Human suffering can be touched by grace, can be borne in

[29] L. Cuénot, *Invention et finalité en biologie,* op. cit., p. 79.
[30] A body, composed of matter and form, can by a *miracle* subsist without its *extension.* Cf. St Thomas, *IV Sent.,* dist. 44, qu. 2, a. 2, quaest. 3, and ad 4; III, qu. 54, a. 1, ad 1; *In Joan. Evang.,* xx, 9. But neither the matter nor the form of chemicals, plants or animals can exist separately. Their solidarity is inevitable.

faith and love, and bear some slight resemblance to the sufferings of Christ. Then, because of the charity which lights it, it is blessed and merits the reward inseparable from the beatitudes in the Gospel : 'Rejoice and be glad, for your reward will be great in heaven' (Matt. 5, 12). And St Paul writes : 'I consider that the sufferings of this present time are not worth comparing with the glory that is to be revealed in us' (Rom. 8, 18).

Animal suffering does not rise above time, but remains immersed in the constant flux of things which are made and unmade each day. It is part of the domain of the merely transient and perishable. As seen by philosophy,[31] it shares the fate of astronomical phenomena and has no *Christian look* about it. The delusion and mistake would be to want to impose a Christian meaning on it.

d. *'The wolf shall dwell with the lamb'*

The prophecy of Isaiah concerning the new age : 'The wolf shall dwell with the lamb, and the leopard shall lie down with the kid, and calf and the lion and the fatling together, and a little child shall lead them. The cow and the bear shall feed; their young shall lie down together; and the lion shall eat straw like the ox. The suckling child shall play over the hole of the asp' (11, 6-8) should not be taken literally. It is a parable, signifying in images the messianic kingdom, the kingdom of grace and truth, of harmony and peace, which will have its beginnings even in this world, but is not

---

[31]From the point of view of animal psychology, F. J. J. Buytendijk justifies Aristotle's remark that laughter is the peculiarity of man: 'All joy and exuberance is essentially *riches,* superabundance, superfluity, that is to say, what goes beyond the necessary. This liberation—apparent even in nature—is the primordial *condition* of mental life; mental life, however, never manages to be developed in animals. The "human-ness" of the young anthropoid is partially human, in a childish, frolicsome and playful way; but it is that of a child which has no tendency to become a man and attain its own adulthood: the "highest" of the animals is like a tragic child, condemned to fall back into an animal nature after appearing to get away from it. This sort of playfulness belongs to the young chimpanzee, which expresses itself in its extravagant mobility and its countless activities with objects; it is gaiety which gradually blurs and fades away, while that of man reaches down ever further till it becomes *joy,* that is to say, interiorized abundance, without exuberance.' *Traité de psychologie animale,* op. cit., p. 312. The italics are the author's own. Again it must be said with Nietzsche, that man is the only being in the world able to lie. Ibid. p. 315.

of this world. In the first half of the twelfth century a young Jew, Judas of Cologne, attracted by Christianity but hesitant about recognizing the fulfilment of the prophecy of the Old Testament, received a sudden illumination in which Isaiah's prediction became immediately clear to him, when in a Rhenish monastery he met two former robbers who had become monks and turned themselves into gentle-natured servants of the poor and of travellers.[32]

e. *Will there be any room in the next world for animal life?*

God can bring a man back to life. When our Lord raised Lazarus from the dead, it was Lazarus' own soul which was infused into a body already starting to rot—it was already a human body no longer—in order to inform it once more, bring it to life and make it once again its own : so that Lazarus after resurrection was identically the same person as Lazarus before it. This was possible because the one and only soul of Lazarus, being spiritual and immortal, had not been affected by its separation from the body, but had remained intact and had survived.

But God who is able to bring a man back to life cannot do so for an animal. Certainly he can give back life to the corpse of a tiger, but if he did, what would be happening? The first soul which gave life to this body was annihilated by death, being incapable of even momentary, fleeting existence without the body. God can give life back to the corpse only by infusing into it a new soul quite distinct from its predecessor—not created out of nothing like the spiritual soul of man, but something which 'emerges' from the matter, 'brought out' from the matter's potentiality; so that the reanimated animal could never be identically the same as the first. So it is not a question of whether the animals in our world might be brought back to life in the next.

But there is a question still unanswered. Will there be, between the world of the bodies of the elect, resurrected and glorified in the likeness of Christ himself, and the mineral world of the new heaven and the new earth (Apoc. 21, 1; II Peter 3, 13), will there be any forms, either of plant or of animal life, with shapes and ways of living which are in this life completely unknown and unimaginable to us?

[32]P.L., vol. CLXX, col. 815.

St Thomas's answer is well known. On the one hand, because of a scriptural interpretation no longer accepted (Apoc. 10, 6 does not mean that *time* will cease but that there will be no more *waiting*), he thought that the movement of the universe, from which the complexity of beings and of biological life now springs, will cease. On the other hand, man's body, being no longer 'animal' but 'spiritual' (I Cor. 15, 44), will no longer have to look for the help or company of plants and animals.[33]

The question has recently been re-opened by Olivier Lacombe in a recent essay on man and the animals.[34] He sets side by side two texts from St Paul: 'To unite all things in him, things in heaven and things on earth' (Eph. 1, 10); and: 'The creation waits with eager longing for the revealing of the sons of God ... in the hope that the creation itself will be set free from its bondage to decay and obtain the glorious liberty of the children of God' (Rom. 8, 19-20), and then asks: 'In this creation which the apostle mentions, would the animal kingdom not be included? The question is not imprudent, but any attempt to answer it must be extremely cautious.' He goes on:

'It should be noted first of all that, in extending to the universe the dogma of the resurrection of the flesh, St Paul takes his stand in the economy of grace and does not appeal to any sense of what is just, nor even of what is fitting, derived from the natural order. And so it is by an overflow of completely gratuitous generosity that the *new earth* of the Apocalypse (21, 1) will be *set free from the servitude of corruption.*

'Since, then, this undreamt of world, brought about by the great eschatological transfiguration, will be subject to new physical laws, measurable by none of the norms of our own physical science, is it unthinkable that the order of infrarational life will also be represented there, although submitted to new biological laws? Perhaps it is not, after all, unthinkable. And without inventing any posthumous destiny for animal life in the sense of one realized in every animal that has ever lived, is living and is yet to live in time, let us not close to irrational life, which ontologically has represented a whole degree of existing beings,

---

[33]St Thomas, *De potentia*, qu. 5, a. 5 and 9.
[34]In *Qu'est-ce que la vie? Semaines des Intellectuels catholiques,* 1957, op. cit., pp. 101-2.

the avenues of approach which the letter to the Romans seems
not to forbid them.'

f. *The suffering of animals can be an opportunity for testing
our faith*

The answer to the problem of the suffering of animals is to be
found, as we have seen, on the plane of philosophical reason, that
is to say, on a pre-Christian level.

For persons incapable of envisaging it under this aspect, and
this is more common than might be thought, this problem will
remain without any direct solution.

The theologian or spiritual adviser they consult should not per-
sist at all costs in trying to convince them. He will know that God
has countless ways of putting faithful souls to the test. The shock
sustained by the sight of animal suffering may well be one
of them.

The solution—and there is always a solution—must therefore
be indirect. It will be to rise above the trial by pure acts of faith
and confidence in the infinite holiness and justice of God.

Their trouble and hurt will be healed by the soothing darkness
of faith.

God expects each one of us, at such a moment in our lives,
when we are faced with such a problem or trial, to give both our
understanding and our fate completely into his hands.

4. THE REASON FOR POSTPONING THE PROBLEM OF SUFFERING
IN THE CASE OF YOUNG CHILDREN

We shall not go into the problem of the suffering of human
beings here. For the theologian, this is not an evil of nature, but an
evil of punishment which results from humanity's initial disaster,
and it can be illuminated by patience and love.

The suffering of young children, who are incapable of giving
any meaning to their trials by the use of reason or faith, is also an
evil of the human person.

A pure philosopher, unfamiliar with or heedless of the light of
revelation, would place the suffering of children on a par with

the evil of the animal world, as an evil of nature revealed on the biological plane.

But for the believer, the theologian, the Christian philosopher, it belongs to another order.[35]

[35]Cf. below, p. 241ff.

6

CHAPTER SIX

Is God Responsible for Sin?

God could have created a world without sin; he permits sin to come about, but he is in no way its cause, either directly or indirectly.

1. THE SUPREME FORM OF EVIL

a. *Sin is hidden from atheists and revealed to faith*

With sin we come to the most troubling point of the mystery of evil.

Those who do not believe in God can certainly suffer, perhaps atrociously, and have personal knowledge of the agonies of despair; but being ignorant of what sin is—the revolt of the creature against the transcendence of that infinite Power who lovingly made it—and rejecting the thought of an after-life and eternal destiny for man, they are incapable of placing the problem of evil in its true perspective and giving it its final terrible dimensions.

The mystery of sin reveals itself to the soul to whom the infinite goodness of God the creator, the wonderful drama of the redemption of the world by the shedding of blood on the cross, and the incompleteness of our temporal life have also been revealed. But it is to contemplatives, illuminated by the gifts of knowledge and wisdom and crucified in their bodies, that it will be given, in so far as they have ascended into the blessed night of God, to fathom the contrary and devastating darkness of the night of sin and, at the price of this stretching of their being, to enter into the secrets of the mystery of the redemption.

b. *Sin is permitted as an offence against God and his creation*

The axiom of St Augustine[1] and St Thomas,[2] according to

[1] *Encheiridon*, ch. XI.
[2] I, qu. 2, a. 3, ad 1.

which God, infinitely good and powerful 'would never permit any evil to exist in his works if he were not sufficiently good and powerful to make good come out of evil itself', is valid still, but in a transposed sense, proportionately the same but essentially different, when the passage is made from the evil of nature to the evil of sin.

The evil of nature is *permitted* in the sense that it is in itself inseparably connected with a good which is intended and directly willed by God. It is tolerated and accepted by God, willed but not intended—it is in spite of, not because of, the element of nothingness which it irremediably contains that a created being is willed and intended by God—and it can be said of the evil of nature that it is willed indirectly and by accident. If God wills the generation of new forms, he must *consent* to the destruction of old ones.

The evil of sin, on the other hand, in itself is inseparably connected to nothing good and acts only to destroy the work of God;[3] so the question as to whether it might, even indirectly or by accident, be willed by God, does not arise. It is *permitted*, tolerated and suffered in a completely different sense from the evil of nature; it is permitted as a rebellion, an offence, *which God cannot will in any way*, which he cannot acquiesce in or *consent* to without denying his own being, which he could certainly suppress by force and eradicate completely, but which also, he can, if he decides to respect even the resistance of our wills, allow to happen and bear fruit indirectly in other things.

When therefore it is said that the evil of sin is permitted, this cannot be taken to mean that it is accepted, consented to and tolerated, in other words indirectly willed, as the reverse side of some good looked for by God. There will always be some mysterious good of which sin is the reverse side,[4] and many splendid things may come of it. The fall of the first Adam called forth the redemption by the second Adam—*O felix culpa*. But to believe sin to have been willed for the sake of the redemption would be to fall into the blasphemy of the Hegelian view of a God immanent in both evil and good and in some undefined way willing the one

---

[3]'Malum culpae, quod privat ordinem ad bonum divinum, Deus nullo modo vult.' St Thomas, I, qu. 19, a. 9.

[4]St Thomas says that God can will two things: to permit evils to exist, and to fit the evils which he cannot will into a higher order: 'Ex quo sequitur quod velit mala facta *ordinare*, non autem quod velit ea *fieri*.' *I Sent.*, dist. 46, a. 4.

or the sake of the other. The human will alone can commit sin, and the divine will alone can bring about the redemption. And it is true that God would never have decided to let man freely stand up against him could he not have brought out of a disaster, which it was metaphysically impossible for him to will, the splendours of the redemption.

Evils, in short, always provide the opportunity for some mysterious good. There are evils which God, without destroying himself, can resign himself to because of this good, and which he *wills by accident*. But as to the evils which strive to destroy God, *only the sinful creature is capable of willing them by accident*, for the sake of some wretched good under whose cloak they hide themselves.

God allows creatures to offend him and to follow the offence to its bitter end. The one and only way of penetrating this mystery is that shown us by the Gospel: to contemplate the outrages suffered by Christ. He was truly the Word made flesh, our Lord and God (John 20, 28), he could have turned for help to his Father, who would immediately have sent him more than twelve legions of angels (Matt. 26, 52); he had only to will it and those who came to arrest him would draw back and fall to the ground (John 18, 6); yet he let himself be buffeted (John 18, 22), spat on in the face (Matt. 27, 65); crowned with thorns, made a mockery of (John 19, 2), and then crucified (John 19, 18). It is their God, come down to save them and to implore their love, whom men outrage to this extent.

2. THE NATURAL CONDITION OF ANY FREE CREATURE

a. *Any free creature is essentially capable of either holding fast to God or not*

Only he who is his own law, only God alone, is essentially incapable of straying from the law; only God alone is by nature infallible and without fault.

Since it is dependent on its Creator, it is of the essence of any creature that its supreme law lies outside itself, hidden in the mystery of the absolute transcendence of the Creator.

It is of the essence of any free, intelligent creature, by an act of choice, to have the capacity to hold fast to its mysterious and absolutely transcendent supreme law or not. To do away with this capacity and suppose a free creature, man or angel,[5] (we are not discussing what God is able to do by his gratuitous interventions and free favours)—which by nature did not possess the possibility or capacity to sin, would be to suppose a creature which was its own supreme law, a creature which was the Creator. 'If there is free will, the creature must be *able* to hold fast or otherwise to the Cause on which it depends. Now to say that it cannot sin would be to say that it is *unable* not to hold fast to its Cause; from which arises a contradiction.'[6]

God is able not to create free beings, but if he does create them, they will be able to fall away. To ask him to make a created will which cannot fall away is to ask him to make one which is the law of its own action, and which therefore has nothing above it by which it can regulate itself, one, in other words, which is at the same time created and uncreated.

St Thomas in the *Summa,* dealing with the angels, puts the question of the basic liability of free creatures to sin : 'An angel,' he says, 'just like any other rational creature, if we consider its nature, can sin; and if it should happen that a creature cannot sin, this results from a gift of grace, not from the condition of its nature ... The only act which cannot deviate from righteousness is the one the law of which is identical with the virtue of the agent. If indeed the hand of the craftsman were the actual law of the cut which he had to make, the craftsman would never be able to cut wood wrongly, his cut would be infallibly correct; but otherwise it can be either correct or incorrect. Now the divine will is the only one which is the law of its own action, having nothing above it ... And so it is only in the divine will that sin cannot exist. In any will of a creature, sin can intervene by virtue of its very

[5]'The angels themselves are not by nature without the possibility of sinning, as the sin of several of them has shown; it is by grace that the good angels are now confirmed in goodness.' St Thomas, *II Sent.,* dist. 23, qu. 1, a. 2, ad 2.

The angel was created in a state of sovereign and inflexibly upright freedom in regard to all the good things which are *at the level* of his nature and constitute his connatural universe. But God is not at the level of the angel's nature or a part of its universe, but *infinitely* above it. Whether we are in the order of nature or grace, God is an infinitely transcendent Good which an intelligent creature, angel or man, must love above all with a *love of free option* and make the basis of his moral life. Cf. St Thomas, *III Contra Gent.,* ch. 109. [6]St Thomas, *II Sent.,* dist. 23, qu. 1, a. 1.

nature.'[7] Consequently if the order of nature is considered, abstracting from the purely gratuitous interventions of God, it must be said that it is as impossible for God to make an impeccable creature as to make a square circle.

b. *The free creature's ambivalence is willed for his good*

It has just been said that God is able not to create free beings but that, if he does create any, they will be able to lapse. It is not possible for God to create a free being without a naturally ambivalent capacity either to conform to the supreme law or to turn aside from it.

It should be noted in passing that these types of impossibility, like that of making a square circle, doubtless denote a shortcoming; but it would be vain to look for this shortcoming in God, since it resides in the proposed object which, being self-contradictory, is self-destructive: 'Things which imply contradiction,' says St Thomas, 'do not fall under the divine omnipotence, since they are not in themselves possible; thus it would be better to say: *they cannot be made,* than: *God cannot make them.*'[8]

In creating a being with a naturally ambivalent capacity, what God intends and wills directly is to give this being the wonderful capacity to turn freely towards the supreme law; but the price of this capacity is, in the same being, the dread capacity to turn aside from the supreme law; this latter capacity is not intended, it is tolerated as inseparable from the former, and it can best be said to be willed only indirectly and by accident.

---

[7] I, qu. 63, a. 1. The thesis according to which an angel, considered in its nature, is, like any other intelligent and free creature, liable to sin in regard to the natural order itself, not merely to a possible supernatural order, is the only one we think to be in conformity with St Thomas's thought and to permit the enigma of the angel's sin to be resolved. From the metaphysical point of view the subject has been reopened in Maritain's authoritative study, *The Sin of the Angel* (Newman Press, Westminster, 1959). From the theological point of view, Fr Philippe de la Trinité, taking note of recent publications, has submitted this aspect of the sin of the angel to a fairly exhaustive investigation in *Études Carmélitaines,* Paris, 1948, pp. 44-85: 'Du péché de Satan et de la destinée de l'esprit', and in *Éphemerides Carmeliticae,* Rome, 1957, no. 1, pp. 45-92: 'Réflexions sur le péché de l'ange'; no. 2, pp. 315-375: 'La pensée des Carmes de Salamanque et de Jean de Saint-Thomas'; 1958, pp. 338-90: 'Evolution de saint Thomas sur le péché de l'ange dans l'ordre naturel?'
[8] I, qu. 25, a. 3. Cf. above, p. 90.

To be able to sin and actually not to sin presupposes an act of free preference and voluntary love. And such acts are so dear to God that in his eyes they justify the whole world of creation, especially that of free beings.

c. *The eminence of the free creature*

'That nature which can sin and yet does not is good,' says St Thomas.[9] From the point of view of *action*, the natures of men and angels, who are *made to surpass themselves* by according with a higher law, a law which unfortunately they can let themselves fall out of accord with, are certainly infinitely below the fullness of the divine nature, which could never know any higher law; but they are far above the indigence of animal natures, which are incapable of even perceiving any call to surpass themselves.[10]

From the point of view of *being,* the natures of men and angels, which, although drawn from nothing, are *spiritual and immortal* are on a level infinitely beneath the unchangeable, divine absolute, which they look up to as a firmament; but they are far above animal natures, immersed in the flux of perishable things with no knowledge of the future.[11]

It is because they are the highest of creatures, drawn out of nothing in order to be brought nearer to God than any others, that free creatures labour under a double tendency and are subject to a sort of distension. On the one hand they are attracted by the Source of their being, whom they are able to know and love. On the other, they are always influenced by the threat and the intoxication of nothingness. In a great passage, where he explains that the tendency to nothingness cannot come from God —who would merely have to cease to intervene in order to destroy and annihilate his creatures—but that it remains essentially inherent in every created being and is inseparable from the very root of its being, St Thomas writes: 'Non-being has no proper cause, no cause *per se*. For nothing can be a cause except in so far as it has being, and being is in itself the cause of being. Consequently God cannot be the cause of the tendency to non-being; but the creature can, *having this inside itself in so far as it comes forth*

---

[9]*II Sent.*, dist. 23, qu. 1, a. 2; *De veritate*, qu. 14, a. 1, ad 16.
[10]*De malo*, qu. 16, a. 2.
[11]The distinction between these two aspects, the one of action or *good*, the other of *being*, is made by St Thomas, I, qu. 48, a. 2.

from nothingness. It is by accident that God can be said to be the cause of the annihilation of things, namely by taking away from them the action by which he preserves them.'[12]

d. *Elevation to the supernatural order does not remove the ambivalence of free creatures during their time on earth*

The nature of men and angels has not been left to itself and abandoned only to its own natural needs, but it has become the vessel into which God has poured supernatural grace. But this has in no way altered the radical ambivalence of this nature so long as it remains in the state of pilgrimage. Raised up by initial grace, men and angels retain the basic faculty of being able freely to hold fast or to refuse to hold fast to the higher law. 'It belongs to the divine providence,' writes St Thomas, 'to lead each being in accordance with its nature, for, as St Dionysius says, providence is not a corrupter but a saver of natures.'[13] To those who thought that had the angels been created with habitual or sanctifying grace none would have sinned, St Thomas replies in the *Summa* that grace, 'coming into a subject, inclines it in accordance with the natural mode of this subject; now the mode of action proper to an intellectual nature is to behave freely in regard to the things it wants; consequently, the inclination of grace does not impose any necessity : he who possesses grace can choose not to use it and to sin.'[14]

3. IN HIS ABSOLUTE POWER GOD COULD HAVE CREATED US FROM THE OUTSET IN STATU TERMINI AND IN BEATITUDE

God cannot create free beings impeccable by nature, but he can make them impeccable by the supernatural dispositions of his providence. This is the teaching of St Thomas : 'If a creature has the privilege of not being able to sin, it owes this to a gift of grace,

---

[12]I, qu. 104, a. 3, ad 1.
[13]*II Sent.*, dist. 23, qu. 1, a. 2: Did God have to permit the temptation or the sin of man? Cf. *Compendium theologiae*, ch. 142, *God in permitting evils does not detract from his goodness:* 'The rôle of providence is not to condemn the nature of the beings it governs but to save them ... If evil were totally excluded from things, *they would not be regulated according to their nature* by the divine providence.'
[14]I, qu. 62, a. 3, ad 2.

not to the condition of its own nature.'[15] Thus the angels and the elect, overwhelmed by the immediate, uninterrupted vision of the divinity, enjoy the happy impossibility of sinning. They adhere unchangingly to God by a consent which is, as it were, beyond our division of acts into necessary and free; they are delivered from themselves and their essential fragility, for they *possess* and *have* more than they *are*. For all that, they are not deprived of free will, for over and above this adhesion to God who fundamentally rectifies their will, 'there exists a multitude of things which they can either do or not do'.[16]

If God does this in the next world for his faithful creatures, after their testing time, why could he not have done it from the outset, creating angels and men in heaven and immersing them immediately in the ocean of his infinite beatitude? From the very start they would have been intrinsically impeccable, 'having in themselves a principle of stability preserving them entirely from sin'.[17]

God could certainly have done this. If we look at his absolute power, or at what he could have done in conformity with his infinite wisdom and goodness, we shall say without hesitation that he *could have* created all angels and men in heavenly beatitude. And it is true that if God had chosen this course, the world would not have known sin, and would have been better. At least, it would have been better from one point of view but there would not have been any room, in a world glorified from the outset, either for the forgiveness of the redemption or for the mystery of a resurrected Christ and a resurrected Church.

Let us, however, not forget that it is an illusion to think that because of his infinite goodness God would have been bound to create, and bound to create this better world rather than that other one, or bound to create the best of all possible worlds.

4. IN HIS SUBORDINATED POWER GOD CREATED US
IN STATU VIATORIS

a. *The meaning of the 'status viatoris'*

In his absolute power, if we think of the world he could have

---

[15]I, qu. 63, a. 1.
[16]St Thomas, *De veritate*, qu. 24, a. 1, ad 16.
[17]Cf. ibid., qu. 24, a. 9.

made in his infinite wisdom and goodness, God could have created us *in statu termini*. But in his *subordinated power*, if we think of the world he has freely decreed to make, still in his infinite wisdom and goodness, he chose another course by which we were to be created, angels and men, *in statu viatoris*, being able to adhere or not adhere to God, in which beatitude would come as the completion of a venture, as an end-product or fruit.

That course is still a good one. From a certain aspect, it may even seem a better one : in order to beatify the creature, it takes account of the law, written into its very heart, by which it wishes to co-operate with God in the task of fulfilling the universe and in that of its own personal fulfilment. In this sense, it has already been said that the privilege of the free creature is to be able to go beyond itself.

This recalls the testimony of Father Eliseus of the Martyrs, stating that on this earth, according to St John of the Cross, 'the supreme perfection of any subject whatsoever in its hierarchy and degree is to *grow and increase* according to its talent and capacities so as to imitate God better, and what is more admirable and divine, *to work with him* in converting and bringing back souls.' And St Paul wrote : 'We are fellow workmen with God' (I Cor. 3, 9).

'A creature would be *better*,' says St Thomas, 'if it adhered unchangingly to God. Yet that creature is *good* which can adhere and not adhere to God.'[18] He refers to St Augustine[19] to explain that in heaven now there are creatures who adhere unchangingly to God, and on earth other creatures who can still choose, and that a universe in which these states of a creature are both represented, both the flower and the fruit, is seen in a better light.

Only *in statu viatoris*, where the ambivalence natural to every free creature is respected, so that it can either adhere or refuse to adhere to the transcendent Source of its being, can the supreme act of free option and preference, in which God is loved by the creature above all things and more than itself, be produced. This act, so dear to God, cannot possibly be imposed, for to impose it would be to put in its place a different sort of act; God looks for it from his creatures, and came to beg it from them.

[18]*De veritate,* qu. 24, a. 1, ad 16.
[19]Cf. *De Genesi ad litteram*, bk. VIII, ch. 20, no. 39.

b. *The mystery of the 'status viatoris'*

This can be stated in two sentences. God wishes to save all men :
if they are saved, the glory is his, and if they are not, the fault is
theirs.

If they are saved, the glory is his. Being as he is the author and
preserver of free creatures, angels and men, he can without doing
them any violence or infringing on the metaphysical structure of
their freedom[20] make them, under an irresistible influence, utter

---

[20]Let us briefly recall that what is true of *being* is true of *action,* which
itself is a form of being. Now it is *by entering into dependence on self-
sufficient Being* that creatures emerge from nothing and take possession
of their own existence; the more they enter into this dependence, the
firmer and richer their being becomes. Likewise it is *by entering into
dependence on the divine Action and Freedom* that beings act at all and
act freely; and the more they enter into this dependence, the firmer and
richer is their action and their liberty. *Thus created freedom is not independence but rather deep and intimate dependence in respect of the
Freedom which is their source.* But being directed towards goodness as a
whole as its proper object, *it remains in a deeply rooted independence,
a fundamental indifference, in regard to all partial goods;* it can accept
them as *good* or refuse them as *partial* and inadequate in relation to goodness as a whole. Only the absolute Good which will fulfil its desires to
overflowing could be a determining object for it. When, in carrying out
a good act, it passes from the power of willing to an act of willing, this can
only come about under a divine influence which does not destroy but
rather actualizes its indifference. God, who made this delicate mechanism
of our free will, is in effect alone capable of influencing it without destroying it. Should the act in question be an evil act, we shall see that nothing
to do with deviation could ever be ascribed to God.

This great metaphysical idea is summed up with assurance by Bossuet,
Traité du libre arbitre, ch. VIII: 'Just as a *created being* does not cease
to be because it is from another, that is, from God: but rather, is what it
is because it is from God; so it must be understood that *created action*
does not cease, if one may speak thus, to be an action because it is from
God: but rather, the more God gives it being, the more it is an action. So
far from God, by causing the creature's action, taking away from it its
quality as an action, he indeed gives it this quality: because he must give
the creature everything it has, everything it is; and the more the action of
God is immediate, the more it will be thought of as giving immediately to
every creature and every action of a creature all the properties fitted to
their nature. So therefore, far from saying that the action of God upon
our actions takes away its freedom we must, on the contrary, conclude
that our action is free *a priori,* because God makes it to be free. Admittedly if we attributed the performance within us of our action to anyone
other than our Maker, it could well be believed that this other would
injure our freedom and would, as it were, in removing so delicate a spring
that he himself had not made, break it altogether. But God would never
need by his action to take anything away from his handiwork, since he
himself makes everything which is in it, down to the last detail; and there-

that assent which raises them infinitely above themselves, draws them into his orbit and opens for them the door to his intimacy and to the beatific vision. Certainly the creature does have the initiative in this assent, without which it would not be free, but it is the *second* initiative. In the line of good, of salutary good, the *first* initiative can only come from God.[21] No angel or human adult can enter or make progress in the supernatural life except by an effect of the sovereign influence of God the Saviour. There is no free creature who does not owe his salvation to the divine goodness.

If we are not saved, the fault is ours. Before he draws us into the sovereign influence of his grace, there is a moment when God comes to stir our souls according to the rule of our nature, which is capable of adhering or not adhering to him. At this moment, it is up to us whether we oppose his universal saving will, erect obstacles to his plans or reject his loving-kindness; in short, before moving us with his sovereignly efficacious influence, God subjects us to an influence which we are able to resist. In this case, the whole initiative of refusal comes from us alone : indeed, while God alone can be the first Cause of being and goodness, the creature alone can be the first cause of evil,[22] and can alone take the initiative in doing what is nothingness and reducing to nothing the divine influx. In God's saving intentions, the influence which can

by brings about not only what we choose but also the very freedom of our choice.' Cf. below, pp. 176-7.

Kierkegaard was certainly right when he wrote: 'The most one can do for another being is to make it free. It needs omnipotence to do that.' But did he realize that man's freedom is not *independence* of God, and that it is only in the *moral order,* not the metaphysical, that man can make himself God's adversary by nullifying in himself all the influence of divine grace? It seems unlikely that he did, when we go on to read what follows: 'The omnipotence which weighs the world down with its heavy hand, can also make itself so light that what has been created may possess independence.' And: 'That God could create free creatures in opposition to himself is the cross that philosophy could never bear, but on which it has remained suspended.' (Quotations taken from Jean Wahl, *Études Kierke-gaardiennes,* Paris, Vrin, 1949, p. 412.)

[21]The will, at the time when it is moved by God to make this decisive assent, neither will nor can refuse *at that actual moment*; this is the *sensu composito*: a man who is seated cannot at the same time be standing. But under another aspect it can refuse, in the sense that, influenced by God to assent, it still reserves, under this influence, the power to refuse: a seated man, *sensu diviso,* has the *power* to stand up.

[22]'Defectus gratiae *prima causa* est ex nobis.' St Thomas, Iᵃ IIᵃᵉ, qu. 112, a. 3, ad 2. Cf. below, p. 178; and above, p. 72.

be resisted is subordinated to the irresistible influence, as the flower to the fruit, as the grain of wheat to the ear; if it is not resisted, it immediately gives way to the saving influence which carries all before it; if it is resisted, the impetus which moves all creatures to act will, through the fault of the free creature, be turned aside towards evil.[23] No angel or adult human being is lost except by having freely refused God's advances.

This is the normal, *ordinary* way in which the subordinated divine will acts. In it grace is given to free creatures *while taking into account* the treatment required by the nature of free creatures, which, being in themselves fallible, are able not to turn to God.

But, in this same world of his subordinated power, God can also, if he wills, give his grace *without taking account* of the treatment required by the nature of free creatures. He can perform *miracles* and send, from the first moment, instead of that influence which

[23]A parallel to the distinction between resistible and irresistible influence can be found in the distinction drawn by theologians between antecedent divine will and consequent divine will, between so called 'sufficient' grace and 'efficacious' grace.

The effect of efficacious grace is to provide the impulse for the saving act. What is the effect of the grace that we are able to resist? Take as an example a man who, gradually turning away from sin, starts by making an act of attrition, before going on to make the acts of charity and perfect contrition which will restore him to God's friendship.

Should we say of the resistible or sufficient influence that it calls forth the *supernatural act of attrition*; and that we call it sufficient and not efficacious because the act of attrition is not enough to justify the sinner? But if so, it is hard to see what the sinner is now resisting, and so we cannot talk of resistible grace but only of 'sufficient' grace. And it is just as hard to see why the sufficient grace of attrition is not always followed by the efficacious grace of justification.

Should we rather say of the resistible influence that it always intends to, and when it is not resisted it effectively does, make a man *actually consider the rule of action,* i.e., at the moment when the will is carried forward by the impetus which urges all creatures to act, it gives him the *power* to take the right direction and afterwards—but then it will be *under the influence of irresistible grace*—to produce the supernatural act of attrition?

If we wish to pay full attention to St Thomas's indications as to the origin of the deformity of sin, which is to be sought in failure to avert to the rule, then I think it is this second line of thought that we must follow, together with Maritain in *Existence and the Existant* (Doubleday, New York, 1948), see especially pp. 101-106, note. The effect of the resistible influence is always to bring us up short against the dilemma: this conforms to the rule, and that goes counter to it. To frustrate the influence is to solve this dilemma by a one-sided consideration of the good which goes counter to the rule.

can be resisted, the sovereign influence under which, admittedly, they will still have to give their consent, to say yes, but no longer to deliberate or to choose between good and evil.

He can do more; he can act, writes St Thomas, 'against what the order of things requires',[24] in his mercy laying low even those who resist him; or as the Liturgy says: 'Though our wills resist thee, press them graciously into thy service'[25]—yet without infringing on the metaphysical structure of our free will, which he alone, as its creator, can move from within.

The ruling of the world always remains that of the subordinated power of God; but this ruling comprises, besides its normal, *ordinary* exercize, one which must be called *exceptional and extraordinary,* however frequent we suppose it to be. The former allows the possible resistances of the free creature to be produced; the latter either prevents these resistances or triumphs over them.

Concerning the distinction between operative and co-operative grace, we may say that the ordinary exercize of God's subordinated power allows first for a general irresistible influence of grace, operative on behalf of supernatural good as seen within the framework of universal good, and by this the will gives its consent without deliberation. Then comes an influence of co-operative grace intended to help the will to deliberate and make a choice: so long as it aims at drawing attention to the rule of action it can still be resisted; if it is not resisted, it is followed by the irresistible influence which causes the salutary act to be performed.

The extraordinary exercize of this subordinated power, however, brings with it from the outset a special irresistible influence of operative grace by which the will consents to the salutary act without having to deliberate.[26]

The distinction between the normal and the exceptional exercize of providence is underlined by Maritain in *Existence and the Existant.* God, he says, can 'if he so wills, transport a created existent at one stroke to the performing of a good act by an unshatterable or infallibly efficacious activation or influence. This is

[24]*III Contra Gent.,* ch. 161.
[25]'Et ad te nostras etiam rebelles compelle voluntates.' Secret of the Saturday after the Fourth Sunday in Lent and of the Fourth Sunday after Pentecost.
[26]For the distinction between *general* and *special* influence of operative grace, see our article 'L'aventure des anges' in *Nova et Vetera,* 1958, pp. 132, et seq. Cf. St Thomas, Iª IIae, qu. a. 6, ad 3. Cf. below, p. 170.

a question of his free predilection and of the price paid for souls in the communion of the saints. How far his own wisdom binds his power, and how far the rule decided by his love binds its impulse to effusion, is the mystery of mysteries. The fact remains that in the order of nature the unshatterable activation is preceded by shatterable activations as the term in which the latter can fructify of themselves, when the nihilating of the created liberty has not rendered them sterile.'[27]

In an earlier work, Maritain had already distinguished these two ways in which the subordinated power may act : God can, if he wishes, activate created freedom towards a good act by an influence which at once precludes any possibility of escaping it. He can also, in the ordinary course of events, activate created freedom towards it by an influence which does not preclude the possibility of escaping. 'And when the creature does not produce nothingness under grace (this is no merit in its part, for not to take the initiative of nothingness is not to do something, it is only not to move under divine action),—when the creature does not take the initiative of nothingness, then divine motion or grace merely sufficient or breakable fructifies of itself into *unbreakable* divine motion or into grace efficacious by itself.'[28]

c. *Two passages from St Thomas*

The two modes of action of the subordinated power of God, one *ordinary*, the other *extraordinary*, are indicated by St Thomas in the *Contra Gentiles*.

He touches upon the first when he discusses : *How it is reasonable to impute it to man if he does not turn towards God, although he cannot do this without grace:*[29] 'If no one by his free will can merit or draw down divine grace, he can still stop himself from receiving it. It is indeed written in the Book of Job (21, 14) : "They say to God, 'Depart from us! We do not desire

[27]*Existence and the Existant,* op. cit., pp. 104-6. (The translator of this version of Maritain's French text has rendered as 'shatterable' and 'unshatterable' the same French words *brisable* and *imbrisable,* which we have thought it better to render, in translating Journet's text, as 'resistible' and irresistible'. *Translator's note.*).

[28]*St Thomas and the Problem of Evil,* op. cit., p. 39.

[29]*III Contra Gent.,* ch. 159.

the knowledge of thy ways' "; and again, (24, 13): "There are those who rebel against the light." And since it is in the power of our free will either to put or not to put an obstacle in the way of the reception of divine grace, he who does erect this obstacle is legitimately considered responsible. God, in whatever concerns him, is indeed ready to give his grace to all men, as it is said in I Tim. 2, 4 : "He desires all men to be saved and to come to the knowledge of the truth." But those alone are deprived of grace who themselves put an obstacle in the way. Thus, when the sun sends its light on to the world, the one who closes his eyes makes himself responsible if any evil should ensue, although he cannot see without the light of the sun.'

And he touches upon the extraordinary exercize of the subordinated power when he explains *How God delivers certain men from sin and leaves others in it:*[30] 'He who sins puts an obstacle in the way of grace, and in the normal course of things, *quantum ordo rerum exigit,* he ought not to receive it. But God can act outside this course of things, *praeter ordinem rebus inditum*—for example, when he gives sight to a blind man or brings a dead man to life—so it happens that, in his superabundant goodness, he prevents with his aid even those who put any obstacle in the way of grace, and turns them away from evil and converts them to good.

'But he neither gives sight to all blind men nor cures all the sick : in those whom he cures the workings of his power appear; in others, the natural order is preserved. Likewise, he does not prevent with his help all of those who close themselves to grace, so as to turn them from evil and convert them to good, but only those in whom he wishes to manifest his mercy; in others it is the order of his justice which appears. "God," says St Paul, Rom. 9, 22, "desiring to show his wrath and to make known his power, has endured with much patience the vessels of wrath made for destruction, in order to make known the riches of his glory for the vessels of mercy, which he has prepared beforehand for glory." '[31]

[30]*III Contra Gent.,* ch. 161.
[31]The same teaching is found in the *Lectura ad Hebraeos,* ch. XII, lect. 3, edit. Marietti, no. 689: 'If anyone puts an obstacle in the way of grace and his heart is then drawn to remove it, this is the effect of a gift of the grace of God who is attracting him by his mercy, according to Gal. 1, 15: "But when he who had set me apart before I was born, and had called me through his grace, was pleased, etc . . ." Where the obstacle is removed

To which it must be added that, though the miracles which bring back the dead to life may be few those which bring sinners back to life are countless. On the miracle at Naïm, St Augustine writes: 'The resurrection of the young man rejoiced the heart of his widowed mother; the spiritual resurrection of sinners each day rejoices the heart of our Mother the Church.'[32]

5. IS CREATION IN STATU VIATORIS, IN WHICH SIN CAN HAPPEN, COMPATIBLE WITH THE INFINITY OF GOD'S GOODNESS?

A very clear-cut answer can be given. Yes, if it is true that God is not responsible for sin in any way whatsoever: either 1) directly and positively by forcing us into it; or 2) indirectly and negatively, by not doing what in his infinite goodness he is bound to do to turn us away from it.[33] Let us here consider the first of these conditions.

a. *It is obvious that God cannot be the direct cause of sin*

How can it be thought that God is positively and directly the cause of sin by forcing us into it? God, if he is the Absolute, cannot turn anything away from himself; and if he creates, that is to say, if he makes beings which depend on him, he cannot wish to turn them away from him, without unmaking them as he makes them; he can neither will not to love himself, nor will not to love, and so set against him, the beings he makes in his likeness.[34]

'There is no good,' says St Thomas, 'that God could prefer to his own goodness, although he can prefer this particular finite good to that other finite good'—he can prefer the good of the whole to that of a part; 'consequently, the evil of sin, which destroys the ordered progress towards the divine Being, is not in

it is the work of God's mercy; where it is not, it is the work of his justice.' In order to ward off any Pelagianism and insist on the rôle of God's helping graces—which we can unfortunately frustrate and set at naught—St Thomas had just written, the moment before, that 'not to put any obstacle (in the way of the salutary act) is itself the work of grace'.

[32]*Sermo XCVIII*, no. 2.
[33]Cf. St Thomas, I^a II^æ, qu. 79, a. 1.
[34]'Omne peccatum est per recessum ab ordine qui est in Deum sicut in finem. Deus autem omnia inclinat et convertit in seipsum sicut in ultimum finem.' Ibid. Cf. above, p. 78.

any way willed by God'.[35] The evil of particular natures is tolerated, that is, willed by accident, in view of the universal good of nature, which remains subordinated to the transcendent good of the divinity; the evil of sin, on the other hand, being the direct refusal of the transcendent good of the divinity, cannot be willed in any way by God.[36]

b. *According to Calvin, 'sins happen not only by God's permission, but also by his power'*

It is absurd to think that God can wish to make us sin. And yet there have been minds which have nourished this folly, in the name of the Fathers and even of the Bible.

Calvin could even go so far as to write : 'So as to carry out his judgments with the aid of the devil, who is the minister of his wrath, God turns where he thinks good the counsels of the wicked, and *moves their wills and confirms their effort.*' He was convinced that this is the teaching of St Augustine : 'St Augustine himself, in the fifth book against Julian, retracting the other opinion, maintains strongly and unwaveringly that sins do not come about merely by God's *permission* or sufferance, but also by his *power,* in order to punish other sins.'[37] The distinction

[35]'Malum culpae, quod privat ordinem ad bonum divinum, Deus nullo modo vult,' I, qu. 19, a. 9.
[36]The metaphysical characteristic of the evil of sin is that it seeks to deny God his prerogative of being the final end: 'Malum culpae in hoc differt a ceteris malis, quod ipsum quantum est ex se, est privativum *boni divini secundum seipsum,* si esset privabile ... Cetera autem mala respiciunt bonitatem divinam *in aliquo particulari effectu.*' Cajetan, *In Iam,* qu. 19, a. 9, no. iv.
[37]What is the teaching of St Augustine in the fifth book of the *Opus imperfectum contra Julianum?* Concerning Rom. 7, 19: 'For I do not the good I want, but the evil I do not want is what I do,' he states that original sin, by way of a penalty, has left in us a 'necessity of sinning, which we can only overcome by grace, stronger than any necessity' (ch. LXI)— and which, let us add, will be offered to all adults. But this necessity to sin is by no means to be traced back to the divine power: 'Does the evil in man,' of which the apostle speaks when he writes that he does the evil he does not want, 'go back to the very Maker of man? *numquid hoc malum hominis ... ipsum hominis pulsat Auctorem?*' (ch. LII). It is clear that this 'necessity of sinning' must be explained, just as the guilt contracted by young children, 'not as the work of God, but by the unforeseen arrival of sin, *non Dei opere, sed peccati origine*' (ch. VII). It is clear also, and this must be stressed once more, that it cannot be a question of anything more than a necessity of sinning, abstracting from the help given by grace which forestalls each of us. The book ends with a warning to

between willing and permitting evil was, in effect, to be rejected by Calvin, as we have already seen : 'Some have recourse here to the difference between *willing* and *permitting,* saying that the wicked perish, God permitting but not willing it. But why should we say that he permits it if we do not mean that he wills it ? How improbable it is in itself that it is only by the *permission* and not by the *ordinance* of God that man has brought damnation on himself.'[38] And a little earlier on : 'What I am saying should not in any way sound strange : it is that God not only foresaw the fall of the first man, and thereby the ruin of all his posterity, but he also willed it.'[39] Even so, the intentions of God remained for Calvin holy and irreproachable.

c. *In what sense does God blind and harden sinners?*

But surely there are passages in the Bible which do support the idea that God himself casts man into sin.[40] For instance, Exodus 4, 21; 7, 3; 14, 4) : 'I shall harden Pharaoh's heart, 'quoted by St Paul, (Rom. 9, 18) : 'He has mercy upon whomever he wills, and he hardens the heart of whomever he wills.' Or Isaiah (6, 9-10) : 'Go and say to this people : Hear and hear, but do not understand; see and see, but do not perceive. Make the heart of this people fat, and their ears heavy, and shut their eyes; lest they see with their eyes, and hear with their ears, and understand with their hearts, and turn and be healed,' quoted by St John (12, 39-40) : 'For Isaiah again said, He has blinded their eyes and

---

Julian: 'But you, if you say there is no foolishness in you, consider whether it is not foolishness to maintain that God is the author not only of the evil of punishment, which is justice, but also of the evil which bears the name of *iniquity?*' (Ch. LXIV). As can be seen, Augustine is far from taking back what he had previously said, e.g., in the third and fourth of the *Eighty-three Questions,* viz., that man becomes evil by the perversity of his own will, not by the divine will, *est ergo vitium voluntatis quo est homo deterior; quod vitium ... longe abest a Die voluntate.*

[38]Ibid., bk. III, ch. 23, no. 8. Cf. above, p. 84.

[39]Ibid, no. 7. This in connection with the first sin which, it should be noted, could not be willed 'in order to punish other sins'.

[40]St Augustine, in the fourteenth of the *Seventeen questions on St Matthew,* proposed instead to read the last words as: 'That they may understand with their hearts and turn and be healed'; and he explains that the Jews must have been blinded, then criminal; then staggered by their crimes, and finally overcome by love, *flagrantissima dilectione conversi.*

hardened their heart, lest they should see with their eyes and perceive with their heart, and turn for me to heal them.' Surely these passages prove that God causes men to hurtle into final impenitence, which is the worst of sins?

The immediate answer is that there are obvious passages which have the opposite meaning. That, for example, in Ezechiel (33, 11): 'As I live, says the Lord God, I have no pleasure in the death of the wicked, but that the wicked turn from his way and live.' Or that of St James (1, 13): 'Let no one say when he is tempted, I am tempted by God; for God cannot be tempted with evil and he himself tempts no one; but each person is tempted when he is lured and enticed by his own desire.' The most telling answer is that what is a metaphysical impossibility could never be either evident or proved.

What, then, can be the meaning of the first set of texts? 'When God blinds and hardens,' St Thomas explains in the *Commentary on St John* (12, 39-40), 'it must not be imagined that he puts wickedness into men or throws them into sin. It means that he ceases to infuse into them his grace. When he gives grace, it is his mercy. When he refuses it, it is our fault and happens because he finds in us an obstacle, *causa hujus quod non infundit est ex parte nostra, inquantum scilicet in nobis est aliquid gratiae divinae repugnans*. God for his part gives light to every man coming into this world (John 1, 9), and desires 'all men to be saved and to come to the knowledge of the truth' (I Tim. 2, 4). It is only when we have turned aside from him that he withdraws his grace from us, *sed quia nos a Deo recedimus, ideo gratiam suam nobis substrahit*, as it is written: 'Because you have rejected knowledge, I reject you' (Hosea 4, 6); and: 'Your loss comes from you alone, O Israel, it is I alone who come to your help.'[41]

It is the same with a man who closes the shutters of his room and to whom I would say: You cannot see because the sun's light has left you. Is it the sun's fault? No, but the fault of him who shields himself from the light, *hoc non esset ex defectu solis, sed quia ipse sibi lumen solare interclusisset*. When St John says that

[41]For this last verse of Hosea, quoted by St Thomas in the Vulgate version, the text of the Septuagint reads: 'In your destruction, Israel, who will be your help?' and the Hebrew text may be read: 'You are ruined, Israel, but your help is in me,' or: 'The cause of your ruin, Israel, is that you are against me, against your help.'

the Jews could not believe *because God had blinded them,* he means that they themselves had created the obstacle which was to blind them, as is written in the Book of Wisdom (2, 21): 'It is their wickedness that has blinded them.'[42]

In the parallel passage in the *Summa theologica,* St Thomas completes the comparison which has just been quoted. When I close the shutters, darkness is produced without the sun itself having acted at all. But if I put an obstacle in the way of grace, God, who is a free agent, can then withdraw the ray of light which shone all round me; in this sense he blinds me, but this withdrawal of grace is a consequence of my refusal: 'The cause of grace being withdrawn is not only the one who refuses but also God himself who, by his own judgment, no longer sends grace . . . to those in whom he finds an obstacle.'[43] If he leaves them to reap the consequences of their sin, it is they themselves who act to bring about their blinding and hardening.[44]

This is the only meaning which is metaphysically possible—the scriptural passages about God hardening sinners cannot be taken too narrowly and rigidly.[45] 'In order to lose you, O God, it is necessary to abandon you, *Te nemo amittit nisi qui dimittit,* and

---

[42]*Lectura super Joannem,* XII, less. 7, ed. Marietti, no. 1698.

[43]'Deus autem, proprio judicio, lumen gratiae non immittit illis in quibus obstaculum invenit.' Iᵃ IIᵃᵉ, qu. 79, a. 3.

[44]It is *sin* which affects man; blinding and hardening are only the results. Ibid., ad 1.

[45]Exegetes will doubtless have other considerations to put forward. E.g., Mark 4, 11: ' "To you has been given the secret of the kingdom of God, but for those outside everything is in parables, so that their eyes may . . . not perceive . . ." It all becomes clear enough provided that we interpret words spoken in a Semitic language according to the laws governing the spirit of that language . . . God willed to save his people, as is shown by the fact that he raised up a preacher . . . God's purpose is evident: it follows from the very language he employs, which is clear, urgent, compelling the Israelites to make their choice. That choice, however, is foreseen, and it will drag them to destruction. Go then, says the Lord to his envoy, with the angry bitterness of love doomed to disappointment: go and speak to them that they may harden their hearts and may not be pardoned! A strange remark, but one of touching beauty! Now, what happened in the time of Isaias happened also in the time of Jesus. The evangelists could not help seeing it, and they knew quite well that it was not God's fault. We have to try to enter their thoughts and follow their train of ideas.' M. J. Lagrange, O.P., *The Gospel of Jesus Christ* (Burns Oates & Washbourne, London, 1938), vol. I, p. 180.

whoever abandons you, where else can he go but from your friendship to your anger?'[46]

d. *In the sinner's action anything which has positive being can be attributed to God; any deviation goes no further than the sinner*

Sin is an *action*, concrete but *disordered*, in other words, deprived of its due subordination to its rule. Everything which can be called positive *being* in this action can be attributed to God as the only, first and universal cause of being. Anything which is *privation* can be traced back to the free creature as the only, first cause of the nullification of being. St Thomas makes a comparison with limping, which is a disordered walk; whatever is positive about it is due to the centres of locomotion, while whatever is deviation in it results from curvature of the bone.[47]

He develops the same teaching further in *De malo*.[48] The universal influence which leads living creatures to act can be received into a healthy plant, in which it will produce perfect seeds; or into a sickly plant, in which it will produce only sterile ones. Likewise the universal influence which moves all free creatures to act can be received in two ways. Either into a well-disposed and righteously ordered will, in which case the action will be good and entirely attributable to God as its first Cause; or into a will which withdraws itself from the rule of righteousness, in which case the disordered action can be split up into two parts : what positive being there is in it is attributable to God as to its first Cause, while the deviation comes only from the free will.[49]

To the objection that what causes the cause also causes the effect, there is a simple answer. 'The effect which proceeds from the

---

[46]St Augustine, *Confessions,* bk. IV, ch. 9, no. 14.
[47]Iᵃ IIᵃᵉ, qu. 79, a. 2.   [48]*De malo,* qu. 3, a. 2.
[49]The free act stems, in effect, from a twofold influence of God: 1) the general influence which universally activates all beings, notably the physical dynamism of the will; 2) the moral influence, resistible or irresistible, which activates to this or that determined good act. Take as an example, the oath taken in a court of law: where the evidence given is true, it stems from the twofold divine influence, from which it obtains both its physical being and its correct moral orientation; but where the testimony is false, the moral influence has been frustrated, and all that is left of the divine influence is that which gives the act its physical being. Cf. ibid., ad 2. Also Maritain, *Existence and the Existant,* op. cit., pp. 101ff.

intermediary cause goes back to the first cause only in so far as it obeys the direction of the first cause; but not if it proceeds from the intermediary cause rebelling against the direction of the first cause. The master could not be held responsible for what his servant does against his orders. Likewise the sin committed by free will against the divine precept could never be attributable to God as its cause.'[50]

St Thomas's analysis of this is profound and clear. But if we should forget, even for a moment, the definition of sin—that sin is an *action, deprived* of its due subordination to the rule—the distinction between what it owes to God and what it owes to the free will of the creature immediately vanishes, and God, responsible for whatever there is of positive being in the evil action is made to seem responsible for the element of deviation in it. This is to leave the threshhold of mystery and flounder in the absurd.

6. GOD IS NOT, EVEN INDIRECTLY, THE CAUSE OF SIN

We can be the cause of the sin of others either directly, by inclining their wills towards it, or indirectly, by making no effort to deflect them from it or draw them out of it.[51] Can we go on to say that God is the indirect cause of our sins, because he failed to prevent them when he could have done so?

a. *When God is bound to intervene and when he is not so bound, even in the name of his infinite goodness*

With us, the only way in which we can possibly come to the aid of another who is free, is to attract him away, directly or indirectly, so lovingly and with so much tact, that his refusal, should it come, can be imputed only to the refusal of the sinful will. We are bound to do this under pain of sinning ourselves.

In God's case, he can act upon free creatures not only through an external attraction but also through his inward influence. Two courses are open to him : one which our condition requires and to

[50]St Thomas, Iª IIªe, qu. 79, a. 1, ad 3.
[51]St Thomas, Iª IIªe, qu. 79, a. 1.

which he is bound; the other, which goes against the grain of our will and to which we would be the first to agree that he is certainly not in the least bound.

Short of detracting not only from his infinite goodness but also from justice, God is bound to give every man, by means either of external invitations or of inward influence, graces which can be resisted but which, if not resisted, will bear fruit in irresistible graces which will move him to perform the salutary act; graces which may, on the other hand, be so pressing that, should they be resisted, the fault will lie entirely in the refusal of the sinful will. This, according to the theologians, is the normal way in which the subordinated power is exercized : grace is offered to us, taking into account (and this is the heart of the mystery) the treatment required by the inherently fallible nature of the spiritual creature; that is to say, it respects the possible resistance of our free will. It is not said that the divine Goodness, being infinite, needs must give all men equal invitations and marks of affection, that it may not give two talents where it is going to ask for two more, five where it is going to ask for five more, so as ultimately to offer itself, in both cases, as the rewards. All that is said, is that God would not be what he is, would not be infinite Goodness, were he a master who 'takes up what he did not lay and reaps what he did not sow' (Luke 19, 21).

But, it may be objected, in giving his grace, God is surely able to act contrary to the treatment required by the necessarily sinful nature of his spiritual creatures? Surely, without destroying the metaphysical structure of their freedom he could from the start submit them to an influence that would irresistibly draw them towards the salutary act—'though our wills resist thee press them graciously into thy service'—and so save even those who make an effort to resist him. In such cases, he could surely have recourse to the extraordinary and miraculous exercize of his subordinated power. Yes, as has been said already, he both can and does do so, and quite frequently.

· Could he *always* act thus? To ask this of him would be to expect from him a different world from the one he chose to make, in which the extraordinary would become the ordinary, and the exception would be changed into the rule. It belongs to divine providence, as St Thomas reminds us, to govern things according to their natures, to preserve natures, not to do away with them.[52]

But at least, surely, the exceptions could be *more frequent*? Perhaps they could. But the real question lies elsewhere. Can we demand God to cause *even one single exception* to the ordinary rule of his subordinated power? Is the divine goodness, having showered its creatures with such help that, should they reject it, the fault should belong entirely to them (they will agree to this and glory in it) bound, under pain of ceasing to be infinite, to break down the resistance of one who freely wills to rebel against it? Not this question, but another, is the one we find unanswerable : why does God sometimes do what he is in no way bound to do? And why does he do it for one person rather than for another? This is where we should listen to St Augustine : 'Do not judge, if you do not want to err.'[53]

Read, within the framework of the ordinary exercise of God's power, the following passage, in which Kierkegaard explains that the Love of God, in order to save us, may well decree the folly of the Incarnation, but will not destroy in us the possibility of being scandalized at this folly and thereby casting ourselves away :

'God and man are two qualities between which there is an infinite qualitative difference. Every doctrine which overlooks this difference is, humanly speaking, crazy; understood in a godly sense, it is blasphemy. In paganism man made God a man (the Man-God); in Christianity God makes himself man (the God-Man)—but in the infinite love of his compassionate grace he made one stipulation, he can do no other. . . . He can humble himself, take the form of a servant, suffer and die for man, invite all to come unto him, sacrifice his life—but the possibility of the offense he cannot take away. O unique work of love! Oh, unfathomable sorrow of love! that God himself cannot, as in another sense he does not will, cannot will it, but even if he would, he could not make it impossible that this work of love might not turn out to be for a person exactly the opposite, to be the extremest misery!

[52]*II Sent.*, qu. 1, a. 2. Cf. *Compendium,* ch. 142: 'Providentiae non est naturam gubernatorum perdere sed salvare.' Elsewhere St Thomas writes that it would not be fitting for the Word to become incarnate in all men, for that would have done away with the multitude of *supposita* which is connatural to human nature. The result would have been another world in which the passion of Christ, the greatest proof of God's love for us, would not have been possible. III, qu. 4, a. 5, ad 2.
[53]Quoted by St Thomas, I, qu. 29, a. 5, ad 3.

For the greatest possible human misery, greater even than sin, is to be offended in Christ and remain offended. And Christ cannot, "Love" cannot render this impossible. Lo, for this reason he says, "Blessed is he who shall not be offended in me." More he cannot do.'[54]

b. *In the ordinary exercize of his power, God does incomparably more than he is bound to do: he even does things which are extravagant*

In the ordinary exercize of his subordinate power when, touching souls according to the treatment required by their natures, he sends them graces which they can resist if they wish, but which are destined in his own mind to bear fruit in irresistible graces under the influence of which the salutary act will be carried out, God does incomparably more than he is bound to in order to draw us out of sin : urged on by his love, he pursues sinners with his mercy.

In the Gospel, Peter asked Christ : 'Lord, how often shall my brother sin against me, and I forgive him? As many as seven times? Jesus said to him, I do not say to you seven times, but seventy times seven' (Matt. 18, 21-2). This is the forgiveness demanded from men; would God do less for them? 'What man of you, if his son asks him for a loaf, will give him a stone? Or if he asks for a fish, will give him a serpent? If you, then, who are evil, know how to give good gifts to your children, how much more will your Father who is in heaven give good things to those who ask him?' (Matt. 7, 9-11). The divine mercy seems to be attracted to sin as an eagle to its prey. It can shock : 'Why do you eat and drink with tax collectors and sinners? And Jesus answered them, Those who are well have no need of a physician, but those who are sick; I have not come to call the righteous, but sinners to repentance' (Luke 5, 30-2). There is no end to the parables telling us

[54]Kierkegaard, *The Sickness unto Death* (translated Walter Lowrie, Princeton University Press, 1946), p. 207. This passage continues: 'So then he may (that is possible), he may by his love have the effect of making a man more miserable than ever in any other way he could become. Oh, unfathomable contradiction in love!'
It should be made clear about these last lines that it is evidently not the love of Christ which finishes up by making a man's misfortune, but the rebellion of this man against the watchful care of Christ; if there is any contradiction, it is between the saving will of Christ and the perverse will of the sinner. This is the whole meaning of John 15, 22, 24: 'If I had not come and spoken to them, they would not have sin; but now they have no excuse for their sin.'

of the almost paradoxical kindnesses of the Saviour : 'What man of you, having a hundred sheep, if he has lost one of them, does not leave the ninety-nine in the wilderness, and go after the one which is lost, until he finds it? And when he has found it, he lays it on his shoulders, rejoicing ... Even so, I tell you, there will be more joy in heaven over one sinner who repents than over ninety-nine righteous persons who need no repentance' (Luke 15, 4-7). The same chapter shows us the father of the family going up the road towards the prodigal son in order to throw his arms round his neck (Luke 15, 20). And before that, at the meal in Simon the Pharisee's house, when the sinful woman was forgiven, we read : 'He who is forgiven little, loves little' (Luke 7, 47).

c. *Justification by ordinary and miraculous ways*

God does not tire of coming back to knock at the doors of those who have chased him away; consequently, although the justification of sinners is, like creation, the effect of divine omnipotence alone, it is a work so usual that it could never, from this point of view, be regarded as miraculous; only when God intervenes by the extraordinary exercize of his subordinated power, for example by bestowing from the outset an insuperable and intrinsically efficacious grace, can it be counted as a miracle : 'Miraculous works,' says St Thomas, 'present themselves as produced outside the regular and customary course of things : for example, when a sick man suddenly recovers his full health, over and above the processes of healing which are usually found in nature or medical skill. From this aspect the justification of the impious is sometimes miraculous and sometimes not. Justification is brought about according to the *normal, habitual* course when, beneath the interior influence of God, man turns towards God, first by an imperfect conversion in order afterwards to raise himself up to a perfect conversion ... But sometimes God moves the soul with such force that it *instantaneously* attains a certain perfection of righteousness, as with the conversion of St Paul'[55] or the good thief.

d. *The power of the prayers of intercession of Christ and of the friends of God*

We know that all the helping graces by which God, as much by

[55] Ia IIae, qu. 113, a. 10. Cf. III, qu. 86, a. 5, ad 1.

his habitual interventions as by his miraculous initiatives, knocks on the doors of our hearts to tear us away from sin, depend on the mediation of Christ who himself was given as ransom for all (I Tim. 2, 6), raised up to draw all men to him (John 12, 32); that they are an answer to the supreme prayer by which, on the cross, he asked his Father's forgiveness for the world : 'In the days of his flesh, Jesus offered up prayers and supplication, with loud cries and tears, to him who was able to save him from death, and he was heard for his godly fear. Although he was a Son, he learned obedience through what he suffered; and being made perfect he became the source of eternal salvation to all who obey him, being designated by God a high priest after the order of Melchisedech' (Hebr. 5, 7-10).

Our Lord's prayer for the salvation of the world is infinite because of the divinity of the One who prayed, and certainly nothing can be added to it in *intensity*; yet it was not intended to make our own prayer futile, but rather to call it forth, give life to it and raise it up. His is the prayer of the Head, asking to be participated in, to grow in *extension* and to be propagated throughout the whole Body. The Saviour desires to be joined to the members who in their turn will pray for the world and, sustained by him, will be able to be, in their degree, with him, in him and through him, the saviours of others. The mystery of the adhesion to Christ who is the Head is the basis of the mystery of the communion of saints with a view to the co-redemption of the world. 'Now,' says the apostle, 'I rejoice in my sufferings for your sake, and in my flesh I complete what is lacking in Christ's afflictions for the sake of his body, that is, the church' (Col. 1, 24).

This mystery of co-redemption is taught in the Gospel. How can we think that God needs us to extend his kingdom? And yet it is up to us to ask him to send workers into his harvest : 'When he saw the crowds, he had compassion for them, because they were harassed and helpless, like sheep without a shepherd. Then he said to his disciples, The harvest is plentiful, but the labourers are few; pray therefore the Lord of the harvest to send out labourers into his harvest' (Matt. 9, 36-8). When the disciples asked Christ to teach them to pray, he gave them the Lord's Prayer, and the first three paradoxical petitions that they had to address to God were that his name be hallowed, his kingdom come and his will be done. These divine things, therefore, will come about partially in depend-

ence on our human initiatives. It must be concluded that the
fervour with which God's friends pray will decide, to a very great
extent, the outpourings of God's helping graces, be they regular
or miraculous, the advances made by the City of God, and any
progress in the conversion of the world. Had the Curé d'Ars not
been a saint, doubtless many souls would not have been saved; and
yet it is certain that of those who might have been lost, each would
have been lost by his own fault and for no other reason. Within
this setting it is possible to understand the ardour that consumes
the hearts of God's friends, and the vehemence and insatiability
of their desires. St Catherine of Siena felt responsible for the
disorders of her time; Mary of the Incarnation, the Ursuline nun,
called upon the eternal Father to do justice to his Son since he
had promised him the nations as a heritage; St Thérèse of
Lisieux wanted to proclaim the Gospel in all parts of the world at
the same time. It can be imagined also that these contracts of love
which they make with God to ransom sinners are only settled at
the price of unspeakable sufferings and agonies which must resemble those of the Saviour.

e. *The final possibility of salvation for the utterly abandoned*

'First of all, then, I urge that supplications, prayers, interces-
sions, and thanksgivings be made for all men . . . This is good, and
it is acceptable in the sight of God our Saviour, who desires all
men to be saved and to come to the knowledge of the truth' (I Tim.
2, 1-4). The Word 'was the true light that enlightens every man
coming into the world' (John 1, 9). This absolute certainty we
have that God provides for every adult with the superabundance
of his graces, and that he will not reap where he has not sown, is
verified for us, in numberless cases, by our own experience of
Christian sinners. But in other circumstances the facts seem to give
the lie to this certainty; it seems effrontery to maintain it in the
face of the fearful misery in which so many human beings live
and die. The Christian thinks 'of other abandoned beings, whose
lot awakens in the soul an unbearable anguish because of the unrelieved darkness of the night in which death struck them . . . I
am thinking of those poor human beings who had done nothing
except their humble daily tasks, and upon whom in a flash death
pounced like some wild beast. Immolated by the whims of war and
of savagery—persecuted not for the sake of justice about which

they were not even thinking, but for the sake of the innocent fact of their mere existence at an unlucky point in time and space. What are, moreover, their sufferings and their death except the likeness and brief summary wherein we may read the sufferings of millions of the poor and forsaken throughout the course of centuries, ground down without defence by the great mill of pride and greed which is as old as humanity? The conquered who have been reduced to slavery, the untouchables, the classless, the slaves of all ages, the black men sold at auction by merchants of human flesh, women and children labouring in sweatshops, the proletarians of the industrial age, all those whom misery has stripped of their human condition, all the accursed of the worldly community . . . And how many others died completely forsaken. They did not give their lives, their lives were taken from them, and under the shadow of horror. They suffered without wanting to suffer. They did not know why they died. Those who know why they die are greatly privileged people.'[56]

There is only one answer, ultimately, to this problem: 'It all seems to take place as though the death agony of Jesus—being so divinely vast—must be divided into its contrasting aspects in order that some image of it might pass into his members, and that men might completely participate in this great treasure of love and of blood. The saints of their own will enter in Christ's passion, offering themselves along with him . . . The beatitude of the persecuted illumines their earthly existence. The more they are abandoned, the more can they say with John of the Cross: Mine are the heavens and mine is the earth . . . But those wholly and completely forsaken, the victims of the night, those who die as though they were the outcasts of earthly existence, those who are hurled into Christ's death agony without knowing it and without wanting it—all these are making manifest another aspect of the same agony, and surely it is necessary that all be made manifest . . . As a legacy left to his other flock, he said: *My God, My God, why hast thou forsaken me?* The great flock of the truly destitute, of those dead without consolation—would he not take care of those who bear this mark of his agony?'[57]

And if they are not found in rebellion against the Author of

[56]Maritain, 'Blessed are the Persecuted', in *The Range of Reason* (Geoffrey Bles, London, 1953), p. 224-5.
[57]Ibid., p. 225.

their lives,[58] 'how could it happen that their very forsaking itself would not serve as the signature of their belonging to the crucified Saviour, and as a supreme title to his mercy? At the corner of death, in the moment when they pass to the other side of the veil, and the soul is on the verge of leaving a flesh for which the world had no use, is there not yet time enough to say to them: Thou shalt be with me in paradise?'[59] even when, to the very end, no light visible to the eyes of men has shone forth for them, even from God himself?

f. *The great number of the elect*

The meaning of the phrase in Matthew (22, 14): 'Many are called but few are chosen' is well known. It concerns the vocation of the Jewish people. Although all are called upon to receive the Messiah, only a handful will recognize him, and the crowd will go astray either in error or perversity. But there is nothing in revelation that forbids us to believe in the great number of the elect. This is probably what John means when he says (14, 2): 'In my Father's house there are many mansions.' Admittedly a look at the way of the world prompts us to think of some other words of the Saviour: 'Enter by the narrow gate; for the gate is wide and the way is easy, that leads to destruction, and those who enter by it are many. For the gate is narrow and the way is hard, that leads to life, and those who find it are few' (Matt. 7, 13-4).

When we look at the world, how can we avoid saying that it is going in a very foolish direction? But when we look at the value of the blood shed for us on the cross, how can we fail to hope that where sin abounds, grace abounds even more (Rom. 5, 20)? The Apocalypse reveals to us, beside the great number of the elect from the twelve tribes of Israel, the enormous multitude from the Gentile nations: 'Which no man could number, from every

---

[58]'The persecuted and the saints, who are saved by Christ, save as instrumental causes and by virtue of the blood of Christ, the persecutors and the evil-doers. Poor persecutors and poor sinners, poor prodigal sons who are struggling in the experience of evil and the unholy business of the world, will thus be saved, except those who have killed within themselves any divine seed of good will and who prefer Hell to God. With the exception of these men who refuse to be redeemed, that very world which hates Christ and his disciples will be finally reconciled to Christ, but after the end of history.' Maritain, *On the Philosophy of History* (Geoffrey Bles, London, 1959), p. 117.

[59]'Blessed are the Persecuted', in *The Range of Reason*, op. cit., p. 226.

nation, from all tribes and peoples and tongues, standing before the throne and before the Lamb, clothed in white robes, with palm branches in their hands' (Apoc. 7, 9).

7. MAN IS THE CAUSE OF HIS OWN SIN

a. *The suggestions of the world, the flesh and the devil cannot force us to sin*

The outside world entices us to evil by putting in front of us good things which stir our desire, but which are yet illusory, since they deflect us from our final end and we may possess them only by deviating from the rule of reason and the divine law.[60] At such times the reason must intervene, distract our train of thought and neutralize the effect of the temptation. Admittedly it can happen, in certain cases which are plainly pathological, that passion can throw a man into madness and deprive him altogether of the use of reason; but then, given that such passion has not been provoked by some previous fault, the subsequent act would be quite involuntary and consequently without sin.[61]

The devil likewise has no power to force us to sin. The angels, good or bad, can act upon our reason by proposing something external to us, by making suggestions; but they are fundamentally incapable of touching our free will. Can the devil nonetheless excite our imagination and disturb our passions to the point of indirectly involving our reason and completely thwarting its activity? This does not appear impossible, says St Thomas, and might be met with in certain cases of possession. But whatever a man does in such a state can never be imputed to him as sin.[62]

In all these cases, either there is not free will and no sin, or there is sin and our free will is the cause of it.

b. *The initiative in doing evil lies with man*

It is clear that the initiative for his free acts is left to man, but differently according to whether the free act is good or evil.

If the free act is morally good, bringing with it positive new values, the first initiative must surely be attributed to God. Then

[60]St Thomas, Iª IIae, qu. 75, a. 2.
[61]Ibid., Iª IIae, qu. 78, a. 7. See below, pp. 233, 235.
[62]Iª IIae, qu. 80, a. 3.

it is the second initiative which is left to man, that of the assent given under God's influence, to which he commits his destiny. This dependence, far from destroying our liberty, is its cause. Our assent freely given to God is the purest and richest spiritual activity which can come from this world, the holiest answer a creature can make to his Creator; where ultimately would its beauty originate if not in God? He moves all beings from within, according to the nature which each of them receives from him, not by constraining them but by activating them and making them grow. By nature man is directed towards good in all its fullness, towards the absolute good which alone is able to complete him, so that the good things of this life, being limited, find him in a state of indifference in regard to them: he can want them in so far as they are good things, or leave them alone in so far as they are not the absolute good. To say that God moves man according to his nature means that he first gives him the desire for the absolute good then, by leaving him the domination over all particular good things, allows him to choose from among them those which will bring him nearer to his final end.

Thus it must be understood that God knows our free acts in the eternal order by which he moves us to produce them. It should not be said that he knows them in *advance*: a being who knows in advance is by definition a being immersed in time, who himself moves from past to present to future, and who can therefore *remember* the past and sometimes *foresee* the future. Now the great mystery about God is that he is not in time, and there is in him no *memory* of the past, no *foreseeing* of the future. From his exalted viewpoint in eternity he does not see things happening in succession, but he sees them in *one glance,* in their presentness, that is to say, at the very instant when they come into existence to coexist with him. He does not know in advance, he sees from all eternity the initiatives which we take freely *hic et nunc* and which for us happen in the present, or did happen in the past, or will do so in the future. 'What we call God's prescience,' says St Anselm, 'is not strictly speaking fore-knowledge. He, indeed, to whom all things are present, knows future things not by foreknowledge, *praescientia,* but by a knowledge to which everything is present, *praesentium scientia.'*[63] And St Thomas: 'All temporal things have always

[63]*De Casu diaboli,* ed. F. S. Schmitt, O.S.B.: in *Opera Omnia,* vol. 1, p. 267.

been present to God, not only, as some say, because he bears the ideas of them in himself, but because his gaze is always directed upon them as present to him.'[64] Cajetan comments: 'The first instant of this hour is in the instant of eternity, the last instant of this hour is certainly not in the first, but it also is in the very same instant of eternity.'[65] Thus in the successionless instant of his eternity, in which there is no room for memory or foreknowledge and which controls and contains all the fugitive moments of our time, God *sees* all the affirmative responses which he causes us to make.

What happens in the case of sin? This is produced by man alone, without God and against God.

It is produced *without* God. It is man alone who takes the initiative and is the first cause of sin: 'The first cause of the falling away of grace,' says St Thomas, 'comes from us.'[66] Can a creature, then, be the first cause of something? No—God alone is the first cause of everything which comes about in the world. But sin is not a positive being: it is a privation introduced into a positive being.

It is not simply apart from God's will but *against* it that sin is produced. None of the initiatives taken by his love should ever be lost sight of. Sin is always a refusal of his help, a resistance to the hidden and interior urgings of his saving grace. For a free creature, in so far as it has come out of nothing, has this fearful privilege of being able to nullify within itself the influence of God. It is cruel to itself, as St Catherine of Siena says: 'What greater cruelty can it inflict on itself than to put itself to death by mortal sin?'[67] God himself bears witness to this: 'What more was there to do for my vineyard, that I have not done in it?' (Isaiah 5, 4). In the voice of the psalmist he pleads: 'Today, when you hear his voice do not harden your hearts' (Hebr. 3, 8, 15; 4, 7). Jacques Maritain says about the evil act: 'God cannot be the cause of evil itself or privation, or of the mutilation which deforms my act; of this it is I who am the first cause. Evil as such is the only thing I am able

[64] I, qu. 14, a. 13.
[65] *In Iam,* qu. 14, a. 13, no. XII.
[66] Ia IIae, qu. 112, a. 3, ad 2. Cf. above, pp. 156 and 166.
[67] *Prayers of St Catherine of Siena,* Eighth prayer made in Rome, Tuesday, 22 February, 1379.

to do without God, by withdrawing myself, as it were, as if by an initiative emanating from my nothingness, from the current of Divine causality. In the line of evil-doing, the creature is first cause. *Without me you can do nothing* (John 15, 5). This is true in two senses : without God we cannot do anything; we can without him do nothing.[68] The first initiative towards good acts comes always from God, so that there the initiative of created freedom has its origin in the initiative of God. But by reason of the power to *refuse,* which is a natural element of all created freedom, the first initiative to evil-doing always comes from the creature : God has the power but does not will to prevent the creature (when it is so inclined) from interposing its refusal.'[69]

God knows the creature's refusal, certainly not by causing it— since he does not cause anything which nullifies—but in the positive influence towards good which the creature makes void. He does not know it in advance, before the initiative of the creature is taken, because there is in him, strictly speaking, neither foreknowledge nor memory. From all eternity he sees the moment when the refusal is produced; it does not disconcert him. What would surprise him would be a creature which could without him add the slightest atom of being to the fabric of the world. But sin is pure privation. Nonetheless, is it able in any way to disrupt the plans of providence? Not if these plans have been laid from all eternity and take into account all that God sees from all eternity.[70]

---

[68]Peter Lombard, *I Sent.,* dist. 46, writes on John 1, 3: '*Et sine ipso factum est nihil,* id est peccatum.' Cf. St Augustine's commentary on this same text: 'Sin is nothing, and men become nothing when they sin.' *In Joan. Evang.,* tr. I, no. 13.

[69]Maritain, *Freedom in the Modern World* (Sheed & Ward, London, 1935), p. 81-2.

[70]'Is this positing a determination of the divine knowledge by the creature, I mean by the irruption of nothingness of which the creature has the first initiative? But do you then believe that non-being is capable of determining? And furthermore do you believe that created beings are for divine knowledge anything else but a secondary term attained as a mere 'material' or factual datum, in no way formative or specifying? Are you forgetting that only the divine essence is for divine knowledge a formal and specifying object, and that neither the things (other than himself) that God knows, nor the "decrees" nor the "permissions" of his will have the slightest determining role in regard to his act of knowledge? If we do not begin by recognizing the absolute freedom of divine knowledge in regard to its created objects, we had better not discuss these things. Even when it

c. *God, who does not contain the idea of evil, knows only through what is good the limited evil in nature and the unlimited evil contributed by man*

The ideas in the divine understanding are the ways in which the divine essence can be participated in. Thus, on the one hand, they are the principles of knowledge and the explanatory causes of things; and on the other hand, they are the principles of production, the models or exemplars of things.[71]

Are there in God any ideas of evil? This is tantamount to asking whether in the divine essence there is an evil which is perceived by the divine understanding and by which, on the one hand, the evil in things would be explained, and by resemblance to which, on the other hand, it would be produced. The answer, of course, is that in God there are ideas only of things : of good things, or of things ravaged by evil, in which case God knows evil in the good

knows that of which it is not the cause—evil as such—it is never formed by what it knows. If its permissions themselves remain formative, it is in this sense that divine knowledge still lays hold of and assumes the initiatives of refusal of the creature in the designs and the forms through which the torrent of being passes.' Maritain, 'The Freedom of Song', in *Art and Poetry,* (Editions Poetry, London, 1945), pp. 58-9.

Earlier in this essay, he made use of the image of musical creativity to illustrate the creative knowledge of God: 'And it is only when the symphony is made and finished that, in the mind of the composer, its creative idea is itself achieved. I mean as to the *expressibility* of this idea, as to the detail of its determinations and of its contours' (p. 55). 'Let us venture to say that in one sense the same is true for the divine knowledge. For to give us some intelligence about the properties of the creative knowledge, called *scientia visionis,* it is not only the consideration of what is called God's "antecedent will" (by which he wills that all be good, all be saved), which we must add to the consideration of the divine essence infinitely transparent to the divine intellection, it is also the consideration of the "consequent will" of God, by which he permits the evil of the free creature—and by reason of what circumstances, if not of the refusal brought about by the creature. I mean not only by reason of the general possibility of refusal included in created liberty, I also mean by reason of the initiatives of refusal which in effect emanate from it at a given moment. If it is true that in the line of evil the creature is the first cause (deficient, not efficient)—first cause of the privation or nothingness that wounds a given moment of his liberty—then it must be said that evil cannot be known save in the same instant when it thus wounds existence, when the creature escapes voluntarily from the influx of being and goodness that descends from creative love; and it is because time is present in its entirety at the immobile and eternal *nunc,* that from all eternity, the free absence, the voluntary non-regulation, the non-being that is the root of the devious act accomplished by me at a given hour of this clock of the universe or the atom, is and was and shall be known of God' (pp. 57-8).

[71]Cf. above, p. 90.

which these things ought to have and which is lacking.[72] But in him there are no ideas of evil.[73]

Let us recall here the fundamental distinction between the evil in nature and the evil of sin.

The evil in nature is not intended by God. What he intends is the good and all its countless proliferations, which are participations in the divine essence, and realizations of the divine ideas. But this good intended by God inevitably holds an element of nothingness and privation which must be accepted, and which in this sense is willed indirectly. The forms of evil in nature, with their proliferations, are willed indirectly by God in so far as they accompany the forms and proliferations of good which are directly willed by him. They are included in the divine ideas of good and are measured by them.

But the forms of the evil of sin are not willed by God in any way at all. They are not included either as willed indirectly in the creative ideas or as measured by them. They are freely contrived, with all their fearful proliferations, by man as the first cause of sin. On this subject Maritain has this to say :[74] 'I have said that in God there is no idea of evil. He invented Behemoth and Leviathan, and all the terrifying forms which people nature and the world of life—the ferocious fishes, the destroying insects. He did not invent moral evil and sin. It was not he who had the idea of all the defilements and abominations, and contempts that are spat into his Face; the betrayals, lecheries, cruelties, cowardices, bestial wickednesses, refined perversions, depravities of mind which it is given to his creatures to contemplate. Those were born solely of nihilation by human liberty. They came forth from that abyss. God permits them as a creation of our power to make the thing which is nothing.

'He permits them because he is strong enough, as St Augustine says, to turn all the evil we choose to introduce into the world,

---

[72]'Evil, as such, is nothing, since it is a privation, for example, blindness. Consequently there is indeed to be found in God the idea of an evil thing, *rei malae*, certainly not inasmuch as it is evil, *in quantum mala est*, but inasmuch as it is a thing, *in quantum res est;* and the evil itself is known by God though the good which is opposed to this evil and in which the thing subjected to a privation is deficient, *et ipsum malum per oppositum bonum cognoscitur a Deo, a quo res privationi subjecta deficit.*' St Thomas, *I Sent.*, dist. 36, qu. 2, a. 3, ad 1.
[73]'Malum non habet in Deo ideam.' St Thomas, I, qu. 15, a. 3, ad 1.
[74]Maritain, *Existence and the Existant*, op. cit., pp. 126-7.

into a greater good, hidden in the mystery of transcendence and such that nothing in nature allows us to conjecture what it may consist in. The man of faith, who is to have a suspicion of the greatness of that good, and marvel at it, measures the greatness of the evil for which such a good will supercompensate.

'Our misfortune is precisely that there is no scenario written by God in advance (it would be less sinister), and that the ill-omened element of the drama comes from created existents, ourselves, and from the fact that God plays fair. Since the evil of the free act is our creation, it is in letting our monsters proliferate to the very end and allowing the infinite resources of our power of nihilating to develop all forms of degradation and corruption of being, that divine liberty manifests the sublimity of its omnipotence, drawing from that itself the higher good which God designs, not for itself but for us.'[75]

d. *God is hurt by our sin*

Contemplation of the mystery of the redemption brings us to an understanding of the real mystery of the evil of sin. If it was necessary for a God to come and save us, then surely sin must conceal some infinite wickedness? This is the question put by St Anselm in the *Cur Deus homo*. St Thomas says: 'Sin committed against God takes on a certain infinity from the infinite Majesty: for the greater the dignity of the one offended, the greater the offence. Hence satisfaction, if it was to be equivalent, *condigna,* required an act whose efficacity, coming at the same time from God and man, would be infinite.'[76] More violently, St John of the Cross writes of sins that they are 'so hateful to God that they forced him to his death, *que Dios tanto oborrece que obligaron a muerte'.*[77]

Sin is an offence against God, an insult to his infinite Majesty. It affects God by defrauding him of something which was owing to him in justice: it infringes the strict right of the final End to be loved above all things. More concretely, it hurts God *himself,* admittedly not *in himself,* but where he is vulnerable, that is to say, in the love by which he strives to save us. 'What then does this notion of an offence against God mean? . . . One way of put-

---

[75]'Deus gloriam suam quaerit non propter se, sed propter nos.' St Thomas, II^a II^{ae}, qu. 132, a. 1, ad 1.
[76]III, qu. 1, a. 2, ad 2. Cf. Journet. *L'Eglise de Verbe incarné,* vol. II, p. 151.
[77]*Letter X.*

ting it would be to say that sin is *deicide* in the sense that, in so far as it has it in itself to do so, it would destroy God, were that possible.

But that is quite impossible! I hurl myself on a man to kill him, but my knife is made of cardboard. Such a way of expressing it throws light on the nature of our act, not on the way it affects God. Sin destroys something created, but destroys nothing in God.

Another way of putting it, which seems preferable, is to say that sin *deprives* the divine will of something which it actually desired ... In his antecedent will, God wills that all men should be saved, and likewise that all my acts should be good. If I sin, something that God has desired and loved will never happen, and this is due to my first initiative.[78] Thus I am the cause—the nullifying cause—of a privation in regard to God, a privation as to the end or the desired effect (though by no means as to the good of God himself) ... Sin does not only deprive the universe of something good, it also deprives God himself of something which was conditionally but really willed by him ... Moral defect affects God, though not in himself, since he is invulnerable, but in the things and effects which he wills and loves. In this, God can be said to be the most vulnerable of beings. There is no need for poisoned arrows, cannons or machine-guns : an invisible movement in the heart of a free agent is sufficient to wound him and deprive his antecedent will of something on this earth which it has desired and loved from all eternity, and which now will never be.'[79]

It is written somewhere that in the Old Testament man was afraid of God, but that in the New it is God who is afraid of man, afraid of me, afraid of you, and of the evil which I can still do to him by myself and through others. God is indeed afraid of sin, *he is afraid on my account of the evil I can do to him;* that is why he sends his one and only beloved Son to search for me in all the highways and byways of the world and to call me under his cross :

> *Quaerens me sedisti lassus,*
> *Redemisti crucem passus,*
> *Tantus labor non sit cassus.*

[78] Cf. St Thomas, *I Sent.*, dist. 47, qu. 1, a. 2, ad 1; 'Those who are not with God are, so far as in them lies, against God, *from the fact that they go against God's antecedent will.*'
[79] Maritain, *Neuf leçons sur les notions premières de la philosophie morale,* op. cit., pp. 175-6.

CHAPTER SEVEN

The Punishment of Actual Sin

The evil of sin occasions the evil of punishment.[1] It is impossible to run your head against the things of God without hurting yourself. Guilt is followed by punishment as a body by its shadow. It follows that different sins call for different punishments. The punishment of original sin will be discussed later, but something must now be said about the eternal punishment of mortal sin, and then of the temporal punishment of venial sin. This involves a consideration of the mysteries of hell, of afflictive and satisfactory punishment, and of purgatory.

I. THE MYSTERY OF HELL

The mystery of hell is the mystery of the twofold disorder of sin, which continues to be freely willed despite the twofold sanction which it entails.

I. IS GOD RESPONSIBLE FOR HELL?

It is evident that whatever there is of ontological wealth and splendour in hell—the incorruptible natures of the angels, the spiritual souls of men and later their risen bodies—and whatever there is of positive ontological value in the natural desire of the damned for happiness, and even in their free, intelligent activity which never ceases—all these have their ultimate source in God and result from the original and unregretted gift of his mercy which urged him to create all things, the material world, angels and man, not in order to bring them to nothing but to maintain them by his providence in their being and actions.[2]

[1]The expiatory sufferings of Christ are a consequence of our sins.
[2]It is the divine goodness which, for example, by giving man his nature, is at the origin of everything which is subsequently due to this nature:

But it is also evident that whatever there is of sin, rebellion, pride or blasphemy in hell cannot be 'a structural element of the universe', cannot be attributed in any way, either directly or indirectly, to God.

But what are we to think of the evil of punishment inflicted on the damned, the evil of suffering which is inseparable from their rebellion? Surely God is its cause? He is its cause in so far as he wills, and cannot but will, that with which the damned come into collision through their own voluntary and persistent fault. In order to put an end to the insoluble conflict into which they are thrown by their rebellion and to leave the field to them, the twofold obstacle—God, and the order of creation—which they come up against, would have to disappear. God would have to disavow himself by a sort of self-destruction, and disavow also the decree by which he imparted order to the universe. When we speak of the holy Justice of God which is opposed to evil, it must be remembered that this can only mean the twofold Love, both the necessary love by which he cannot but will his own being, and the free love by which he cannot turn aside from the world which in his wisdom he has already decreed. 'Not to punish the damned would mean that God accepted that self-assertion in opposition to him, which is sin.'[3]

God is the light that enlightens every man coming into the world (John 1, 9); only those who close their hearts to him are in darkness, in the same way as a man who closes the shutters and plunges everything in gloom. But, as St Thomas has pointed out,[4] there

---

'Thus mercy appears in all of God's works as their original root, *in quolibet opere Dei apparet misericordia quantum ad primam radicem ejus.*' St Thomas, I, qu. 24, a. 4. In a sense God's love is itself present in hell, but as *something rejected*. In this way must be understood this passage of Isaac the Syrian: 'Those who find themselves in gehenna will be scourged by the flail of love. How bitter and cruel this torment of love will be! Those who realize that they have sinned against love undergo a suffering greater than that brought about by the most fearful tortures. The pain which grips the heart that has offended against love is more acute than any other affliction. It is not correct to say that sinners in hell are deprived of God's love ... But love acts in two different ways: it becomes suffering in the damned and joy in the blessed.' Quoted by Vladimir Lossky, *Essai sur la théologie mystique de l'Eglise d'Orient* (Aubier, Paris, 1944), p. 232.
[3]Jean Hervé Nicolas, 'Amour de Dieu et tremblement', in *La Vie Spirituelle,* October, 1958, p. 239.
[4]Iª IIae, qu. 79, a. 3. Cf. above, p. 165.

is a difference: when a man closes his shutters, darkness is produced without any reaction on the sun's part, but when he closes his heart to God, God freely withdraws the light of his grace.

As for sin, so with punishment: we can be bruised against a wall without any reaction on the wall's part, but when a sinner rises against God, God, who is a free agent, reacts freely against the sinner and abandons him, exiling him from his love. This mysterious reciprocal action can only be understood if it is realized that 'to refuse to love is to refuse to be loved; and to refuse to be loved is to exclude oneself from the love that was offered'. Then the love which came freely to meet us is withdrawn by the one who offered it. The love of friendship 'is reciprocal . . . It would be impossible to reject love without being rejected by love . . . Eternal damnation is first of all that exclusion from God's love which was brought about by refusing to be loved by God. This does not mean . . . that it is a mere ratification on God's part of the refusal made by the sinner. God rejects the one who rejects him and by doing so casts him off.'[5]

The evil of punishment, then, is evidently willed and permitted by God in a completely indirect way.[6] It is not the first Love, as the poet said, but the rebellion against the first Love and its created work which has made hell.[7] Refuse it and the first Love withdraws.

We now see, also, how to answer the question: if evil is permitted and tolerated for some great good, for what great good is the evil of punishment permitted, by what great good is it justified? The revolt against that goodness which is the infinite holiness of God brings with it what is called the pain of damnation; and the revolt against that goodness which is the finite holiness of creation brings with it what is called the pain of the senses.[8]

[5] Jean Hervé Nicolas, loc. cit., pp. 231-2.
[6] While God in no way wills the evil of sin, writes St Thomas, he may be said to will 'the evil in nature and evil of punishment, inasmuch as he intends a good which this evil seizes upon: in willing justice he wills punishment, in willing the conservation of the natural order he wills the corruption of certain beings', I, qu. 19, a. 9.
[7] This may not be the place to mention it, but a very dear friend of mine was converted, not by the triplets Dante engraved on the door of his Inferno, but by the sudden bursting upon him of the frightening certainty that hell is where love is mutually refused. Cf. below, pp. 188 and 192.
[8] Cf. below, p. 255.

2. CARICATURES OF HELL

It is absurd, unworthy and hateful to think that God can draw pleasure from the sufferings endured in hell and that he can seek and find in revenge a means of satisfying his justice—and yet is any blasphemy about hell more common than this?

a. *Vindictive punishment*

Even from a purely philosophical point of view, the justification of sanctions by the theory of vindictive punishment is unacceptable; it offers only a pseudo-explanation which is both anthropomorphic and irrational. In such a theory, writes Maritain: 'Punishment is essentially a retort, *arbitrary* and purely voluntary at that, determined solely by the free decree of the one who inflicts it (as with human punishment, the punishment of the positive law, which are *discretionary* punishments, at the legislator's discretion). And above all, in this theory punishment intends *primarily* the evil produced in the one who is punished. It is as though the misery and suffering of the guilty gave satisfaction to nature or to the gods. A superior strength would enjoy pleasure in revenge after the offence. Such a theory is not merely anthropomorphic. The human pattern on which it is based, revenge, is something in itself illicit and wicked. St Thomas, II^a II^{ae}, qu. 108, a. 1, explains that revenge, inasmuch as it principally intends the evil inflicted on the offender and is satisfied by this evil, is entirely illicit and unforgivable: one sin following on another. *Vindicatio* can be licit—*aliis debitis circumstantiis servatis*—only if the intention of the agent is principally a good to which the penalty inflicted on the guilty is a means, e.g. the rehabilitation of the guilty, the protection of other people or the upholding of justice. *Justitiae conservationem:* hence the justice of the penalty is in itself something other than revenge, just as it is in itself something other than a cure. The theory, or rather the confused and vaguely imagined idea of vindictive punishment, simply poses more questions and aggravates the problem of sanctions. If a murderer's death were able to give back life to his victim, then it could be understood as some compensation for his crime. But as it is, it merely adds death to death, and suffering to suffering. What joy can there be in men's suffering or in evil added to evil? And who is there who could take pleasure in this addition of evil to evil, what is the power to which this doubling of evil could be attributed? Nature does not care; God takes no pleasure in evil; the world-order feels neither pleasure nor displeasure. Vindictive punishment is a mockery. There must be another theory with more ontological depth . . .'[9]

b. *Berdyaev*

Berdyaev has a few extremely lucid and penetrating flashes when he sees in the religious idea of hell 'a profound affirmation of personal being',[10] and when he connects this idea with the mystery of man's freedom : 'Man is free to choose torment without God rather than happiness in God; he has a right to hell, as it were. But hell means the impossibility of loving God because of a certain orientation of human freedom, of a certain estrangement from God and separation from him, through self-isolation.'[11] 'If we logically affirm personality and freedom we are bound to assert the possibility of hell. It is easy to get rid of the idea of hell, but it is at the price of personality and freedom.'[12]

But he immediately goes on to neutralize and destroy the implications of these ideas : 'On the other hand, our personality and freedom cannot be reconciled with eternal punishment . . . It is still possible to admit punishment from man's standpoint, but not from God's.'[13] Hell, for him, is ultimately only a myth born of the experiences we have of suffering here on earth : 'The idea of eternal punishments was born of experience in virtue of which all suffering felt in this life appears to us as eternal. Torment which was not eternal would not be the torment of hell. Hell is precisely this sense of infinity, this ignorance of the end, this eternity of suffering contained not in its prolongation but in a single instant.'[14] He is trifling when he makes use of Dante's *Inferno* to accuse Christianity of 'reducing spiritual life to the sphere of naturalism'.[15] He deludes himself and puts the blame on the

---

[9]Maritain, *Neuf leçons sur les notions premières de la philosophie morale,* op. cit., pp. 180-2. Cf. above, p. 77.
[10]Nicholas Berdyaev, *Freedom and the Spirit,* op. cit., p. 325.
[11]Ibid., p. 324.   [12]Ibid., p. 325.
[13]Ibid., p. 325.   [14]Ibid., p. 324.
[15]Ibid., p. 324.

Gospels when he asserts that 'the doctrine of posthumous sanctions is only the product of a cruel and barbaric age which saw earthly justice in terms of punishment, and torture'.[16] Moreover, the flood-tide of his Gnosticism sweeps away the whole of Christian eschatological teaching.[17]

[16]Ibid., p. 324.

[17]'The modern Christian attitude cannot reconcile itself with primitive eschatology on moral grounds. It is very difficult to accept a metaphysical system which makes the eternal destiny of the soul dependent on this temporal life, which exists merely from the cradle to the grave. According to this point of view our brief life on earth is a mere trap, and our fitness for eternity is determined by an experience whose duration is entirely insignificant' (the 'religious nightmare'). Ibid., p. 323. For Berdyaev, freedom, being anterior to God, is not a gift which comes from him. The human soul is not created at the moment of conception, but pre-exists in the spiritual world (Plato). It is destined neither to be endlessly re-incarnated (as against Plato: 'the occultist and theosophical nightmare'), nor to lose its individuality in God ('the nightmare of mysticism'), but to enter one day into eternity and the Kingdom of God. Berdyaev is here unfaithful to Dostoyevsky, cf. below, p. 192.

We may well compare what Kierkegaard has to say on the subject: 'And since now in our enlightened age when people find all anthropomorphic and anthropathic conceptions of God improper, yet do not find it improper to think of God as a judge in likeness of an ordinary civil judge or solicitor general who cannot get at the rights of such a prolix affair—they conclude then that it will be exactly so in eternity. Therefore only let us hold together and secure ourselves by seeing to it that the parson preachifies in this way ... The thing to do is to become many, a whole lot of us, if we do that, then we are secured against the judgment of eternity. Yes, doubtless they are secured if it was only in eternity they became individuals. But they were and are before God constantly individuals. A man seated in a glass case is not put to such embarrassment as is a man in his transparency before God. This is the factor of conscience. By the aid of conscience things are so arranged that the judicial report follows at once upon every fault, and that the guilty one himself must write it. But it is written with sympathetic ink and only becomes thoroughly clear when in eternity it is held up to the light, while eternity holds audit over the conscience. Substantially everyone arrives in eternity bringing with him and delivering the most accurate account of every least insignificance which he has committed or has left undone. Therefore to hold judgment in eternity is a thing a child could manage; there is really nothing for a third person to do, everything, even to the most insignificant word is counted and in order. The ease of the guilty man who journeys through life to eternity is like that of the murderer who with the speed of the railway train fled from the place where he perpetrated his crime. Alas, just under the railway coach where he sat ran the electric telegraph with its signal and the order for his apprehension at the next station. When he reached the station and alighted from the coach he was arrested. In a way, he had himself brought the denunciation with him.' Kierkegaard, *The Sickness unto Death* (translated Walter Lowrie, Princeton University Press, 1946), pp. 201-2.

c. *The difficulties of Ivan Karamazov*[18]

'Oh, Alyosha, I'm not blaspheming! I understand, of course, what a cataclysm of the universe it will be when everything that lives and has lived cries aloud : "Thou art just, O Lord, for thy ways are revealed." ' And yet Ivan does not want the eternal harmony.

Even if he is invited, he will refuse for love of humanity : ' "We cannot afford to pay so much for admission. And therefore I hasten to return my ticket of admission ... It is not God that I do not accept, Alyosha. I merely most respectfully return him the ticket."—"This is rebellion," Alyosha said softly.'

Alyosha is right. It is not for us, drawn out of nothing by the divine goodness, to fix the conditions for this voyage whose destination 'no eye has seen, nor ear heard, nor the heart of man conceived' (1 Cor. 2, 9). Because of this destination St Paul could say : 'I consider that the sufferings of this present time are not worth comparing with the glory that is to be revealed to us' (Rom. 8, 18).

Ivan will not accept that he is a rebel. ' "One can't go on living in a state of rebellion, and I want to live." ' He wants to have right on his side against God : ' "Imagine that it is you yourself who are erecting the edifice of human destiny with the aim of making men happy in the end, of giving them peace and contentment at last, but that to do that it is absolutely necessary, and indeed quite inevitable, to torture to death only one tiny creature, the little girl who beat her breast with her little fist, and to found the edifice on her unavenged tears—would you consent to be the architect on those conditions? Tell me and do not lie!" "No, I wouldn't," Alyosha said softly.' Here again he is right. (1) God created us in a state of harmony in which neither suffering nor death existed. (2) If he had created us and left us in the state of nature, death and suffering would not have been spared us, but even then the final happiness of the just would have been built on the faithfulness of their hearts, not on suffering or injustice. How could it be thought without blaspheming that, for this happiness to exist, it should be necessary for a single being to be put to the torture, or that it should or could be built on a child's tears?

[18]Dostoyevsky, *The Brothers Karamazov,* bk. VI, ch. 4., 'Rebellion' (trans. David Magarshak, The Penguin Classics, 1958).

But 'what is the use of a harmony which includes hell?' Ivan's question gives real trouble only to those who try to justify human suffering by declaring it to be required for the smooth running of the universal order of the cosmos,[19] or those who see in hell 'a structural element of the universe'.[20]

Ivan realizes quite well the solidarity of sin and punishment. He also thinks that there are sins which no one has the right to forgive. ' "I do not want a mother to embrace the torturer who had her child torn to pieces by his dogs! She has no right to forgive him! . . . She can forgive the torturer for the immeasurable suffering he has inflicted upon her as a mother; but she has no right to forgive him for the sufferings of her tortured child. She has no right to forgive the torturer for that, even if her child were to forgive him!" ' But if the mother cannot forgive, how may she find peace? She is unhappy and full of resentment, there is no heaven for her and she in her turn is also in hell. ' "If they have no right to forgive him, what becomes of the harmony?" ' The sophism is apparent. In this world or in the next, will the mother be required to see the torture of her child as anything but abominable sin? No—in the eyes of men, of the angels and of God sin is eternally hateful. But can she not wish the murderer suddenly to realize his crime and pray that his heart be changed, so that his sin becomes as hateful to himself as it is to God? To forgive is to conform oneself to God even as far as that. With God's grace all men can and must forgive. God, the source of forgiveness, can give us the strength to forgive—but the sinner may still refuse forgiveness. This is Alyosha's answer: ' "You said just now, is there a being in the whole world who could or has the right to forgive? But there is such a being and he can forgive everything, everyone and everything and *for everything*, because he gave his innocent blood for all and for everything." '[21] Indeed, God alone has the supreme right to forgive, for it was against him that sin ranged itself in the first place, and it is he who is first of all offended : *Tibi soli peccavi et malum coram Te feci.*

---

[19]Cf. above, p. 52.

[20]Cf. below, p. 212, note 69.

[21]A little further on Dostoyevsky recalls the legend of the Blessed Virgin imploring the Father to pardon even her Son's executioners and obtaining a respite each year for the damned, from Good Friday to Pentecost. For the question of a possible mitigation of the pains of hell, cf. my *Destinées d'Israel* (Luf, Paris, 1945), pp. 416-27.

How could the elect remember their sins and not hate them? And how could they ever be happy? The answer is that the conditions of life will be changed: 'The detestation of sin is accompanied by sorrow in those who are susceptible to sorrow, as is man here on earth. But in the next life the saints can no longer be touched by sorrow: they are displeased by their past sins, and they disclaim them, without there being in them the least shadow of sadness, as is said in Isaias 65, 16: 'For the former troubles are forgotten.'[22] They will look on evil and even on hell with the eyes of God, and their wills will be nothing other than God's. But we cannot now see with those eyes.

Further on Alyosha remarks on the thoughts of the elder Zosima about hell: ' "Fathers and teachers, I am thinking, What is hell? And I am reasoning thus: The suffering that comes from the consciousness that one is no longer able to love." '[23]

Earthly life, within the confines of time, is offered to a spiritual being so that he can make a gift of his love. Now this being ' "rejected the priceless gift, prized it not, loved it not, looked scornfully upon it and remained indifferent to it . . .

' "Men speak of material hell fire: I do not go into that mystery and I dread it, but I think that even if there were material fire, they would be genuinely glad of it, for I fancy that in material agony the much more terrible spiritual agony would be forgotten, even though for a moment. And indeed, it is quite impossible to take that spiritual agony away from them, for it is not outside but within them . . .

' "They feed upon their wicked pride, like a starving man in the desert sucking his own blood from his body. They will never be satisfied and they reject forgiveness, and curse God who calls them . . . and demand that God should destroy himself and all his creation. And they will burn eternally in the fire of their wrath and yearn for death and non-existence. But they will not obtain death . . ." '[24]

3. IS THERE AN ETERNAL SANCTION FOR A MOMENTARY FAULT?

God could in his infinite goodness either create or not create:

[22]St Thomas, III, qu. 84, a. 8.
[23]This, as has been seen, is the idea taken up by Berdyaev.
[24]*The Brothers Karamazov*, op. cit., bk. VI, ch. 3, 'From the Discourses and Sermons of Father Zosima'.

he could also create a more or less good world. He could produce
free creatures in their final state or simply *in statu viatoris*. He
chose, and we have tried to give a reason for this, the latter course.
With us as with the angels the way ends in the final state, both for
the good and the wicked.

a. *The passage from time to eternity*

Merely from the point of view of philosophical reflection, and
for anyone who has any grasp of what man really is in his undivided unity of mind and body, reason and sense, death reveals
itself as such a stumbling-block, such a dislocation of our substance,
that it is probable that by setting a final point to our activity it
introduces us to some new and definitive state, approaching that
which theology calls the *status termini*. None will deny that at
death everything seems over and done with.

At the same time there would seem to be imposed another
certainty about the soul's condition. The spiritual values accumu-
lated in it during the course of its pilgrimage—either light-bringing
and connected with the beatitudes of the Sermon on the Mount,
like poverty of spirit, patience in tribulation, hunger and thirst
after justice, mercy, purity of heart, the peace of heaven; or dark
and connected with pride, rebelliousness, hatred—these values
could never in themselves be affected by the touch of death; and
so the soul must take them with it as an eternal heritage of happiness or misery.

The Scriptures are full of warnings about the irrevocable outcome of this journey which we make only once. They ceaselessly
insist on the shortness of our lives and on how fatal the stakes are :
'And do not fear those who kill the body but cannot kill the soul;
rather fear him who can destroy both soul and body in hell' (Matt.
10, 28). 'If your hand or your foot causes you to sin, cut it off and
throw it from you; it is better for you to enter life maimed than
with two hands or two feet to be thrown into the eternal fire.'
(Matt. 18, 8). The same call is made by St Paul : 'I consider that
the sufferings of this present time are not worth comparing with
the glory that is to be revealed to us' (Rom. 8, 18). 'For this slight
momentary affliction is preparing for us an eternal weight of glory
beyond all comparison, because we look not to the things that are
seen but to the things that are unseen; for the things that are seen
are transient, but the things that are unseen are eternal' (II Cor.

4, 17-8). 'Do not be deceived; God is not mocked, for whatever a man sows, that he will also reap. For he who sows to his own flesh will from the flesh reap corruption; but he who sows to the Spirit will from the Spirit reap eternal life' (Gal. 6, 7-8). 'The point is this : he who sows sparingly will also reap sparingly, and he who sows bountifully will also reap bountifully' (II Cor. 9, 6). 'It is a fearful thing to fall into the hands of the living God' (Hebr. 10, 31).

b. *Eternity beginning here on earth*

The first truth given us by Scripture is that there is a passage from the provisional to the definitive, from here to eternity. And certainly there is an infinite disproportion between the duration of the *status viatoris* and the *status termini*; so that if justice were to be sought in an equality of duration there would be no possible justice for either the good or the wicked in their passage from the present to the future state. But the other teaching of Scripture is that there is a sowing and germination in time of what ultimately comes to fruition in eternity. Thus between the two states there could be no difference in kind; rather there is the continuation of the same life, first set in motion beneath the veil of sense-life and later revealed in its issue. The very substance of eternal life is sown in time. Consequently it is here on earth that grace, by which we become 'partakers in the divine nature' (II Peter 1, 4), and which is offered to all—God our Saviour desiring 'all men to be saved and to come to the knowledge of the truth' (I Tim. 2, 4)—is once for all either accepted or rejected; here on earth the supreme decisions are made either with or against the light of God's helping grace; here on earth, as a result, there are built up in the depths of every soul the ultimate realities of heaven or hell : 'Truly, truly, I say to you, he who believes has eternal life' (John 6, 47). 'He who believes in (the Son of God) is not condemned; he who does not believe is condemned already . . . and this is the judgment, that the light has come into the world and men loved darkness rather than light, because their deeds were evil' (John 3, 18-9). The Gospels reveal to us as no prophecy had ever done before the terrifying value of this poor life, which withers like grass (Isaiah 40, 6), its fearful ambivalence, its unimaginable power for either good or evil, which will astound all at the hour of judgment. Pascal, commenting on the Gospels, says : 'The elect will not know their virtues, nor will the damned the greatness of their crimes :

"Lord when did we see you hungry ... or thirsty ...?" ' (Matt. 25, 37, 44).[25] Julien Green echoes him : 'Your sins are in themselves nothing, but they will become great when they snatch you from heaven, and it is you who give them this power, simply because you are great yourself. If you were not so great you could not damn yourself.'[26]

c. *Transmigration of souls and the overwhelming thought of the after life*

Although the Hindu idea of transmigration of souls runs counter to certain fundamental philosophical positions by denying man's substantial unity, which cannot be reduced either to angel or to animal, and by denying that the soul and the personality are inseparably joined—this personality, this soul; that soul, that personality—how does it come about that such an idea 'remains a permanent temptation for the religious consciousness of humanity? Why is there this temptation to metempsychosis?' Jacques Maritain answers : 'In my opinion it results from the conflict between the idea of retribution for human acts and the idea of the shortness and unhappiness, the inconsistency and folly of human life. How is it possible for an unhappy human life, with all its insignificance, delusions and miseries, to end up all of a sudden in eternity? How is it possible for an eternal retribution, an eternal and unchanging end, to be fixed for us in virtue of the good or bad motions of a free will as weak and whimsical and sluggish as our own? The disproportion between End and Means is too great. It seems that Indian thought was seized with discouragement and fear before such a perspective, and that it fell back, as it were, on the infinity of time, as if a series of new lives offered to the same soul had any hope of narrowing the disproportion just indicated between the precariousness of the journey and the importance of the destination.'[27] He goes on : 'Certainly, but in that case there is neither end nor destination. The mind finds itself placed in front of the horror of endless reincarnations. The very law of transmigration becomes a terrible and unbearable law of new sufferings, trials and punishments incessantly assumed in the midst of a

[25]Pascal, *Pensées,* ed. Brunschvicg, no. 515.
[26]Théophile Delaporte, *Pamphlet contre les catholiques de France,* no. 131.
[27]Maritain, 'L'immortalité du soi', in *De Bergson à Thomas d'Aquin* (Maison Française, New York, 1944), pp. 143-44.

perpetual resurgence of vanishing and tormenting new appearances . . .'[28]

Where is the solution to be sought? Not in 'the pursuit of immortality by a horizontal movement throughout endless time'; but
in 'the vertical attainment of immortality by the fruition of a final
and infinite end'. This is the Judæo-Christian conception. What
makes it possible 'is not merely *a true appreciation of the relation
between time and eternity* : extend time as much as you like, add
years to years, pile lives upon lives, time will remain without any
common measure with eternity ... But what makes the Judæo-
Christian solution possible is above all the fact that *the philosophy
of the final end is part of the whole complex of its truths
and mysteries revealed by God*. It must be realized that God is
personal, and that he is Life, Truth and Love in person (or
persons); that there is a supernatural order and that the slightest
degree of grace, or participation in the intimate life of God, is
worth more than all the splendour of this starry universe; that God
took flesh in the womb of a virgin of Israel in order to die for
humanity and to infuse into us the life of his own blood; that the
free initiatives, the resources, the patience and the inventiveness
of God's mercy are infinitely greater than the weakness or wickedness of our human free will. From this it will also be realized that
the disproportion between the precariousness of the journey and
the importance of the end, which was insisted on just now, is truly
made up for, excessively and superabundantly, by the generosity
and *humanity (philanthropia)*, as St Paul called it, of our Saviour.
It is God and Christ who save man by the power of the cross and
divine grace, and by faith and charity bringing forth fruit in good
works.'[29]

d. *Man's decision is made 'in his eternity'*

Reflecting on the precariousness of our decisions and the eternity
of their sanctions, it is true that we are scarcely conscious of any
objection when it is a question of a happy outcome and the beatitude of the chosen ones. But as soon as we start to think of the
eternity of hell, giddiness seizes us. And yet the conditions are no
different on either side. It cannot be doubted that, in the final
analysis, to the eternal life proposed to him on earth a man responds
by an affirmation or negation which reveals what is most sealed

[28]Ibid., p. 144.   [29]Ibid., pp. 144-6.

and secret in the very depths even of his unconscious self; this consists less in what he expresses about himself, either to himself or to others, or in what he thinks of himself and believes himself to be in his own estimation, than in what he really is before God, whose word 'is living and active, sharper than any two-edged sword, piercing to the division of soul and spirit, of joints and marrow, and discerning the thoughts and intentions of the heart. And before him no creature is hidden, but all are open and laid bare to the eyes of him with whom we have to do' (Hebr. 4, 12-13).

To an observation of St Gregory the Great, in which the unrepentant sinner is said to want to make his fault eternal,[30] St Thomas adds a penetrating comment : 'Anyone who sins in his own eternity (*in suo aeterno*) against God, will be punished in the eternity of God (*in aeterno Dei*). And man sins in his own eternity not only by the continuation of one and the same act throughout his whole life, but from the very fact that if he sets his end in sin his will is to sin eternally.'[31]

e. *The patience of God*

Yet we should be far from imagining that God spies out our failings or can find joy in catching us out in any sort of treacherous way, watching carefully for the exact moment of our denials. Under the laws of contingence which apply to all without difference of distinction, under the sun which rises indifferently on the good and the wicked and the rain which falls on the just and unjust alike (Matt. 5, 45), his solicitude silently and lovingly follows the children of men, each of whom is worth more than many sparrows (Matt. 10, 31). He knocks insistently on the door of each soul (Apoc. 3, 20); he is not a master who comes to reap where he has not sown (Matt. 25, 26); he demands five talents where he has lent five, two where he has given two, one where he has only lent one, so as to bring these humble servants, stewards of so few things, equally into the ineffable joy of their Lord. There is room

---

[30]*Magna Moralia*, Lib. XXXIV, ch. 19 (16), no. 36 (P.L., vol. LXXVI, col. 738): 'The wicked only sinned for a time, because they only lived for a time; but their wish was to live for ever so as to remain for ever in their iniquities. Their desire is to sin rather than to live: if they wish to live always it is so that they may not have to put an end to their sin as long as their lives last.' Cf. the parallel passage in *Dialogorum*, Lib. IV, cap. 44 (P.L., vol. LXXVII, col. 404).
[31]St Thomas, Iᵃ IIᵃᵉ, qu. 87, a. 3, ad 1.

for trembling—but also for hope. *Teme con confianza,* says St John of the Cross.[32]

Last of all, it should not be forgotten that on the last day, far from blaming God for not having helped them enough, the damned will themselves glory in the resistance they have put up against the advances of his goodness.

f. *The parable of Dives and Lazarus*

It is fitting in this connection to dispel the idea that the damned could repent. The parable of Dives and Lazarus (Luke 16, 19-31), must not lead us astray here. In the dramatic stories of the Gospel parables the exegetes tell us to look for what they call the 'point' of the account, its purpose, finality or orientation. The parable of Dives and Lazarus was told to warn us that there is a time when it is possible to listen to Moses and the Prophets, and a time when it is unfortunately too late to be guided by them. Its aim was not to depict for us the inner dispositions of the damned or the nature of the torments of hell, but simply their irremissibility.[33] If any of the damned could feel compassion for sinners who are causing their own ruin here on earth, wish for their conversion and do anything to turn them from the punishments which threaten them, he would be transformed by that very act of love and immediately leave hell.[34]

Let it not be said then that the fault is momentary and the sanction eternal : the fault continues, taking its sanction with it.

If it will never occur to anyone in hell to put the blame on God for his rebellion and damnation, neither will any of the elect think of thanking him like the Pharisee who prided himself on his righteousness (Luke 18, 11-2). The only thought that could come into their hearts at the last moment will be that of the publican : 'God be merciful to me a sinner!' (18, 13). The prayer which all

[32]'Spiritual Sentences and Maxims', in *The Works of St John of the Cross,* op. cit., vol. III.

[33]The explanation given by St Catherine of Siena is different. According to her, Dives was acting not out of charity but out of fear of seeing his torments increase when his brothers are damned in their turn. *Dialogue* (English trans. by Algar Thorold, Kegan Paul, London, 1907).

[34]'God can forgive as he wishes, and he does not cease doing so. But the sin which set the creature up against him is not susceptible for forgiveness, because it is refusal of forgiveness as well of submission. Forgiveness is an act of love ... and the damned soul obstinately places himself outside love.' Jean Hervé Nicolas, *La Vie Spirituelle,* Oct., 1958, p. 239.

just men find on their lips was made in this way by a Sufi: 'O my God, you know that I cannot bear hell. And I know that I am not good enough for paradise. What ruse can I employ except your forgiveness?'[35]

4. THE MYSTERY OF HELL ANTICIPATED IN MORTAL SIN

There is no substantial discontinuity between our life in time and our life in eternity. The passage from the one to the other involves a change of level. The riches of heaven are anticipated in those of grace; the privations of hell in those of mortal sin. Anyone who understood mortal sin would understand the mystery of hell which makes it eternal.

a. *Twofold disorder and twofold punishment: one infinite, the other finite*

To sin is to desire a good which turns one away from God; it is to sacrifice the infinite for the finite, the Creator for the creature. There are two aspects of sin: a breaking with God, the uncreated and infinite Good, and a disordered fixing of the will on a created and finite good.[36]

The sinner breaks with God. He resists the influences of helping grace which invites all men in secret to turn towards a God who reveals himself as the final end beyond everything the mind can conceive: 'What no eye has seen, nor ear heard, nor the heart of man conceived, what God has prepared for those who love him' (I Cor. 2, 9). This is the formal element, the very heart of mortal sin, its most spiritual and hidden aspect, and its supreme perversity.[37]

It is to attach himself inordinately to some created good, spiritual or sensual, that man turns away from God; this is the immediate or 'material' element of sin. Such an attachment, in effect, inasmuch as it is disordered, introduces a disturbance into

---

[35]Yahya (died 872).
[36]In peccato mortali sunt duo, scilicet *aversio* ab incommutabili bono, et *conversio* ad commutabile bonum inordinata.' St Thomas, III, qu. 86, a. 4.
[37]'In quolibet autem peccato mortali principalis ratio mali et gravitas est ex hoc quod (homo) avertit se a Deo.' St Thomas, II[a] II[ae], qu. 20, a. 3. Cf. our study written some time ago: 'La peine temporelle du péché', in *Revue Thomiste,* 1927, pp. 20-39; and pp. 89-103.

the very heart of the universe, of which man forms a composite part together with the angels and the cosmos. He brings disorder into the laws by which the created universe must progress towards the ends assigned to it by God. What is directly involved, directly opposed and injured, is the relation of the sinner, not with the transcendent and infinite good, but with the immanent and finite common good of the universe, the internal order of creation.

In this twofold collision with an order which transcends him, the sinner causes himself a twofold injury.[38]

Corresponding to the rebellion against the transcendent and infinite Good—the beatific vision to which God's grace was helping him—is the privation of the vision of this same transcendent and infinite Good, in other words, a punishment *infinite in value*; this is the 'pain of damnation'.

Corresponding to the rebellion against the immanent and finite order of the universe which, being desired by God, is good, is a punishment finite in value, called figuratively, by synecdoche, 'pain of sense', because it extends as far as repairing the order of sensible nature itself in so far as this has been injured.[39]

b. *The reason the punishment is made eternal*

He who blinds himself, as Oedipus did, remains blind always. He who takes away his own life disappears for ever from the scene of the world. There is no possible remedy, apart from a miracle of divine power.

The same thing applies to the supernatural order. He who destroys in himself the principle of life, which is grace and divine charity, falls headlong into a misfortune which in itself is without remedy. St Thomas explains here that any order flows from its principle; we can only participate in an order by participating in its principle. Now sin, by turning us away from God destroys the very principle by which man's will is able to tend towards his final

[38]Cf. St Thomas, Iª IIae, qu. 87, a. 1: 'Utrum reatus poenae sit effectus peccati?' Resp.: '... Quicumque peccat, contra aliquem ordinem agit; et ideo ab ipso ordine consequens est quod deprimatur.' And further on, Ibid., a. 3: 'Manente autem causa, manet effectus; unde quamdiu perversitas ordinis remanet, necesse est quod remaneat reatus poenae.'

[39]Cf. St Thomas, Iª IIae, qu. 87, a. 2: 'Utrum peccato debeatur poena *infinita secundum quantitatem?*' To which is answered: 'Ex parte *aversionis* respondet peccato *poena damni*, quae etiam est *infinita*; est enim amissio infiniti boni, scilicet Dei. Ex parte autem *inordinatae conversionis* respondet ei *poena sensus*, quae etiam est *finita*.'

End; that is, grace, charity and the love of God. Thus, if God has not intervened by his mercy before the sinner's death, if he finally leaves him to his own desires and abandons him to his own ways, the sinner will never *be able* and, let it be quite clear, will never *want* to regain possession of himself. The disaster in itself is irreparable. The twofold punishment of mortal sin, the infinite pain of damnation, and the finite pain of sense, are both in themselves endless, *eternal in duration*.[40] The eternity of the punishment does not result from the *gravity* but from the *irremissibility* of the fault.[41]

c. *Do the damned wish to be as they are?*

It has just been said that the damned go on willing the rebellion which causes their misery. Yet it is not possible to desire misery— it is always something good that the free creature seeks; yet this good may be bound up with some great disorder which causes the misery.

St Thomas gives the example of a man in prison who, in order to gratify his revengefulness, thinks only of killing his enemy and nourishes himself on the very hatred which consumes him and takes away his hope.[42]

To the common, trivial form of despair, that of the man who does not want to be himself and for consolation takes refuge in dreams, Kierkegaard opposes a supreme form which he calls demoniacal, in which man stands up against everything which is not himself and *wants* to be himself despite the universe and even despite God, seeking to be a thorn in God's side; or, to use another comparison, to be a fatal misprint in the divine work, put right time and again by the author, but obstinately reappearing in order to destroy the whole sense of a beautiful poem.[43]

Other images are used by Nietzsche. 'The force which urged him to wound himself,' says Lou Andreas Salomé, 'was a form of

---

[40]Cf. St Thomas, Iª IIae, qu. 87, a. 3: 'Utrum aliquod peccatum inducat *reatum aeternae poenae?*' Resp.: '... Si per peccatum corrumpatur principium ordinis quo voluntas hominis subditur Deo, erit inordinatio, quantum est de se, irreparabilis, etsi reparari possit virtute divine ... Et ideo quaecumque peccata avertunt a Deo, caritatem auferentia, quantum est de se, *inducunt reatum aeternae poenae.*'

[41]Ibid., a. 5, ad 3: 'Aeternitas enim poenae non respondet *quantitati* culpae, sed *irremissibilitati* ipsius.'

[42]I, qu. 64, a. 2, ad 3.   [43]*The Sickness unto death,* passim.

the instinct of self-preservation. He could only escape suffering by plunging himself entirely into a new suffering.'[44] Nietzsche was the 'Don Juan of experience', depicted in *Aurora,* who revels in wild flights of experience 'to the point where at last there was nothing left to pursue except the absolutely *painful* elements of experience, like the drunkard who ends up by drinking absinthe and spirits. This is why he came to desire hell—the last experience which remained to *seduce* him.'[45]

The damned who desire a good which is bound up with their misery would prefer, however, *not to exist*. It would be better for them, and they know it, not to exist than to exist. For non-existence, in so far as it does away with suffering, can take on the aspect of good.[46] Hence the complaint of Job : 'Why did I not die at birth, come forth from the womb and expire?' (3, 11); and the terrible words of the Saviour : 'It would have been better for that man if he had not been born' (Matt. 26, 24).

But in the fact that it is not able to cease being lies the dignity of the spiritual creature. Kierkegaard says : 'Socrates proved the immortality of the soul from the fact that the sickness of the soul (sin) does not consume it as sickness of the body consumes the body. So also we can demonstrate the eternal in man from the fact that despair cannot consume his self, that this precisely is the torment of contradiction in despair. If there were nothing eternal in a man, he could not despair; but if despair could consume his self, there would still be no despair.'[47]

Since they must live, the damned prefer to be as they are, and to desire their own will. Jacques Maritain writes about the condition of the fallen angel : 'He has made himself his beatitude and he will remain in this attitude, at the price of all the pains of hell, which he has accepted in advance. He prefers this sort of beatitude —solitude in his own nature and self-sufficiency in evil and negation, and pride in being able to impose privation on the (antecedent) will of God—to the true beatitude which he rejects and which, from the moment he does not love God, can

[44]Lou Andreas Salomé, *Frédéric Nietzsche* (Grasset, Paris, 1932), p. 29.
[45]Ibid.
[46]'Sic, non esse accipit rationem boni.' St Thomas, *IV Sent.,* dist. 50, qu. 2, a. 1, quaest. 3.
[47]*The Sickness unto Death,* op. cit.

no longer be true beatitude for him. He has what he wanted.'[48]

5. STRICTER DEFINITIONS OF THE PAIN OF SENSE

The damned come into fatal collision with God, the infinite Good, in whom their beatitude was to be found : that is the pain of damnation. They also come into fatal collision with the universe of creation : that, according to the theologians, is the pain of sense.[49]

a. *The law by which balance is restored to being*

The most thorough explanation of the origin of the pain of sense known to me has been made by Maritain in the course of an attempt to define the difficult philosophical notion of sanction.[50]

The Indian theory of *Kharma* can point us in the right direction. On many points it is certainly wrong, particularly in its belief that the moral act produces its own physical reward, as the seed produces the fruit; but it is right in saying that within the universe, moral good and evil bring as their consequence happiness or unhappiness, and this is the true element which must be disentangled from the theory. The guilt-punishment nexus is certainly concerned first and foremost with the relation of man to God; but in one aspect it is also immanent in the world.

From this viewpoint 'ontological evil—suffering—is a natural *fruit* of moral evil. It is the theory of punishment as the fruit borne as opposed to that of punishment as a rejoinder',[51] to the theory of punishment dictated by vengeance, to the idea of making him who caused suffering suffer himself. Ontological evil can in effect result from moral evil 'coming back upon the very doer of the evil action. This is punishment. Not only in the sense that to commit evil is to give oneself over to it and to undergo in oneself a deterioration or deviation; but in a deeper sense which it is our task to explain.'[52] It must be remembered that the universal order of

[48]*The Sin of the Angel* (Newman Press, Westminster, 1959), pp. 91-2.
[49]For St Thomas's teaching on the pain of sense or fire, see 'Les anges et le cosmos,' in *Nova et Vetera*, 1953, pp. 146-7.
[50]Maritain, *Neuf leçons sur les notions premières de la philosophie morale,* op. cit., pp. 72, et seq.; 173; 182, et seq.
[51]Ibid., p. 183. Cf. above, p. 187.   [52]Ibid., p. 184.

creation, governed by the infinite power and goodness of the transcendent God, comprises two worlds : the world of nature and the world of freedom.[53] Man can set a check on God, even eternally, in the moral world of freedom. But the universal order is always realized, in virtue of what may be called 'the law by which balance is restored to being'. An important quotation must be given here :

'There is an ontological law of equal force between the universal whole and the particular whole which is a centre of free activity. A sort of metaphysical Archimedes' principle. This means that the moral agent must not be considered in isolation but in his relation to the whole.

'Sin of itself signifies death, a triumph of nothingness. Non-being has been injected into the whole from the very fact that a particular part of the whole has freely defected, and the balance has thereby been disturbed. It will be restored by the fact that non-being will come upon the subject as a privation suffered by him.

'This privation is merited, it is due. Due to what? To the whole? Certainly since it has been deprived, and since balance is a good due to it (in the broad sense of the term). But this coming back of nothingness is also due, primarily to the subject himself. Inasmuch as he is simply *something which exists,* it is due to the human being *to be on the same level as the whole, to be homologous with the whole* (in proportion to his capacity as a part), and to be in his true place in the whole. This is due to his very being. It is a fundamental requirement of the internal consciousness of the being. Otherwise the subject would be like the centre of a circle which was not in the middle, or like a right angle in a triangle which was not equal to the sum of the other two angles.

'The first thing which is due to me, not inasmuch as I am a person, but simply inasmuch as I exist, is to be *situated* within the whole. This is a basic requirement of existence and is due both in the order of good (reward) and in the order of evil (punishment). The ultimate good due to the devil, as a being who *exists,* is to be chastized and put in line with the whole, by suffering as an intelligent being.'[54] By my moral acts I raise the level of moral good or evil in the universe and break up my original balance

[53] Ibid., p. 75. Cf. above, p. 50.
[54] Ibid., pp. 185-6.

in relation to the universe; and the universe will requite me, *setting me in the new place which as a result is due to me,* by making the moral good or evil of which I am the source flow back on me, but under the form of ontological good, or evil, happiness or misery.[55] Thus God can be held in check, even eternally, by the perverse creature, in the particular order of morality; but not in the universal order of creation.[56]

b. *The pain of sense designates the whole range of finite punishment for sin*

The expression 'pain of sense', used by theologians to designate the finite punishment of sin, the requital of the universe for the disorder produced in the world of freedom, can be misleading and give us to believe that the pain of sense could have nothing to do with devils who are incorporeal, and that it will not be experienced by the damned till after the resurrection of their bodies. But, as has already been said, it is only figuratively, taking the part for the whole, that the punishment which results from the pressure exerted on the violations of the moral order by the whole universe, even the visible and sensible universe, is called pain of sense.

The angels, good or evil, are present in our visible world; they maintain relations, good or bad, with it, and to this extent they have a place in it.[57] It is evident that hell, for the devils and the damned, is above all a condition of life, a *spiritual state*; yet it is also for them a place. But let us not, as in earlier times, hastily conclude that it is in the centre of the earth. Exactly to the extent that the rebellious spirits enter into conflict with the whole sensible and visible part of the universe, with the whole world of nature,

[55]Ibid., pp. 73-4.
[56]Cf. Jean Hervé Nicolas, *La Vie spirituelle,* October, 1958, pp. 237-8: 'Sin is an abuse of liberty. A free being must by his own decision enter into an order which is greater than himself and enfolds him completely. By doing so he makes this order his own as well as the Good which develops this new life within him, creating for himself a right to receive his own share in it. This is merit. But this privilege has a formidable counterpart: with this same power he can remove himself from this order and seek to impose his own order in which he will be at the centre and in which his own particular good, the one he has chosen for himself, will be the guiding principle. Such a disorder especially affects the sinner himself: the order imposed by God is not arbitrary, it is the one, and the only one, in which a free creature can find his own fulfilment. Eternal damnation sanctions the sinner's loss by setting himself up outside God.'
[57]See 'Les anges et le cosmos', in *Nova et Vetera,* 1953, p. 139.

hell is thereby localized and becomes for them a *place* of suffering. This place is nothing less than the whole visible cosmos, with all its splendour, to the extent that they have, by their fault, made it hostile to themselves and uninhabitable.

6. THE CONDITION OF THE DAMNED

a. *The tragedy of hell*

The tragedy of hell is summed up by Maritain in a page of very exact theology : 'In the final analysis, being punished is simply having what one wanted, gathering the fruit that grew from the act. It is true that—unlike what happened with the sin of the angels—we did not know quite what sort of fruit was to grow from the act (this was due to the weakness of our intellect and will; what we explicitly wanted was the act, not the fruit), and we can also change our minds and repent. But if it is a question of the final act of the will, at the moment when the soul is separated from the body, then it can be said that a man has really wanted the fruit as well as the act. For the blessed prefer God and eternal life; and the damned prefer hell.

'The will of the damned is divided and torn. They suffer a capital punishment which they do not desire and which horrifies them : indeed they tend naturally towards God in virtue of the structure of their being; and this from the very fact that eternal life—which they reject—has been offered them; in short, from the very fact that a happiness which infinitely satisfies their capacity to desire has been shown to be possible—in the very instant that they refuse it—and has awakened the hunger of their whole being, supernatural beatitude has become for them the only end in which their natural leaning towards God can be satisfied; it has become for them a good craved for by their being, a *bonum debitum* (ontologically, not morally, due); a good whose absence is a *privation,* and the worst privation of all.

'But at the same time, having freely rejected God as their supernatural end, they have also freely rejected him as a natural end. They detest him through a free act in which they are set, and *prefer* the false beatitude they have chosen, their pride, to their true beatitude. That is the ultimate end they desire above all, even at the price of all sorts of suffering and privation—*their* beatitude is to be gods by their own strength. They cannot take back this choice, because this has to do with their last end and has been made in the full light of the mind, fixing the will in it in such a way that all subsequent acts of will can only be effected in virtue of that act. And so there is remorse but no repentance, they ask no forgiveness and would refuse it if it were given them—they *wish* to continue in this state.[58]

'Thus eternal justice must be designated, if we are looking for human comparisons, less as the mysterious anger than as the mysterious patience of God, who suffers his mercy to be finally refused, and allows a creature to be for ever, by his own free choice, his own god.'[59]

The thought of this is enough to make anybody stop in the chapel of Saint Zeno, at Saint Praxede's, to implore the little mosaic Virgin, inside her niche: *Sancta Maria, libera nos a poenis inferni.*

b. *The intense activity of the damned*

A perpetual agitation, a prodigious activity, a formidable expenditure of energy, such is the condition of the damned. The devils do not lose the original wealth and resources of their angelic nature, nor the damned the dignity of their immortal soul created in the likeness of God. And the original impetus which carried them to desire and seek happiness could never be jeopardized or taken away from them. These are the irrevocable and indestructible gifts of the Creator's goodness. They can abuse them, but they cannot reject them without denying their own being.

Their will, certainly, is unchangeably fixed in evil, as is that of the elect in good. But within the fatal decision which tears them from their true glory and their final end, the free will remains intact; for free will has to do with selection and has a bearing on the choice of means to an end.[60] It goes without saying that if the end ultimately intended is evil, the whole activity it commands will be perverted.

Thus St Thomas distinguishes in the damned between a will of

---

[58]Cf. St Thomas, *IV Sent.*, dist. 50, qu. 2, a. 1, quaest. 2: 'Mali igitur non poenitebunt per se loquendo de peccatis, quia voluntas malitiae peccati in eis remanet...'
[59]Maritain, *Neuf leçons...*, pp. 189-90.
[60]Cf. St Thomas, *Compendium theologiae*, ch. 174.

nature and a deliberative will. The will of nature, which persists
in them, comes from God himself; it is good and tends towards
being and happiness. But the deliberative will, by which they definitively turned themselves away from God, is irremediably perverted in them, with the result that the good which they can desire
they do not desire in a good way or for good reasons, and that,
even then, their will is not good.[61]

What can be the nature of the extraordinary fury of activity
in which the damned are engaged? How could it be anything
but anarchic, since each of them seeks, in the last resort, to turn
all things to his own glory? One end alone will be capable of co-
ordinating them: the common hatred they bear God and the
universal order of creation.[62] It ceaselessly collapses, but is
ceaselessly reborn. It is necessary to them, and deceives their black
despair by its ever new attempts. The theological virtue of hope,
for ever destroyed in them, gives way to a swarm of vain hopes.
It is not quite the same as Sisyphus in the *Odyssey*, who is forever
setting himself to the same task of pushing his stone up to the top
of a mountain and failing at the last moment; it is more accurate
to think of an intelligent and inventive activity, fertile in discoveries and resourceful in every contingency, exerting itself in
ever new conditions and means. Think of the senseless enterprises
which Milton wished to give us some idea of, when at the beginning
of his *Paradise Lost* he tried, though not very successfully, to describe the conspiracy of the rebellious angels. Hell has an 'historical
course', not a cyclical repetition of the same events. The age-old
myth of eternal recurrence, which intoxicated the Nietzsche of
Zarathustra, according to which the number of possible exchanges
between beings can be exhausted and start all over again, is an
absurdity. In effect, free beings continually introduce new elements into the course of events, in such a way that circumstances
will never reproduce themselves unchanged. The activity of hell
is not to be compared with the functioning of a machine: it is an
historical process with discoveries and new unfoldings, an attempt

---

[61]*IV Sent.*, dist. 50, qu. 2, a. 1, quaest. 1.
[62]'There may be not peace but an agreement among the demons. This
does not result from any friendship among themselves but from their
common wickedness which makes them hate men and oppose the justice of
God. . . . The superiors gain no advantage by being obeyed by their in-
feriors, for doing evil is misery, and commanding evil only increases it.'
St Thomas, I, qu. 109, a. 2, ad 2 and 3.

to remake creation, to construct, govern and unceasingly modify factitious worlds, some idea of which we may perhaps get from the effort of Joyce in *Finnegan's Wake* to shuffle and reset the time, history and language of men, so that, as has been said of him,[63] he might carry off the supreme victory, that of the writer dethroning God.[64]

7. 'GOD IS TOO GOOD TO ALLOW HELL'

'God is too good to allow hell : he is too good to tolerate a hell which goes on for all eternity!'—yet it is *man* who is responsible for hell, not *God*. However willing God in his infinite goodness may be to help us, *he can tolerate man's desire to resist him,* even his eternal desire to resist him. 'God is too good, it is said, not to forgive. That is exactly what he does : everything, he forgives everything the moment the heart repents. If the devil repented he would immediately be forgiven. But sin without repentance *cannot* be pardoned, any more than God can annihilate himself; sin postulates a world of its own, deprived of God as it is itself, a fire of its own nearly as hard as that of charity—and where nevertheless God's pity, which is absent from nothing, makes it so that one suffers less than one deserved.[65] Love created everything in order to diffuse the divine beauty; it cannot be vanquished. If I refuse to manifest it in mercy I shall manifest it in justice. It is this refusal which is obscure.'[66]

At the end of his *Souvenirs d'enfance et de jeunesse,* Ernest Renan writes : 'Several times a year I receive an anonymous letter, containing these words, always in the same handwriting : "Yet suppose there was a hell after all!" The pious person who writes this must surely have the salvation of my soul at heart, and I am very grateful. But hell is an hypothesis which scarcely fits in with what we know from other sources about the divine goodness.' And he goes on in the same amused tone : 'The infinite goodness which I have met with in this world inspires in me the conviction that eternity is filled with a goodness which is hardly less and in which I have an absolute confidence.'

[63] Jean Paris, *James Joyce par lui-même* (Seuil, Paris, 1957), p. 188.
[64] Cf. below, p. 255.   [65] Cf. St Thomas, I, qu. 21, a. 4, ad 1.
[66] Maritain, 'Answer to Jean Cocteau', in *Art and Faith* (Philosophical Library, New York, 1948), pp. 81-2.

'The divine goodness' . . . : Renan admits in the same book to having entered German philosophy as a temple and to having desired to be a 'Christian' like Herder, Kant and Fichte.

'What we know from other sources of the divine goodness' . . . But what do we know of the divine goodness? What book or message, apart from the Gospels, has made known to us its infinite depths and even its folly? And at the same time, what book has made known to us so clearly the terrible sternness of God?

One can open the Gospels and turn the pages almost at random : 'If your right eye causes you to sin, pluck it out and throw it away; it is better that you lose one of your members than that your whole body be thrown into hell' (Matt. 5, 29). 'Enter by the narrow gate; for the gate is wide and the way is easy, that leads to destruction and those who enter by it are many' (Matt. 7, 13). 'On that day many will say to me, "Lord, Lord, did we not prophecy in your name, and cast out demons in your name, and do many mighty works in your name?" And then will I declare to them, "I never knew you; depart from me, you evildoers" ' (Matt. 7, 22-3). 'Whoever denies me before men, I also will deny before my Father who is in heaven' (Matt. 10, 33). 'He who finds his life will lose it, and he who loses his life for my sake will find it' (Matt. 10, 39). 'The Son of Man will send his angels, and they will gather out of his kingdom all causes of sin and all evildoers and throw them into the furnace of fire; there men will weep and gnash their teeth' (Matt. 13, 41-2). 'Then two men will be in the field; one is taken and one is left. Two women will be grinding at the mill; one is taken and one is left. Watch therefore . . . for the Son of Man is coming at an hour you do not expect' (Matt. 24, 40-4). 'To everyone who has will more be given and he will have abundance; but from him who has not, even what he has will be taken away' (Matt. 25, 29). The same warnings are to be found in St Luke : 'The ones along the path are those who have heard; then the devil comes and takes away the word from their hearts, that they may not believe and be saved' (Luke 8, 12). 'Woe to you, Chorazin! woe to you Bethsaida! . . . it shall be more tolerable in the judgment for Tyre and Sidon than for you' (Luke 10, 13). 'Temptations to sin are sure to come; but woe to him by whom they come! It would be better for him if a millstone were hung round his neck and he were cast into the sea, than that he should cause one of these little ones to sin' (Luke 17, 1-2). And in St John :

'Did I not choose you, the twelve, and one of you is a devil?' (John 6, 70). 'For judgment I came into this world, that those who do not see may see, and that those who see may become blind' (John 9, 39. 'He who loves his life loses it and he who hates his life in this world will keep it for eternal life' (John 12, 25).

There is the parable of the man who was cast out because he had not wanted to beg for the wedding garment (Matt. 22, 11-14). Against the hypocritical scribes and Pharisees comes the series of seven curses which are the counterpart of an immense Love refused, unable to contain itself any longer: 'Jerusalem, Jerusalem, killing the prophets and stoning those who are sent to you! How often would I have gathered your children together as a hen gathers her brood under her wing, and you would not!' (Matt. 23, 13-31, 37). And there is the disturbing parable of the wise and foolish virgins: ' "Lord, Lord, open to us." But he replied, "Truly, I say to you, I do not know you" ' (Matt. 25, 11-12). Finally there is the overwhelming scene of the last judgment, the terrible weighing of sentences and punishments: 'Come, O blessed of my Father, inherit the kingdom prepared for you from the foundation of the world'; 'Depart from me, you cursed, into the eternal fire prepared for the devil and his angels' (Matt. 25, 34 and 41).[67] And then: 'They will go away into eternal punishment, but the righteous into eternal life' (Matt. 25, 46). [68]

[67]It is the horror of hell in its entirety, comprising especially the pain of the senses as well as the pain of loss, which Christ means by fire in the Gospel. Cf. 'Les anges et le cosmos', *Nova et Vetera*, 1953, pp. 143-5.

[68]Many other passages of the New Testament could be quoted. E.g., St Paul, 'Do you suppose ... you will escape the judgment of God? Or do you presume upon the riches of his kindness and forbearance and patience? Do you not know that God's kindness is meant to lead you to repentance? But by your hard and impenitent hearts you are storing up wrath for yourself on the day of wrath when God's righteous judgment will be revealed. For he will render to every man according to his works ...' (Rom. 2, 3-6); the Lord 'will bring to light the things now hidden in darkness and will disclose the purposes of the heart' (I Cor. 4, 5); 'Do you not know that the unrighteous will not inherit the kingdom of God? Do not be deceived; neither the immoral, nor idolaters, nor adulterers, nor homosexuals, nor thieves, nor the greedy, nor drunkards, nor revilers, nor robbers will inherit the Kingdom of God' (ibid., 6, 9-10); 'For we must all appear before the judgment seat of Christ, so that each one may receive good or evil, according to what he has done in the body' (II Cor. 5, 10); and most explicit of all: 'When the Lord Jesus is revealed from heaven with his mighty angels in flaming fire, inflicting vengeance upon those who do not know God and upon those who do not obey the gospel ...

And there is yet more. If it is true that the Word was made flesh, and that the eternal Son of God desired to come into our midst to die on the cross, is it possible that such an undertaking, such an inconceivable emptying of himself, as St Paul says (Phil. 2, 7), a sacrifice whose value, since it is that of a God-man, is absolutely infinite, should have been proposed to him by his heavenly Father and that he should have freely wished to go through with it, except to remedy some evil, itself infinite in its own way, by saving men from the folly of sin? The mystery of an infinite redemption could surely not be explained unless it were an answer to some infinite distress. These are the two infinities which are contending for the heart of man.

8. CONCLUSION

We have touched on the terrible mystery of hell, but not in order to explain it away, for that would be foolish.[69] It is inextricably bound up with the revelation which is given us from above and to which we must try to open our hearts and minds.

They shall suffer the punishment of eternal destruction and exclusion from the presence of the Lord and from the glory of his might ...' (II Thess. 1, 7, 9).

The same teaching is to be found in the Apocalypse: 'But as for the cowardly, the faithless, the polluted, as for murderers, fornicators, sorcerers, idolaters, and all liars, their lot shall be in the lake that burns with fire and brimstone, which is the second death' (Apoc. 21, 8).

[69]We could not make this passage of Fr Teilhard de Chardin our own: 'You have told me, O God, to believe in hell. But you have forbidden me to hold with absolute certainty that any single man has been damned. I shall therefore make no attempt to consider the damned here, nor even to discover—by whatsoever means—whether there are any. I shall accept the existence of hell on your word, as a *structural element in the universe,* and I shall pray and meditate until that awe-inspiring thing appears to me as a strengthening and even blessed complement to the vision of your omnipresence which you have opened out to me.' *Le milieu divin* (Collins, London, 1959, tr. Bernard Wall), p. 141. Quite apart from the fact that these lines seem to be too like a subterfuge, I do not believe, according to the words italicized by Teilhard himself, that hell, which results from mortal sin, can be a *structural element of the universe.* I find such an assertion unconsciously blasphemous. It has been seen above, p. 78, that evil *is not* a part of the universe; this applies *a fortiori* to hell where the evil of sin is perpetuated.

We must remain very close to God and, in the words of St Paul, 'become one spirit with him' (I Cor. 6, 17), if our minds are to be enlightened about mysteries; and in order that the mystery of evil, considered here in its extremity, may no longer trouble us or be a stumbling block : but rather a trap door put in our way by God to make us fall into the trap of faith and love. The saints have sometimes had things to say about the mystery of hell which seem too much for us to assimilate. Taking up the invocation in the Litanies : 'By thy holy judgments, deliver me, O Lord', Angela of Foligno said : 'I do not find God's goodness any more in a good and holy man or in many good and holy men, than in one or many souls in hell. This was only shown to me once in all its depth, but never will I lose the memory or joy of it. And should it ever happen that everything depending on faith were to fail me, yet would I cling to this one unique certainty about God, concerning his judgments and the justness of his judgments. But, O! how deep this is! Everything can be turned to the advantage of the good : for any soul which had or will have knowledge of these judgments will, by this knowledge of God's name, gain fruit from it all.'[70]

For us the revelation of hell and its eternal coexistence with the infinite goodness of God remains a mystery which terrifies us by the light it throws on the hidden places of our hearts. But we know that mystery does not have anything in common with absurdity or contradiction; and that the one is to be revered, the other detested. Those who refuse the revelation of hell by calling it nonsensical always begin by disfiguring it and then they are criticizing mere caricatures of the real thing.

In the end, the light which will make all clear is unknown to us here on earth. It is hidden behind a veil of silence, in the very heart of the Trinity. Only in the next life will the ultimate questions be resolved, the 'stumbling-block' be no more, and the divine goodness appear infinite to us not simply in everything it has created but even in the forbearance with which it is able to tolerate the rebellion of its free creatures.

As long as we live the thought of hell will overwhelm us. It is a thorn in our sides. It forces us to tremble before the judgments

[70]*The Book of Blessed Angela of Foligno,* end of the first part, towards the middle of the seventh step.

of God, to implore a purer faith and pray that our rebellious wills may be constrained, so that no man may resist the loving grace of the infinitely good God, of whom St Paul writes that we deceive ourselves if we think he is mocked (Gal. 6, 7).

II. THE TEMPORAL PUNISHMENT OF SIN

The pain of sense, which has already been discussed, can in two cases coexist with charity, and thereby cease to be irreparable and eternal, and become expiable and temporal : in the case of venial sin, and in the case of mortal sin which God has forgiven.

The sinner may not have destroyed in himself the charity which orders him towards his true final End : only his fault, by its inconsistency, has affected the means conducive to this end, like the sick man who, without ceasing to desire health above all things, allows himself occasionally to take liberties with the treatment prescribed. This is venial sin : there is no turning away from the final end (*aversio a Deo*), but simply a disordered attachment to creatures (*conversio deordinata ad bonum creatum*).[71]

Charity allows the sinner to disclaim and purify his *fault* here on earth.[72] He then opens himself fully to the divine forgiveness. Yet it remains for him to restore his balance with the order of creation, which is good in itself and which he has disturbed. This is the *pain of sense*.

The charity which is in him will, moreover, make him desire to restore this balance through punishment. If he is still *in statu viatoris,* the penances he imposes on himself and the sufferings he lovingly accepts will take on a compensating, satisfactory char-

---

[71]'Quando vero fit deordinatio citra aversionem a Deo, tunc est peccatum veniale.' St Thomas, Iª IIᵃᵉ, qu. 7, a. 5.

[72]Particularly at the moment when he feels the approach of death. Cf. St Thomas, *De malo,* qu. 7, a. 11. Otherwise the disowning of his venial faults would be his first act on entering purgatory, Ibid., qu. 7, a. 11, obj. et resp. ad 16.

What St Catherine of Genoa calls the 'blight of sin' is only the pain of the senses. 'The souls in purgatory are without the guilt of sin. Consequently there is no obstacle between God and themselves, except this pain which holds them back ...' 'Traité du purgatoire', in *Sainte Catherine de Gênes,* translated from the French version of Pierre Debongnie (Desclée de Brouwer, Paris, 1960), p. 205.

acter;[73] they will also be meritorious and make charity more intense in him. If he has already entered the *next world,* or purgatory, he will continue to call ardently for this restoration of balance, which will then be for him purely expiatory and satisfactory, although no longer capable of raising in him the level of grace.

But the sin may have been mortal and destroyed charity in him. God, however, has forgiven him. 'The universe cannot forgive. It knows neither pity nor mercy. But God can; his mercy does not go contrary to his justice; it is above his justice, but not opposed to it. "By being merciful," says St Thomas,[74] "God does not go against his justice, but above it ... For to remit or forgive is to make a free gift ... Mercy does not remove justice, but is the fullness of justice." It is a free gift, and there is no more guilt, hence no more punishment or restoration of balance, due as far as God is concerned.'[75] The charity which God had freely taken away from me at the moment when I refused it, is now restored to me, so that I am once more directed towards him. There is no more turning away from God, no more obligation to the pain of damnation.

But a pain of sense, or the restoration of harmony as far as the universe of creation is concerned, can remain due in the normal way. It is consented to by the man who is forgiven and united to God, who wills what is still required by justice. If it is accomplished here on earth it is satisfactory and meritorious; if put off or left uncompleted it will be purely expiatory in the next life.

The way in which God cures bodies throws light on the way he saves souls.[76] Sometimes the cure is sudden, as for Peter's mother-in-law (Luke 4, 39); sometimes gradual, as for the blind man of Bethsaida (Mark 8, 22-5). The same thing happens in conversions.

Sometimes they are exceptional and, in this sense, *miraculous*; charity in regard to God, who does away with guilt and the pain

[73]Satisfactory pain, as suffering, when against the will, is an evil (physical or ontological); as something freely chosen or borne, it may become a great (moral) good. St Thomas, I^a II^ae, qu. 87, a. 6. 'The pain of *affliction* restores the balance of creation by a *minus* (which is introduced into the perpetrator of the evil). The pain of *satisfaction,* or voluntarily accepted pain, restores the balance of creation by both a *minus* and a *plus,* which is love. It has in itself, therefore, an element of over-compensation.' J. Maritain, *Neuf leçons* ..., p. 186.

[74]I, qu. 21, a. 3, ad 3.

[75]Maritain, *Neuf leçons* ..., p. 188.

[76]Cf. St Thomas, III, qu. 86, a. 5, ad 1; and I^a II^ae, qu. 113, a. 10.

of damnation, is accompanied, in regard to the disorder of sin, by so intense and sorrowful a contrition that it is enough to compensate in a moment for all the strayings of the past,[77] as it did for the sinful woman at the feet of Christ (Luke 7, 47) or the good thief (Luke 23, 43).

But *normally* conversions are gradual; the influence of grace adapts itself to the processes of human action which bear first on the ends and then go on successively to the use of the necessary means. Under the influence first of operative grace, where man consents without the need for deliberation, the soul, at the first stage, both *makes good, once for all,* his turning away from God (*aversio a Deo*) by an act of charity (theological virtue) and contrition (moral virtue of repentance); and *begins to restore* the balance in the universe (*conversio inordinata ad creaturas*) by an act of satisfaction (moral virtue of repentance). Then, at the second stage, still under the impulsion of grace, which is now co-operative grace alone, it undertakes its deliberations and actions with a view to acquitting itself fully of the pain of sense.[78]

The idea of a temporal pain due to sin—rejected by Luther because of his teaching of righteousness being imputed to man[79] —is to be found in scripture. The penalties incurred by the first man after his sin go on after God forgave him (Gen. 3, 16 *et seq.*). Miriam, the wife of Aaron, had to be isolated even after the intercession of Moses on her behalf (Numbers 12, 14). Moses and Aaron, because they hesitated to strike the rock, were not to enter the promised land (Numbers 20, 12). David was forgiven his

---

[77]'When the mind turns away from sin, it happens that its disowning (displicentia) of the sin and its adhesion to God are so vehement that all obligation to the pain disappears.... The love of God suffices to establish man's mind in what is good, especially if it is vehement, and the disowning of the past fault, when it is intense, is accompanied by great sorrow. It follows that the vehement love of God and hatred for past sins liberate from the obligation to pain of satisfaction or of purification. If the intensity is not such that it entirely dispels the pain, at least it effects a proportionate diminution of it.' St Thomas, *III Contra Gent.,* ch. 158.
[78]'Sometimes God converts the heart of man by such a sudden shock that a perfect spiritual cure is immediately effected: not only is the guilt remitted but even the traces of sin as well; as in the case of Mary Magdalen. Sometimes, though, it is the guilt which is first remitted by operative grace; and then, by co-operative grace, the last traces of sin disappear one after the other.' St Thomas, III, qu. 86, a. 5, ad 1. Cf. also Ibid., a. 4, ad 2.
[79]Cf. 'La peine temporelle du péché', in *Revue Thomiste,* Jan.-Feb., 1927, p. 21.

adultery, but his sufferings were not to be escaped (II Sam. 12, 13-14).

Repentance, ceaselessly preached in the New Testament, which consists primarily in a conversion of the heart, calls on man, even when justified, to deny himself temporal goods, by almsgiving, bodily goods by fasting, and spiritual goods by humility in prayer.

Our Saviour redeemed us by a love which condescended to actions, and even to the acceptance of privations, suffering and death—not to dispense us from these but to urge us to follow his example.

In themselves the forms of temporal punishment restore our harmony with the universe to our own detriment, diminishing us by suffering. But he who accepts them with love provides the universe with a good action, increasing the being of the universe; the universe in its turn will increase the being of the agent so that the balance of both may remain steady. To compensation by punishment there is a corresponding over-compensation by love.[80]

---

[80]Cf. Maritain, *Neuf leçons . . .* , pp. 73, 186.

CHAPTER EIGHT

The Trials of the Present Life

But when we have dealt with the evil in nature, with the supreme evil which is sin, and the evil of its eternal or temporal punishment, we have still not said everything. There remain countless evils for man, among them suffering and death, which a pure philosopher would consider as natural but which, from the viewpoint of the Christian faith—and hence of Christian philosophy and theology—take on a penitential character to the extent that they are the result of sin. What is the primary origin of these evils?

I. THEIR PRIMARY ORIGIN

All the trials in our human lives are due to sin, though not all in the same way: some are attributable to original sin, others to our personal sins.

a. *Original justice and its prerogatives*

Important theological truths are contained in the naïve yet mysterious accounts of creation. Certainly, in his infinite goodness, God could, in creating man, have left him simply to the resources of his sensible and rational nature, but he did more than that: he poured out on him the gifts of original holiness and justice. The first of these gifts, sanctifying grace, was *supernatural*: it gave man a share in the divine nature and prepared him for the beatific vision. This grace, unlike ours, was also transfiguring. It strengthened powerfully the threefold but fragile natural domination of the soul over the body, of reason over the emotions, and of man himself over the external world. From this followed three *preternatural* gifts: exemption from sickness and death, from ignorance and emotional troubles, and from conflicts with the external world, which for man was like a garden, not because it was any different from what it is today, but because man's relationship with it was

218

different from what it is today. Thus the condition of the first man was not the dramatic one connatural to a being made up of mind and body, of reason and emotions, but a condition of harmony, and Adam should have passed it on to all his descendants.[1]

b. *The irremediable effects of the fall*

We could consider the effects of the fall in young children who die before baptism.[2] Instead, we shall try here to define its repercussions on men who live in time.

The fall happened, and irremediably deprived man of original grace and the prerogatives attached to it. At once there arose the conflicts, until then under control, of soul against body, reason against emotions and man against the exterior world. If we consider, as a pure philosopher would do, simply the *essential constitution* of man, mind and body, situated at the joining of two worlds, these conflicts might seem *normal and natural*, at any rate at first sight. But if we believe in the Judæo-Christian revelation and consider the true *existential condition* of man, fallen for ever by his own fault from an earlier state of happiness, these same conflicts will clearly bear a *penitential character*. From this follow the sanctions of Genesis 3, 17-9 : 'Cursed is the ground because of you ... In the sweat of your face you shall eat bread[3] till you return to the ground, for out of it you were taken.' And also the teaching of St Paul : 'Therefore as sin came into the world through one man and death through sin, so death spread to all men because all men sinned' (Rom. 5, 12). And further on : 'For the wages of sin is death' (6, 23).[4] This shows the real meaning

---

[1]Cf. 'De la condition initiale privilégiée de l'homme', in *Nova et Vetera*, 1954, p. 210.

[2]Cf. Charles Journet, *La volonté divine salvifique sur les petits enfants* (Desclée de Brouwer, Paris, 1958).

[3]Work itself is something blessed; it is the pain that may accompany work which is a punishment.

[4]'Death is *natural* in regard to our bodily condition; it is *penal* in regard to the loss of the divine privilege which preserved us from it.' St Thomas, II^a II^{ae}, qu. 164, a. 1, ad 1.

Cf. Bossuet, *Sermon on Death*: 'Do not persuade yourselves that we ought in accordance with the reasonings of medicine, to look on death as a natural consequence of our being a composite and a mixture. We must raise our minds higher and believe, according to the principles of the Christian faith, that what involves the flesh in the necessity of corruption, etc. ...' But the remainder of the passage seems to limit the vast prospect put before us by St Paul.

of the faith which sees in sickness a sort of conquest or empire of the devil; and it can be well be thought that it was the vision of the whole disaster of humanity which troubled Christ when he wept over the death of Lazarus (John 11, 35).

Certainly sanctifying grace was to be once more offered to men on the very morrow of the fall, but without the transfiguring prerogatives of the state of innocence, which were lost for ever and which will give way to more mysterious virtues, capable of conforming men to their crucified Saviour. The time of Christ's grace was to follow that of Adam's. St Thomas writes that at baptism Christ immediately delivers man 'from everything which affects his *person*, i.e. the guilt of original sin and the pain which follows it, the privation of the divine vision. But the penalties of the present life, such as death, hunger, thirst, etc. affect *human nature*, from which they flow as from their source since it was stripped of original justice; and that is why these miseries, *defectus*, will only disappear at the time of the ultimate repairing of our nature by the glorious resurrection.'[5]

c. *Can reason arrive at the fact of an initial disaster?*

From the viewpoint of faith and of the theological and philosophical thought inspired by it, the trials of the present life appear, therefore, as punishments. Do they seem the same from the viewpoint of reason alone?

If, as has already been said, the life of man, on the dividing line between two worlds, is by nature dramatic, the threefold conflict, between soul and body, reason and emotions, and man and the external world, which now distresses us, may appear normal and natural, at least at first sight; and the fact of an initial fall, far from being evident, as Pascal maintained, may well remain hidden.

Upon more attentive reflection, however, both on God's general plan of subordinating lower realities to higher ones and on the outstanding dignity of our spiritual soul, it may well seem that the weight of body on soul, emotions on reason and the whole universe on man is too heavy and overwhelming, too often fatal, for there not to be any inkling of an earlier condition of happiness destroyed by some mysterious disaster.

[5]III, qu. 69, a. 3, ad 3.

Such is the idea of St Thomas : 'The miseries or defects of the present life, if human nature is considered absolutely, with all its elements of weakness, appear natural to man. Yet by consideration on the one hand of divine providence, and on the other of the dignity of the superior part of our nature, it can be established with sufficient probability, *satis probabiliter probari potest,* that these miseries have a penitential character. And, since punishment follows upon sin, it may be concluded that the human race was originally tainted by some sin.'[6]

d. *The great number of our miseries*

The pains of this life are bodily and spiritual.

'Among bodily pains,' writes St Thomas, 'the foremost is death, to which all the others like hunger, thirst, etc. are directed. Among spiritual pains, the foremost is debility of reason, by which man only with difficulty comes to knowledge of the truth[7] and lapses easily into error, and through which he does not succeed in controlling completely his animal appetites, but is often blinded by them.'[8]

The sphere of human miseries is boundless : the evil of ignorance and error, the evil of temptation and scandal, the evil of pain and death which does not spare even little children, the evil of moral suffering—loneliness, mourning, anguish, agony.

The reflections which will be put forward in this chapter could hardly be exhaustive. Their only purpose will be slightly to increase our knowledge of the mystery of evil which, as has already been said, can be considered only in the light of the mystery of God. Attention, however, must first be drawn to two facts.

[6]*IV Contra Gent,* ch. 52. For a comparison of the teachings of Pascal and St Thomas on original sin, cf. Charles Journet, *Vérité de Pascal* (Saint-Maurice, Switzerland, 1951), pp. 88-155.
[7]A certain *spontaneous* knowledge of God is inherent in humanity: 'For what can be known about God is plain to them, because God has shown it to them. Ever since the creation of the world his invisible nature, namely, his eternal power and deity, has been clearly perceived in the things that have been made. So they are without excuse ...' (Rom. 1, 19-20). It will require all the efforts of atheistic propaganda and its myths to stifle this instinct. But an explicit and developed knowledge of God, what St Thomas calls the *truth about God,* 'when it is sought for by reason (alone), comes only to a few men, after a long time and mingled with many errors,' I, qu. 1, a. 1.
[8]*IV Contra Gent.,* ch. 52.

e. Pains of this life are aggravated by our wickedness but may be transfigured by faith

The pains of this life are innumerable and tormenting, they strike so brutally and blindly, confuse our reason so completely and so often leave our minds without light, that the only way out is to believe that in the next life they may call for infinite compensations. This is the answer given by faith. St Paul says : 'I consider that the sufferings of this present time are not worth comparing with the glory that is to be revealed to us' (Rom. 8, 18).

But the first point to be made is that in the enormity of our misfortunes, the pains which come to us from original sin would in themselves count for very little. The sea of suffering which breaks upon humanity is not simply the result of what we have inherited from Adam, but incomparably more is it the result of man's own wilful actions, his pride, his ambitions, his jealousies, his hatreds, his cruelties and his follies.[9]

We have already shown that sin can in no way be attributed to God; the other side to the problem of sin reveals the endless train of physical and moral disasters which it brings down on man. When Dostoyevsky sets himself to describe the suffering of children in order to make the vision of evil unbearable for us, he chooses his examples from the little victims of men's cruelty and sadism. And the one thing worse than doing harm to the body of a child is to harm its soul : 'Whoever causes one of these little ones who believe in me to sin, it would be better for him to have a great millstone fastened round his neck and to be drowned in the depth of the sea' (Matt. 18, 6).

Men's sins begin by offending God and go on to increase their own misfortunes so tragically. And we know that his forbearance with them comes from his being 'strong enough to turn all the evil we choose to introduce into the world into a greater good,

[9]'Dieu est ce qu'il y a de plus terrible au monde ... Il Châtie.' In these words of one of the characters in his novel *Jeunesse sans Dieu,* Odon de Horvath suggests the infernal dialectic in which the creature who rebels against the One for whom he is made is involved, from the time of his coming into the world. The same character adds: 'On ne doit pas renier Dieu, même quand on ignore pourquoi il nous punit.' And again: 'Dieu va par tous les chemins.' We have only to think of the *Deus excelsus terribilis* of the Psalms; and also of the phrase Jean Wahl uses summing up Kierkegaard: 'Christianity is not terrible, but only the world into which it comes.' *Études Kierkegaardiennes* (Vrin, Paris, 1949), p. 413.

hidden in the mystery of transcendence and such that nothing in nature allows us to conjecture what it may consist in. The man of faith, who is to have a suspicion of the greatness of that good, and marvel at it, measures the greatness of the evil for which such a good will supercompensate.'[10]

The second fact, the full significance of which we cannot even imagine, is that the sufferings of this world, whether they come from original sin by way of our inheritance or whether they are a consequence of the personal sins committed by ourselves or by others, can be transfigured : then they will cease to be merely afflictive and become satisfactory or compensatory, and even merit greater love and eternal life.

The evils of the present life can be amplified indefinitely by our personal sins, yet they are also capable of being illumined by grace.

2. THE EVIL OF IGNORANCE AND ERROR

It was the weakness of our reason, both practical and speculative, which so saddened St Thomas when he thought of the miseries of the present life.

a. *Man's first innocence lacked knowledge but was not ignorant.*

It must not be imagined, as some, like Hegel or Kierkegaard, have done, that in the state of innocence man lacked the power of discernment between good and evil :[11] in that case sin, being a conscious rebellion against the divine order, would not have been possible. The knowledge of good and evil which man was forbidden (Gen. 2, 17), was not that knowledge which is able to discern good from evil, but that which claims the right to decide and experience what evil is for oneself.[12]

Certainly Adam was not omniscient, there were many things he did not know; but if lack, meaning mere absence of knowledge,

[10]Maritain, *Existence and the Existant*, op. cit., p. 126.
[11]For Hegel, see *The Philosophy of Mind* (trans. W. Wallace, Oxford, 1894), pp. 196ff; for Kierkegaard, see *The Concept of Dread* (trans. W. Lowrie, O.U.P., 1944). Cf. 'De la condition initiale privilégiée de l'homme', in *Nova et Vetera*, 1954, p. 227.
[12]Cf. R. De Vaux, 'La Genèse' (Cerf, Paris, 1951), p. 45.

is distinguished from ignorance, meaning privation,[13] then there was no ignorance in him, he knew what he needed to know. 'As to his intelligence, because of the stable harmony and the perfect subordination of faculties, which human nature enjoyed by grace on the morn of creation, it must be thought of as incomparably strong in its vitality and its powers of development, at that time spoiled by no defect. As regards the mode of human knowledge, this virgin intelligence was founded in a state of simplicity and inexperience which is hard to imagine; and yet its ideas were full of immense potentialities.'[14] The sin of the first man, like the angels' sin, did not require in him any kind of ignorance, but merely the absence, at the moment of action, of the necessary consideration of the rule.[15]

Ignorance is a consequence of original sin;[16] it has grown over the ages by the accumulation of our negligences, emotions and errors. It has become a patrimony of misfortune for humanity. It is only blameworthy in any of us when it is wilful, and altogether ceases to be so when it is invincible.

b. *Error and illusion*

St Thomas is very hard on error : 'To err is to approve the false as true. This presupposes an act ... Error is manifestly a sin : to make a pronouncement about something which is not known, particularly in dangerous matters, could not be done without presumption.'[17]

St Thomas here is thinking less of the inheritance of errors passed on to us by education than of minds whose temerity opens the paths of seduction to others. The understanding is made for truth as the eye for light, and it is impossible for it to attach itself to pure darkness; only under the cover of some truth will it adhere to an error which has insinuated itself.

[13]'Nescientia dicit simplicem scientiae *negationem* ... ignorantia vero importat scientiae *privationem*.' St Thomas, Iᵃ IIᵃᵉ, qu. 76, a. 2.
[14]Raïssa Maritain, *Histoire d'Abraham ou les premiers âges de la conscience morale* (Desclée de Brouwer, Paris, 1947), p. 57.
[15]St Thomas, I, qu. 63, a. 1, ad 4.
[16]'Once original justice was withdrawn from the will there came about an impairing (*defectio*) of the knowledge of truth in the understanding and of rightful moderation in the irascible and concupiscible emotions; thus ignorance and concupiscence are as it were the material aspect of original sin.' St Thomas, *De malo,* qu. 3, a. 7.
[17]*De potentia,* qu. 3, a. 7.

The consequences of an intuition which is both basic and true becoming adulterated at the outset of a major trend of thought, through the use of a defective conceptualization to express it, can be disastrous. 'At the heart of every great philosophical system there is thus a very simple and yet inexhaustible insight—Bergson has singled it out in a celebrated passage—which on some occasion has overwhelmed the mind with its certitude. With every great philosopher and every great thinker there is a central intuition which in itself does not mislead. But that intuition can be conceptualized, and in fact in a great number of cases is conceptualized, in a mistaken, perhaps even pernicious, doctrine.'[18]

Reflecting on Marx's initial misconception of the analogical richness of being, Georges Cottier writes: 'We have spoken of *option*, when the subject under discussion is a certain original *vision* by the intelligence of being because we believe that genuine vision reveals the innate generosity of being; if meanness seems inherent in being, it is only because an option, which strictly speaking lies in the moral order, has interfered with the original intuition. The understanding and the will are wrapped up with each other; the decisions of the one can project upon the other's pure transparency shadow-lines which will then accompany thought in all its successive stages ... To state that creation is not possible because it goes against the will to autonomy is to make a postulation.'[19]

In what sense is it permissible to speak of option in the perception of primary truths? Olivier Lacombe analyzes the question : 'The word is dangerous because it seems to imply that each person's liberty—using liberty in an arbitrary, voluntarist sense—opts for such and such a view, as if the will dictated to the understanding what it ought to see. But this is not possible. Yet *option* does have a meaning because of the condition of man, since man's reason and understanding is not a divine, nor even an angelic, understanding. Human reason, whatever the idealists may think, is not transparent to itself; and, more serious still, not only is it not always transparent to itself in all its stages of thought, but it is resolutely obscure to itself in the first and decisive step by which it initiates

[18]Maritain, 'The Metaphysics of Bergson', in *Redeeming the Time* (Geoffrey Bles, London, 1943), p. 53.
[19]*L'athéisme du jeune Marx, ses origines hégéliennes* (Vrin, Paris, 1959), p. 345.

any philosophical doctrine. Herein is the root of the relativity of human thought. And without grace, it might well be wondered whether any philosophy would ever see the light which had sufficient contact with reality to be more than partial, in both senses of the word. The first perception of the very first principles, the point of departure of any philosophy, lies buried in the unconscious and preconscious. This moment is not transparent even to the mind of the philosopher, yet it is the point of departure from which he must set about building his system, and against which he can do nothing. So it is permissible to speak of option, because the influence of individual factors does play a considerable role; I do not think that it is sufficient to destroy or distort our reason, but it is enough to make the actual plurality of philosophies inevitable, man being what he is.'[20]

All that has been said of philosophies is even more tragically true of the great aberrant religions and of the dissidences within Christianity. The fomenters of schisms availed themselves initially of some distorted Christian truth.[21] In the end they let themselves be carried away by the Messianic illusions and false hopes against which Christ himself put us on our guard (Matt. 24, 23). They passed on to their disciples not the sins of schism or heresy, which are always personal and hence not transmissible, but a legacy of confusions, misinterpretations and errors which in the course of time were to become for their followers genuinely invincible and thus not blameworthy.

c. *Invincible ignorance*

Ignorance, even when it is invincible, is the cause of incalculable evils. We have only to think[22] of the host of men of good faith, good men who have not refused the divine invitations in their hearts and therefore belong invisibly and spiritually to Christ and form the Church in its initial, imperfect and developing state, yet in whom misapprehensions, for them insurmountable, restrict the

---

[20]'La pluralité des philosophies est-elle une richesse?' in *Nova et Vetera,* 1959, p. 25. Also in *Chemins de l'Inde et philosophie chrétienne,* Paris, Alsatia, 1956, p. 165.
[21]Cf. Journet, *The Church of the Word Incarnate* (Sheed & Ward, London and New York, 1955), vol. I, pp. 32ff.
[22]Ibid. Cf. the conclusion of volume II. This volume has not been published in English translation. Its French title is *L'Eglise du Verbe Incarné* (Desclée de Brouwer, Paris: *Translator's note*).

spontaneous motion of grace and prevent it from attaining the only place where it could flourish properly. Visibly and physically they belong to religious formations which to a greater or lesser extent are seriously deficient : to the pre-Christian religions, Brahmanism or Buddhism, or to Islam or Judaism. Closer to ourselves, some belong to those different sects which seem to have destroyed the divine unity of the Church and divided its indivisible essence. How scandalous this rending of the seamless robe![23]

Perhaps all this may be swept away before the end of the world, and perhaps all the just will gather together visibly in Christ and into the fold which he entrusted to Peter in order to confront the terrible onslaughts of Gog and Magog.[24] Christ's words allow room for hope, without being definite : it was primarily to point out that his Church was to overflow from the world of the Jews into that of the Gentiles and that the faithful of both worlds would in future form but one people that he announced : 'And I have other sheep that are not of this fold; I must bring them also, and they will heed my voice. So there shall be one flock, one shepherd' (John 10, 16).[25] As for the great prayer in which Christ asked that his disciples should be one, 'even as thou, Father, art in me, and I in thee, that they also may be in us, so that the world may believe that thou hast sent me' (John 17, 21), must we think that it has not yet been granted, that it will be granted only if all the just in the world are one day visibly and bodily assembled around Christ and his Vicar on earth? Surely it is more likely that this prayer has been infallibly granted since the time of Pentecost, in that place where the Saviour himself reaches men with sacramental and jurisdictional powers and pours into them the grace

---

[23]'In its Office for Good Friday, when the Church beseeches God to take away the evils that oppress the world, it is of every error that she first begs deliverance: *Oremus Deum Patrem omnipotentem, ut cunctis mundum purget erroribus; morbos auferat; famem depellat* ...' Maritain, *Freedom in the Modern World,* op. cit.

[24]We know that the thousand years in Apoc. 20, 7-9, represent the whole duration of the messianic era which extends from Christ's first coming as Saviour to his second coming as Judge. The beloved city is the Church, gathered round Christ and assailed with him. Gog and Magog symbolize all the successive attacks of the Beast which will no doubt reach their climax at the end of the world.

[25]Cf. D. Mollat, S.J., *L'Evangile de Saint Jean* (Cerf, Paris, 1953), p. 129, who refers to John 11, 51-2: 'He (Caiaphas) prophesied that Christ should die for the nation, and not for the nation only, but to gather into one the children of God who are dispersed.'

by which they may become fully conformed to him, so as to make of them by vocation not simply members *saved* by and in Christ, but also, if they are faithful to him, members who, by and in Christ, *themselves save* other men.

And furthermore, through the hidden graces of supplication, which draw every man coming into the world to Christ and his Church, the same great prayer for unity is again realized, although this time in an incipient way, in all the good men who begin invisibly and spiritually to belong to Christ, and in whom the Church exists in potentiality. But the more we believe in the reality, the extent and the splendour of the Church thus potentially constituted, the more also we suffer at the thought of so many men of good will who are prevented from seeing the fullness of the Church, because 'a veil lies over their minds' (II Cor. 3, 15). The evil is worse than might be imagined. In a letter to Gerard Manley Hopkins, Newman confided that despite those who claim that cultivated men have no excuse for invincible ignorance, it is precisely cultivated men who have this excuse more than any others.[26]

What a great resurrection for the whole world it would be if, all of a sudden, the Church potential, with all its resources, could pass over into the full light of the Church actual : if what St Paul proclaims of Israel—cut off only for a time, to be one day included again (Rom. 11, 12-15)—could come true for all the sects and all good men on earth. But this may be no more than a dream. We may well need to be reproved by adversaries for a long time yet, many of them perhaps of good faith, so as to learn not to confuse our habits of worship and our narrowness with that Church without stain or spot to which we have given our hearts, but into which we are far from being fully integrated; so as not to be found wanting in vigilance for the treasures of truth which are entrusted to us; and so as to remind us, like the Jews at the time of Christ, that 'many will come from east and west and sit at table with Abraham, Isaac and Jacob in the kingdom of heaven, while the sons of the kingdom will be thrown into the outer darkness' (Matt. 8, 11-2).

Only later, in the next world, will all ignorance be removed.

[26]Gerard Manley Hopkins, *Letter to Robert Bridges,* 22 September, 1866. On the question: *When can faith be considered to be adequately proposed?* see Journet, *L'Eglise du Verbe Incarné,* op. cit., vol. II, pp. 852-9.

Pascal writes: 'This land is not Truth's; she wanders here unknown amongst men. God has covered her with a veil which lets her go unrecognized by those who do not hear his voice.'[27] Alas, it is we ourselves who cover her with a veil which may cause her to go unrecognized, to some extent, even by those who are beginning to hear the voice of God.

Error can be blameless; but the same cannot be said for making the great number of errors in existence an excuse to despair of ever finding the truth. As we have just seen, the *de facto plurality* of philosophies, even Christian ones, could never be raised into a *de jure pluralism*, and the contingency of philosophical inventiveness 'is rather a sign of human weakness than of intellectual freedom'.[28] The same observation has been made at the theological level: 'This diversity is not in itself something good, not an intrinsic wealth, even if we take into account our human nature and the nature of our human intelligence. It is the price to be paid for the weakness of our intelligence, affected by sin, and for the non-rational elements involved in any speculative enquiry.'[29] Pascal's words should not be forgotten: 'Those who do not love the truth make a pretext of all the points at issue and of the great many people who deny it; hence their error comes solely from their loving neither truth nor charity. Hence they have no excuse ... Many certain things are contradictory but contradiction is not a mark of falsity any more than the absence of it is a mark of truth.'[30] He echoes St Paul's words about those 'who will listen to anybody and can never arrive at a knowledge of the truth' (II Tim. 3, 7).[31]

---

[27]*Pensées,* edited Brunschvicg, no. 843.
[28]Olivier Lacombe, *Chemins de l'Inde et philosophie chrétienne,* op. cit., pp. 154, 167.
[29]Louis Gardet and M.-M. Anawati, *Introduction à la théologie musulmane, Essai de théologie comparée* (Vrin, Paris, 1948), p. 468.
[30]*Pensées* (Edit. de Cluny, Paris, 1942), no. 163.
[31]Cf. the well-known thesis of Kierkegaard, for whom sin has so radically disorganized man that he is no longer capable of objective doctrinal truth and his only salvation lies in his subjectivity and the sincerity of his belief. Christ, Kierkegaard was fond of saying, did not teach, he lived. But first of all, what would be left of Christ, his Incarnation and Redemption, and of Christianity as a whole if these facts were shorn of their objective significance and truth content? And then, how are we to be sure of our sincerity? 'Nowadays,' writes Georges Cottier, 'a conscience is authentic if it is spontaneous, and to be sincere, therefore, it is sufficient to see things as one sees them at the moment when one sees them. At that moment

We have very little idea of the evil error wreaks in each one of us and of the extent to which we are responsible for it. A host of practical judgments which we apply to ourselves, to our relations with our neighbours and to the things of God and their requirements, and by which we reassure ourselves, are inspired by our egoism, our self-esteem, our instinct of self-preservation and our cowardliness. In the end we poison ourselves. Even the supreme truths we are attached to cease to be thought of with sufficient purity of heart and lose their transparency. We become so used to the signs, we forget the splendour of what they signify. This is what St John of the Cross meant when he said: 'Be thou never willingly satisfied with that which thou understandest of God, but rather with that which thou understandest not of him . . . For this is to seek him in faith.'[32]

3. THE EVIL OF TEMPTATION AND SCANDAL

Temptation is not an effect of original sin: it made its appearance in the earthly paradise. But since then it has gained in power, exciting our wounded sensibility and troubling our emotions.

a. *The temptation of the first man*

What brought about the temptation of the first man? Was it necessary? And did God have to allow such a disastrous trial?

The first thing to be said about this is that the temptation was not inevitable. So long as man's mind remained subject to God and his emotions to his reason, no conflict or trouble of the senses could have arisen in him.[33] The first sin of all could only be a spiritual one and had to begin by a revolt against God. The only possibility

---

one could hardly see them otherwise! The error of such an outlook lies in the supposition that conscience is an absolute, whereas our conscience is something obtained by a struggle—it must be moulded and educated. We may be responsible *before* our conscience only after we have been responsible *for* it.' 'Pauvreté et amour de la vérité', in *Nova et Vetera*, 1960, no. 3, p. 169. And finally, for Subjectivity to be identical with Truth we should have to be Christ himself: 'I am the Truth' (John, 14, 16).

[32]*Spiritual Canticle,* in *Complete Works,* trans. and edited by E. Allison Peers (Burns Oates, 1943), vol. II, p. 200.

[33]Cf. St Thomas, IIa IIae, qu. 164, a. 1.

open to the devil was to act by way of persuasion and suggestion.[34] The entire decision was left to man's free will.

The devil's suggestion did not presuppose any previous complicity on the part of the first man. It did not cause him any surprise
or bewilderment. St Thomas reminds us of this when he says that
it remained something external to him, that it did not have any
penal character and that it was easy to repel.[35] In one way, in
so far as it was purely external, it resembled the temptation of
Christ in the desert. But in other ways it was profoundly different :
for if the confrontation with the prince of this world was incapable
of giving rise to any faltering in the Saviour, yet such an encounter
must have caused him unspeakable suffering; the mystery of the
Temptation with which his public life began resembles the mystery
of the Agony which ended it.

The devil's suggestion to man was so far from inevitable that
the choice between adoration or rebellion might well have
presented itself to the first man independently of any external intervention, as it did with the angels. Yet, while it was not the decisive
element, this intervention was effective. Might it not have been
prevented? Certainly God might have performed a miracle. He
might have made the first man impeccable by grace. He might,
in his infinite goodness, have made another world. But he was
also able to make the world he actually did make. And then 'it
belonged to man's nature to be able to enter into society with
other creatures and to be helped or hindered by them. And so it
was fitting that, in the state of innocence, God should both permit
the first man to be tempted by the wicked angels and arrange for
him to be assisted by the good ones.'[36] To make allowance for
the treatment required by the nature of free beings like ourselves,
it was good for us to be left to the decision of our own wills, as is
said in Ecclesiasticus 15, 14 : 'It is he who in the beginning made
man and left him to the decision of his own counsel.'[37]

There were two possible outcomes to the temptation put before
the first man. It might have led to an act of fidelity and growth
in love. Someone may reply : 'But God knew beforehand that
Adam would sin!' But God did not know *in advance,* he was seeing
it in his eternity. The eternal plan was not made in advance :
God, who knows all things not by *foresight* or memory but by pure

[34]I{a} II{ae}, qu. 80, a. 1.   [35]II{a} II{ae}, qu. 165, a. 1; also ad 3.
[36]St Thomas, II{a} II{ae}, qu. 165, a. 1.   [37]Cf. Ibid., ad 2.

vision, only gave his plan effect once he had already made allowance from all eternity for all the free refusals of his creatures.[38] And from all eternity he decided to remedy the folly of the original disaster by the folly of the redemptive Incarnation.

b. *The penal character of our temptations*

Unlike that of Eden, the temptations we know have a penal character. They may come from the perverting action of the devil or of men who seek to beguile us.

They may arise also, says St Augustine, simply from the beauty of things, which is a gift of God, and therefore good; a beauty which can be loved by us in a good way or a bad way—good if due order is preserved, bad if due order is set aside.[39]

They may incite us to revolt against the injustices and miseries which oppress us.

They may, and this for Kierkegaard gives them their terrible seductive power, take the form of what he calls dread, that inexplicable attraction exercized by the unknown, that desire to step at least once over the frontiers of the forbidden zone and explore the infinity of the depths of evil, in order to forget for a moment, in the intoxication of danger and adventure, our limits and our incurable wretchedness.[40]

---

[38]'This feeling for *unforeseeableness* . . . in itself is a highly philosophical feeling and one which we should not let lie quiescent within us. . . . Certain too elementary expositions of theodicy might seem to compromise it. In reality the God of Saint Thomas safeguards as much as the God of Bergson the unforeseeableness of concrete becoming. If he knows all things from all eternity, and the feather which tomorrow will fall from the wing of a certain bird, it is not because the history of the world should be only the unfolding of a *ready-made scenario*. It is on the contrary, that all the moments of the whole of time are present for the divine Eternity, who sees in its own instant, and hence always, everything creatures do, have done, will do in the very instant that it *happens,* and hence in an eternal freshness of life and newness.' Maritain, 'The Metaphysics of Bergson', in *Redeeming the Time* (Geoffrey Bles, London, 1943), p. 72-3.

[39]*De civitate Dei,* bk. XV, ch. 22.

[40]'For him dread is the most terrible type of temptation. In his *Diary* of 1832 he showed that all sins start with fear, and adds that they end in a sort of impotent despair. In 1836 he discussed the astonishing anxiety which follows upon moments of elation. In 1837 he wrote that he was in danger of delivering himself over to Satan so that he might learn from him all the forms of sin in all their horror. Although love of good was in him, he felt in himself also this inclination towards the mystery of sin. Like

In all these cases temptation receives unseen help from our wounded nature, agitates our emotions, disturbs our judgment and shatters our inner harmony. So long as we struggle against it and withhold from it the consent of our free will, it can never turn into sin; on the contrary, it may be the occasion of growth in faith and love: 'We rejoice in our sufferings, knowing that sufferings produce endurance, and endurance produces character, and character produces hope ...' (Rom. 5, 3-4). Yet these temptations are still not without risks and dangers and they are great miseries, which had no place in the integrity of the earthly paradise and will have none in the world to come.

c. 'Irresistible' temptations

There are temptations which, when allowed to eat into the self, are irresistible. They distract the emotions, and have the power of an elemental force. They sweep away the tardy resistance of the free will. St Thomas specifies the emotions of love and anger.[41] There are others like ambition, or jealousy, by which souls are twisted just as a bar of iron is bent when taken red-hot from the fire. We have only to think of Othello or, worse still, of Judas. It was said that 'he was a thief and as he had the money box he used to take what was put into it' (John 12, 6). But afterwards, when Christ had gone, he was to throw the thirty pieces of silver down in the temple (Matt. 27, 5). Avarice is not a sufficient explanation of his tragedy, but rather, it would seem, a sort of mysterious jealousy: jealousy at seeing another disciple preferred, or perhaps jealousy of Christ himself?

Why are such terrible evils to be seen, which can violently attack each one of us? An immediate answer is given in the Gospel warning: 'Watch and pray that you may not enter into tempta-

---

Lehnau's Faust he wanted to know the truth which lies in evil. We read in the *Diary*, 1841-2: "The fundamental category has been passed by in silence; this is dread ... Dread is a desire directed towards what one fears, a congenial antipathy ... What one fears is also what one desires; and so the individual weakens and the first sin is produced in this weakness." In 1843, speaking of his period of worldly life and, to take him at his own word, of dissoluteness, he wrote: "It is dread which has led me astray." '
Jean Wahl, *Études Kierkegaardiennes* (Vrin, Paris, 1949), pp. 222-3.
[41] Ia IIae, qu. 10, a. 3; qu. 77, a. 2.

tion' (Matt. 26, 41). And we know that God never comes to reap where he has not sown. St Augustine says: 'God does not command the impossible, but his commandment calls on you to do what you can and to pray for what you can not.'[42] The Council of Trent adds: 'He aids our ability'[43] and I John 5, 3: 'His commandments are not burdensome.'

For the end of time are foretold temptations capable of leading astray, if it were possible, even the elect (Matt. 24, 24). But it is said also that only those will be lost who 'refused to love the truth and so be saved' (II Thess. 2, 10). St Thérèse of Lisieux desired to confront these terrible trials.[44]

d. *Scandal*

Scandal is the cause of fearful destruction. Think of the scandal given to adults which can wound them beyond cure.

Think of the outrage of the little girl in *The Possessed* who repeated in her delirium that she had 'killed God', and who powerlessly threatened Stavroghin with her little fist before going to hang herself in a corner near the water-closet.[45]

Then there are the great collective scandals at the end of the world : 'Then if anyone says to you, "Lo, here is the Christ!" or "There he is!" do not believe it. For false Christs and false prophets will arise and show great signs and wonders, so as to lead astray, if it were possible, even the elect' (Matt. 24, 23-4). It will be too late to think then of preparations, man must be found ready : 'Blessed are those servants whom the master finds awake when he comes' (Luke 12, 37).

Now is not the time of glory but of questioning : questions which, because of things that scandalize us, our hearts ask God ceaselessly; and the unique and decisive question which God asks each one of us by putting us, always watched over by his grace, in the thick of a world seemingly overrun by scandals and outrages. But all these together will never be able to extinguish love : in souls of great stature they will cause love to burst into flame.

'Woe to the world for temptations to sin! For it is necessary

---

[42]*De natura et gratia*, ch. 43, no. 50.
[43]Session VI, ch. 11; *Denz.*, no. 804.
[44]*Autobiography of a Saint* (Harvill Press, London, 1958), pp. 233-4.
[45]But God could hardly have failed to take this child immediately into his paradise.

that temptations come, but woe to the man by whom the temptation comes!' (Matt. 18, 7). In the soul of the Saviour there was an
unspeakable pain and an intense love both for the glory of God and
for poor humanity, when he uttered that terrible curse against
the bringers of scandal.

e. *The temptation to suicide*

There are creatures who seem to have been born too weak to
bear the weight of misery or moral suffering which piles up on
them and who end up by taking their own lives. One hears, perhaps, of some girl, a practising Christian but torn by anguish, the
support of her ageing mother, who one morning, just before she
would have gone off to work, hangs herself with the sash-cord; her
rosary is found in her bed. The theological virtue of faith is undoubtedly more powerful than any discouragement, and when a
man is really seized by faith and led through the trials of what St
John of the Cross calls the night of the senses, it completely dis-
sipates all melancholy. But, however genuine and precious it may
be, faith is not always so firmly entrenched. It is not always strong
enough to dispel neuroses, although it certainly does ward off a
great many. Others it helps people to bear with, as they might
bear tuberculosis or cancer, in a holy way. But it does happen that
the intensity of despair can unbalance the mind to the point of
making certain suicides innocent in the eyes of the merciful God
who knows what is in each man's heart. Yet even from a purely
philosophical viewpoint suicide is essentially folly.[46] It must be
even more so from the viewpoint of faith. 'To the suffering man
who is tempted to suicide, we can only say: remember what
Christ and the martyrs suffered. You, like them, must carry your
cross. You will not cease to suffer, but the cross of suffering will
itself become sweet to you by an unknown power which comes
from the very heart of divine love. You must not kill yourself,
because you must not *throw away your cross*. You have need of it.
And so, ask your conscience whether you really are innocent. You
will find that, though you are perhaps innocent of a thing which
the world blames you for, you are to blame in a thousand other

[46]It is condemned by Plato in the *Phaedo* (62 B.C.); and later by Plotinus,
Enn. I, 9, 'even if it is realized that madness will come.' But he justifies it
in *Enn.* I, 4, nos 7 and 8: if pain is prolonged the wise man 'will decide on
what he ought to do; for his free will has not been taken from him'.

ways. You are a sinner. If Christ, who was innocent, suffered for
others, and, as Pascal said, shed for you also a drop of his blood,
have you, a sinner, the right to refuse to suffer? Perhaps it is a sort
of punishment. But divine punishment is special and incomparable in this, that it has nothing vindictive about it and is, of its
very nature, purifying. Whoever rebels against it is really rebelling
against the very meaning of his own life. Unquestionably there is
no justice here on earth. Monsters have fantastic success and no
one suffers more than the saints. Here we touch upon the mystery
of iniquity, which is closely allied to that other mystery—that the
meaning of life is fully realized in and through suffering. Man, it
used to be said, is a being who can kill himself and who must not
do so. This statement now takes on a more precise meaning. The
temptation exists, and so does the refusal. When the refusal is
genuinely Christian, it gives proof of an act of the love of God, and
of suffering; though not for its own sake—that is impossible, for
algophilia is pathological and Christ himself hesitated before the
ultimate suffering and prayed God to spare him from it—but of
suffering in so far as it contains a remedy willed by God.'[47]

f. The trials of the mystics

There exist other mysterious temptations, exceptionally harrowing ones, which God keeps for his most faithful servants when he
wishes thoroughly to purify their understanding by faith, their
memory by hope and their will by charity. The three theological
virtues coming down upon them throw them into unspeakable
anguish, described by St John of the Cross in the Dark Night of
the Soul. Their agony is a renewal of that of the Blessed Virgin
abandoned by her Child: 'Son, why have you treated us so?
Behold, your father and I have been looking for you anxiously'
(Luke 2, 48). It makes them repeat the very prayer of Christ:
'Abba, Father, all things are possible to thee; remove this cup from
me; yet not what I will, but what thou wilt' (Mark 14, 36).

It was of these holy temptations, to be both desired and feared,
that Fr de Caussade was thinking when he depicted the trials of
the state of abandonment: 'Souls that walk in the light sing the
canticle of the light; those that walk in darkness sing the songs of
the darkness. Both must be allowed to sing to the end the part

[47]Paul-Louis Landsberg, Essai sur l'expérience de la mort, followed by
Problème moral du suicide (Seuil, Paris, 1951), pp. 145-6.

allotted to them by God in the great Oratorio. Nothing must be added to the score, nothing left out; every drop of bitterness must be allowed to flow freely at whatever cost. It was thus with Jeremiah and Ezechiel, whose utterances were broken by tears and sobs, and who could find no consolation except in continuing their lamentations. Had the course of their grief been interrupted we should have lost the most beautiful passages of Scripture. The Spirit that afflicts can also console : these diverse waters flow from the same source.' Afterwards will come the day of glory : 'At this awakening, those who, like Jeremiah and David have been in their grief, will see that in their desolation they have been a subject of joy to the angels and of glory to God.'[48]

g. *The different meanings of temptation*

To tempt is to test. But the two words mean different things.

It is possible to test someone by trying to drag him into disaster. The devil, the 'ancient serpent' (Apoc. 12, 9), tempted the first man in the garden of Eden (Gen. 3). He is furiously determined to deceive us, as Paul wrote to the Corinthians : 'I am afraid that as the serpent deceived Eve by his cunning, your thoughts will be led astray from a sincere and pure devotion to Christ' (II Cor. 11, 3). He may tempt us through our lack of self-control (I Cor. 7, 5). He even came up to Christ to tempt him in the wilderness (Matt. 4, 1-11).

Creatures tempt us, both by their beauty, which, by captivating our senses, is liable to darken our reason, and by the suggestions of the wicked and the sight of their disorderly lives.

God tempts man in another way : 'After these things God tested Abraham, and said to him, "Abraham!" and he said, "Here I am." He said, "Take your son, your only son Isaac . . ." ' (Gen. 22, 1-2). It is said of the righteous in the Book of Wisdom : 'God subjected them to the test and found them worthy of him; as gold in the crucible he has tried them . . .' (Wisdom 3, 5-6). If he permits us to be solicited by all sorts of appearances and crushed by all sorts of evils, it is not to find out our reactions—he knows these in his eternity. It would be silly to imagine that he wants to lay traps for us; St James writes : 'Let no one say when he is

---

[48] J. P. de Caussade, S.J., *Abandonment to Divine Providence* (English trans. from 10th complete French edition, by E. J. Strickland, The Catholic Records Press, Exeter, 1921), pp. 76-7.

tempted, "I am tempted by God"; for God cannot be tempted with evil and he himself tempts no one' (James 1, 13). But God permits temptation which has two meanings and which can help us to become aware of our wretchedness, to pray more intensely for the assistance of his grace and to go forward in faith and hope.

'God tempts no one.' Yet we are bound to ask the Father in heaven not to lead us into temptation, or more accurately, not to put us to the test (Matt. 6, 13). We know that God tempers the wind to the shorn lamb. We must ask him, in his infinite goodness, not to allow us this day to come up against any temptation greater than our powers of resistance; or if he does, to strengthen us with a further granting of his grace. And also that he may not put us so greatly to the test as to expect from us all that he has a right to claim . . . and that he may take our weakness into account. For anyone who prays with humility in this way St Paul's words will ring true : 'No temptation has overtaken you that is not common to man. God is faithful, and he will not let you be tempted beyond your strength, but with the temptation will also provide the way of escape, that you may be able to endure it' (I Cor. 10, 13).

4. THE EVIL OF SUFFERING AND DEATH

Now we come to the suffering and death of human persons; not the suffering and death of animals, which comes under the evil in nature.[49]

a. *Its enigmatic character*

It is clear that the human soul is immortal; since it is spiritual, how could it be affected by decomposition and death? The real enigma, however, is whether man himself is mortal or immortal.

Had he from the very beginning been created to occupy a middle station between spiritual and corporeal creatures, between

---

[49]Kierkegaard says: Death is most terrible in the degree that the organism is more perfect. Thus, whereas the death and decay of a plant diffuses an odor almost more delicious than its spicy breath, the decay of an animal, on the other hand, infects the air. It is true in a deeper sense that the more highly we value man, the more terrible death appears. The beast cannot properly be said to die; but when the spirit is posited as spirit, death appears terrible. At the instant of death man finds himself at the extremest point of the synthesis; the spirit cannot, as it were, be present, and yet it must wait, for the body must die.' *The Concept of Dread* (English trans. Walter Lowrie, Princeton University Press, 1944), pp. 82-3.

the angel and the material universe,[50] the death that is every day seen to sunder his essential union of soul and body, a union nonetheless created to last for ever, might indeed provide a stumblingblock.

On another level, the primitive myths about the survival of the dead, burial rites in which we can see a revolt against death, the primitive notion of a recurring time-cycle and their refusal to accept history and its degradations, in short their whole attitude cannot be explained except by their possession of an instinctive intimation of immortality which is not disposed to see in death the end of man.

More profoundly still, reflexion shows that life here on earth rests upon a paradox. It can be maintained and can progress only if at every moment man risks his personal life, his most treasured possession here below. Nature could have no reason for imposing such a strange condition on us unless it was obscurely aware that our personal lives do not finish with death. 'We come up against a paradox here. On the one hand there is nothing on earth more precious than a single human person, yet on the other nothing on earth is more wasted than human life, or more exposed to all sorts of dangers—and this is a basically normal condition. What can the point of this paradox be? It is perfectly clear. What we learn from this is that man very well knows that death is not an end but a beginning. He very well knows, in his innermost being, that he can run all risks, expend his life and scatter his goods and gifts, because he is immortal. The chant of the Catholic liturgy over the bodies of the dead corresponds to this instinctive knowledge which is rooted in us: *vita mutatur, non tollitur.* Life is changed, not taken away.'[51]

It has already been observed[52] that the suffering and death of human persons are an enigma for the pure philosopher.[53] He may think he can account for them sufficiently by making appeal, as for the suffering and death of animals, to the laws of biology, and by explaining that what is an evil in relation to the individual is a good in relation to the order of the universe; but this is to forget

[50]Lateran Council, ch. 1, *De fide catholica; Denz.,* no. 428.
[51]Maritain, 'L'immortalité du soi', in *De Bergson à Thomas d'Aquin* (New York, 1944), p. 126.
[52]Cf. above, 'The Forms of Evil', ch. III; 'The Evil in Nature', ch. V.
[53]We are opposing *pure philosophy* to *Christian philosophy* which takes into account the data of revelation concerning man as he is.

from the outset that man, as a person, is not simply a part of the world of nature, a fragment of the cosmos, but an irreducible whole, a world apart, in a direct relation with others of his kind and with the divine Persons of whom they are the likenesses. The problem of the suffering and death of the human person, which the pure philosopher must leave hanging in the air, will only find a sufficient answer in revelation, which makes known to us that they had no place in the original plan of creation and have come into the world by the sin of the first man, who dragged all others with him into disaster.

The individual in the animal, vegetable and mineral kingdoms is called a *suppositum,* but the individual man is called a *person.* What is a person? It is an 'I', which can think and love.[54] The idea of 'person' is realized in the angel : every angel is a person. It is realized in each of the three divine Persons. It is therefore used analogically, being applied to spheres of existence which are essentially different; it is proportionately discernible on planes as far removed from one another as those of man, angel and God. But on the angelic plane it is natural for the person not to know death; and even more so on the divine. Why, then, on the human plane, does the person know death? Certainly it is not because it is a *person* but because it is a *human* person, a person closely allied to a body, compound of spirit and flesh and thus liable to decomposition, subject to death. As a person it desires immunity from death; it could hardly escape this desire to avoid death. But as a human person it cannot avoid death. It is pulled in opposite directions, carrying within it a *natural* necessity of dying and a *transnatural* desire not to die.

The only conclusion to be drawn is that the state of innocence cannot be demanded in justice but that it corresponds to the *transnatural* longings of the person, concerning the human person not in so far as it is *human,* but in so far as it is a *person* and shares, in its own imperfect degree, in the transcendental perfection of personality.[55] 'We see there the most profound reason of suit-

---

[54]It should be added: *and which possesses the totality of its nature.* The separated soul, being only a part of human nature, is not a person. It is not 'personality' or 'subsistence' which it lacks, but the totality of its specific nature. 'Person' does not designate personality but the subject in this condition of *wholeness.* Cf. St Thomas, I, qu. 75, a. 4, ad 2.

[55]Maritain, 'L'immortalité du soi', op. cit., p. 133.

ability for the elevation of the intelligent creature to the super-natural order; I say reason based on fitness! Not on necessity, nor on justice. God could, without the least injustice, have created man in a state of pure nature, man would have been de-frauded of nothing which his *nature* as such demands; but in actual fact God has created man in a state of grace; let us say that in actual fact he would not have created nature if he had not destined it for grace—but this word carries us very far. Very far from Leibniz. Any good belonging to the order of grace, St Thomas says, is greater than all the good nature is capable of.'[56]

b. *Young children*

Consider the mystery of the suffering and death of young children, baptized or unbaptized.[57]

What answer can pure philosophy give? It will say that they come under an aspect of the great wholeness of the universe to which life and sensibility bring incomparable riches, even though they have pain and death as an inseparable counterpart. It will say that as a whole it is better that pain and death should exist than to want to do away with them and thereby do away with life and sensibility. That is true, and St Thomas says as much;[58] but he does not leave it at that.

The mistake lies in making this answer out to be sufficient. 'This philosopher, then, will tell us it is a good thing for a mother to bewail the death of her child, because the machine of the world required it in order to be more perfect. *Rachel plorans filios suos, et noluit consolari . . .* (Rachel bewailing the death of her sons and refusing to be consoled). Explain this Leibnizian position to the mother in question, tell her this thing was necessary in order that every degree of being should be filled, and she will answer that she cares not one whit for the machine of the world—let them give her back her child! And she will be absolutely right; for such questions are not resolved by the machine of the world but in the darkness of faith, and by the cross of Jesus.'[59]

As for St Thomas, he does not forget, and frequently repeats,

[56]*St Thomas and the Problem of Evil,* op. cit., p. 13. Cf. above, pp. 54 and 56.
[57]Cf. Charles Journet, *Les sept paroles du Christ en croix* (Seuil, Paris, 1952), pp. 93-6.
[58]I, qu. 48, a. 2.
[59]Maritain, *St Thomas and the Problem of Evil,* op. cit., pp. 8-9.

that man is a person. 'The suffering of a man is the suffering of a person, of a whole. Here he is considered no longer as a part of the universe, but insofar as he is a person he is considered as a whole, a universe to himself; to suffer that pain as part of the universe in the perspective of nature or of the world taken as God's work of art, does not do away with the fact that as far as the person is concerned it is an utter anomaly.'[60]

Clearly philosophy cannot have any firm basis here without borrowing higher truths from theology. And what will theology say about the suffering and death of young children? It will certainly say that suffering and death are natural to them, composed as they are of spirit and flesh, but that God, in his infinite goodness, had provided for them a condition of pure happiness; and that it is as the consequence of an original offence that pain and death have come into our world.

It will say that Rachel's cry is so to speak, a demand for the earthly paradise, and that she did not wish to be consoled because she had an obscure inkling of our first condition.

It will say that one day young children, raised from the dead by the power of Christ, will not know suffering any more, neither in heaven if they are baptized, nor in Limbo if they died unbaptized.

And it will also tell Rachel that some sufferings must remain without consolation in this life, that Christ sheds light on them without consoling them, and that their consolation will come only in heaven.

It may also tell Rachel that to the young unbaptized children who were massacred out of hatred for Christ, Christ gave the baptism of blood and took them immediately into his glory.

c. *Some observations by Jacques Maritain on the paradox of suffering, the attitude to be taken towards it, and the dialectic of suffering in the Christian world*[61]

Three points will be examined, concerning the nature of suffering, the attitude it asks of us, and the way it is accepted in the Christian world.

1. *The paradox of suffering:* how, while being an evil, it can be something good. In itself suffering is not a good but an evil. Yet

---

[60]Ibid., p. 12.
[61]With his permission I transcribe here notes taken during a talk given by Jacques Maritain at Kolbsheim in the summer of 1950.

as to its *effects* it is ambivalent. By consideration of the concomitance of sin with beings inclined to evil, as we all of us are, one
might formulate the law that pain tends both to impair the free
agent's physical resources, in themselves good, and to hinder the
evil use he made of them and thus to make good and give some
redress for what was evil in him. It lessens the biological element
in man, but can strengthen and purify the moral element.

From this follows the enormous part played by pain in the
education of humanity, since by and large we are more wicked
than good. The paradox lies in the fact that a (physical) evil can
act as a remedy for a greater (moral) evil. Suffering then appears
as a good. The poets have understood this. In the words of
Baudelaire: 'May you be blessed, O God, who gives suffering as a
divine remedy for our impurities ...'[62] Or again: '. . . Blessed
be your scourge, O Lord, and may pain, O Father, be blessed!
In your hands my soul is not an expendable toy, and your prudence
is limitless.'[63]

The words of Bloy may be recalled: 'Man has places in his
poor heart which have yet to exist, and therein sorrow enters so
that they may come into being.' And the negress in *Requiem for
a Nun* says that God cannot prevent us from wanting evil, but that
to make up for it a little he invented suffering, which is the true
light of our poor world.

Sayings like these, it is true, have been touched by a ray of faith
in the mystery of the Redemption of the world on the Cross of
Christ. In this spirit Pascal wrote his *Prayer to God for the right
use of sickness.*

But suffering remains an evil. It is an evil, and intrinsically
detestable, *in the natural order:* here it is only necessary to think
of the fearful havoc wrought by sickness, old age and death; it
can hinder the use of reason, darken even prayer, and change
people's personalities. It remains an evil—a physical evil—*from
the viewpoint of faith,* since the order of grace does not destroy the
order of nature. From the same viewpoint, as has already been

---

[62] 'Soyez béni, mon Dieu, qui donnez la souffrance
Comme un divin remède à nos impuretés ...'

[63] '   ... Que béni soit ton fouet,
Seigneur, que la douleur, o Père, soit bénie!
Mon âme dans tes mains n'est pas un vain jouet
                    Et ta prudence est infinie.'

said, all human suffering, due as it is to guilt, original or personal, takes on a penal character and is a *malum poenae*. From this viewpoint pain, when it is accepted, will always appear as medicinal, a remedy to the evil of a will too often beguiled by the world and the emotions.

We must always adopt the central viewpoint of faith if we are to have an integrated view of human suffering and the way in which God permits it : just as there is no perfection except a supernatural one, so there is no *ultimate* reason for pain except a supernatural one.

2. *What attitude is to be taken towards suffering?* Naturally each one of us must bear it. But granting this, what attitude can we adopt towards the suffering of others, the suffering which afflicts the human race ?

In the natural order, we must fight it, we must strive to lessen its extent in the human race as far as possible, since it is an evil. No one could fail to approve man's enormous effort to defend himself against sickness, misery and physical suffering. There exists a false, pseudo-Christian moralizing which preaches resignation to suffering, just as, in Proudhon's time, it preached resignation to misery. Suffering is an enslavement of nature. One of man's tasks, on the cultural level, is progressively to win his autonomous freedom by detaching himself ever more perfectly from the grip of the material universe and all its servitude. The rational use of anaesthetics, the procedures of painless childbirth, are a step in the right direction; there is nothing un-Christian about them.[64]

---

[64] In a *Discourse* given on 24 February, 1957, on the religious and moral problems of analgesia, Pius XII speaks very concisely about three important topics:

(1) *On the general moral obligation of bearing physical pain:* The *fundamental principles* of anaesthesiology, both as a science and as an art, and the end it pursues, do not give rise to any objections. It combats forces which, in many respects, produce harmful effects and hinder greater good. The *physician* who makes use of these methods runs counter to neither the natural moral order nor the specifically Christian ideal. He seeks, in accordance with the order laid down by the Creator (Gen. 1, 28), to make pain subject to man's power, and to that end uses the discoveries of science and technology, in accordance with the principles stated by the Church, which will guide his decisions in particular cases. The *patient* who desires to avoid or quieten pain may, without any trouble to his conscience, make use of the means made available by science and which, in themselves, are not immoral. Particular circumstances may suggest another line of conduct, but the duty of inner self-denial and **purification**

In the supernatural order also suffering is an evil, but an evil which God uses for our good and which he alone can use safely and surely. So when it is our own lot it must be blessed, because in God's hands this evil can become a good. But it must never be desired for others, since it is an evil. In this way the paradox of Christian life can be explained : pain is something good, not of itself, but as an instrument of God, yet we must seek to ward it off from those we love. To listen to some pietistic clichés, it might be thought that we should desire contagion and hunger for those who are dearest to us. It is not for us to be able to transform sorrow into light, or a physical evil into a moral good : this is for God.

3. *The dialectic of suffering in the Christian world.* Three progressive stages can be discerned in the way of accepting suffering among Christians.

The first stage is the most common. Suffering is regarded from the viewpoint of pure nature, *as if* man were a purely natural being and, like the animals, suffered simply because he has been created and made a part of the mechanism of the world, and thus subject to physical evil. Or perhaps, if it is realized that suffering exists because the human race is being punished for original sin,

incumbent on Christians is no obstacle to the use of anaesthesia, because it can be fulfilled in another way. The same rule applies also to the superogatory demands made by the Christian ideal.

(2) *On narcosis and the deprivation, total or partial, of consciousness:* Within the limits indicated, and with observance of the required conditions, narcosis which brings with it a diminution or suppression of consciousness is permitted by natural morality and compatible with the spirit of the Gospel.

(3) *On the use of analgesics:* Is the suppression of pain and consciousness by means of narcotics (when medical indications require it) permitted by religion and morality to the physician and patient (even at the approach of death and when it is foreseen that the use of narcotics will shorten life)? The answer must be that if no other means exist and if, in the given circumstances, this does not prevent the carrying out of other religious and moral duties, it is permissible. As the Pope had already explained, the ideal of Christian heroism does not, at least in general, impose the refusal of a justified narcotic, even at the approach of death; everythings depends on individual circumstances. The more perfect and heroic decision may be found in acceptance just as well as in refusal.

In a previous *Discourse* given on 8 January, 1956, Pius XII had pronounced on the legitimacy of painless childbirth: 'Is this method morally irreproachable? The answer, which must take into account the object intended and the motive, can be briefly stated: taken in itself, it contains nothing reprehensible from the moral point of view.'

this state of suffering is regarded simply as a state of submission to the laws of the physical world. Suffering is a fact of nature, something inevitable and accepted with painful resignation. And finally there is the added recognition that this state must be supported patiently for love of God and for a supernatural motive. This is the stage of Christian suffering *in its infant state,* i.e. (to borrow St Paul's words concerning childhood Gal. 4, 3), we are here 'slaves to the elemental spirits of the universe'.

In the second stage it is realized that for man suffering is not like that. It is an irregularity of the personality and its aspirations. This is quite true. But it is taken to greater lengths. Men act as if the condition of innocence were something to which the human person has a *right*. Then it looks as if human suffering is penitential not merely *de facto,* but also *de jure*. To put it differently, to say that human suffering, partially explained by our nature, which is a composite of mind and body, is only sufficiently explained by an original offence, does not go far enough. It would have to be said that it is strictly inexplicable and absurd without some offence. And since no one is thinking of an original offence, but only of the guilt of some particular person, they go on to say that it is not merely a scandal but an absurdity that an innocent should suffer. Some such perception must have been in Dostoyevsky's mind when he wrote of the tears of a child. This second state represents a Christian position gone astray, and is found in Christians in revolt. It may be called the stage of *outraged Christian suffering*.

Finally there is a third stage. Here it is realized that innocent suffering is the consequence of original sin, and that it is not a penalty *de jure* inexplicable and absurd, but, in fact, one due to the loss of certain gratuitous privileges. At the same time it is not held to be simply a fact of nature, something inevitable and to be endured, but rather a co-redeeming force in so far as it is a participation in the suffering of Christ and in the pouring out of his blood. If the original fall was permitted only with a view to the Redemption of the world by Christ's sufferings, innocent suffering is likewise permitted in conformity with Christ's sufferings. Then the whole picture is transfigured. It is no longer a question of the *problem of suffering,* but of the *mystery of suffering* and our participation in it. It is no longer necessary to talk of resignation to suffering but of assuming the circumstances and the work of the

Saviour. Suffering is no longer accepted because of any submission to the laws of the physical world; it is taken on because it unites us to the person of God made man. Suffering was cherished by Léon Bloy, precisely because it is a union with the suffering Christ : 'I have often meditated long on suffering. I have arrived at the conviction that it is the only supernatural thing here on earth. The rest is human. In every Christian there is a man of sorrow, and God was that.'[65] 'The cross of the needy and vagrant, the sweet cross of the ancient country roads, the welcoming cross of the wretched and the lame, with bleeding feet and sorrowing hearts, of those who have been bitten by serpents in the wilderness and who are cured of their wounds by looking upon this cross of distress and triumph!'[66] Suffering like this is *the suffering of the fully-grown,* the royal way of the saints.

Christ did not choose suffering because it was good. Suffering was an evil for him in so far as he was a person. But he willed to undergo it so as to save the world. And in this way, as Christ's chosen instrument in his redemptive work, suffering has become good. And therefore, in so far as they believe their suffering to be a sharing in Christ's sufferings, the saints love and cherish it as a treasure *because of him,* as the suffering of Christ shared by them —not in any way just as suffering, for as such it is always hateful. Christ found it hateful, and this explains his prayer during the agony : 'Abba, Father, all things are possible to thee; remove this cup from me; yet not what I will, but what thou wilt' (Mark 14, 36).

d. *The dialectic of suffering in God's plan*

Why do human persons have to undergo suffering and death? St Paul says that because of one man's trespass death reigned (Rom. 5, 17), and that death is the wages of sin (6, 23).

And why did the Son of man have to undergo suffering and death? The answer is given in the Gospels : 'The Son of man came to seek and save the lost' (Luke 19, 10). What reason can be found for this folly? 'God so loved the world that he gave his only Son, that whoever believes in him should not perish but have eternal life' (John 3, 16). Could proof of love be carried any further? It

[65]*Chosen Passages* by Albert Béguin (Luf, Paris, 1943), p. 36.
[66]Ibid., p. 283.

could : 'Greater love has no man than this, that a man lay down his life for his friends' (15, 13). Suffering and death were in the world. The Son of God came down into the world to share in this suffering and death 'to be made like his brethren in every respect' (Hebr. 2, 17) and to be 'in every respect tempted as we are, yet without sinning' (4, 15), and also to become wedded to humanity at the deepest point of its distress and to transform for it the meaning of suffering and death.

Thus the wonderful dialectic of Christian suffering unfolds. Suffering and death are evils which God detests and which he did not will for the first man. But man brought them into the world by his rebellion and was overwhelmed and crushed by them. At that moment, suffering and death changed their aspect in God's eyes. They had been hateful to him, but they were now to become desirable and enviable since they were human. He came down from heaven to take them upon himself; he did not do away with them, he did something more : he gave them a meaning and lit them up from within, transfiguring them and making them God-like. And then they could be desirable for man himself. They became what Christ prophetically called crosses, recollections of his own cross; and blessed are those who will to carry them with him, for they will be carried there where they do not wish to go, but where, all the same, it is better for them to be.

The dialectic of Christian suffering is complete : God, who did not desire either suffering or death for us, envied them when they had become ours; he transfigured them by making them his own through his Son, so that we also in our turn could long for them.

e. *Illumined suffering*

Suffering was an evil for Christ as for us. But charity, which illumined it with God's light in the crucified Christ, can be diffused from him and illumine it even for us. To St Catherine of Siena it was said : 'Your sacrifice must be of both body and spirit together, like the cup and the water offered to the master : the water could not be given him without the cup, and the cup without water would cause him no joy. And so, I tell you, you must offer me the cup of many bodily trials, and in the way in which I send them to you : without choosing the time, the place or the trial according to your own desire but conforming yourself to mine. But this cup must be full of love and true patience, so that you may bear with and support the defects of your neighbour, having hatred and sorrow for your own sin. Then . . . I shall receive this present from my sweet spouses, from all the souls who serve me.'[67] St Paul called upon the Colossians 'to share in the inheritance of the saints in light' (I, 12).

With the thought of illumined suffering in mind, Léon Bloy could write : 'All suffering has two pains : the pain of damnation and the pain of sense. Only the Redemption of Christ delivers us from the first, the one which drowns all hope.'[68]

5. CONCLUSION

Only a few aspects of the evil of punishment have been touched on, but they are enough to depict the life of men on earth as a long trial. How could it be otherwise ? This is the *status viatoris*, not the

---

[67]*Libro della divina dottrina*, ch. 12 (Bari, 1912), p. 29.

[68]Nothing appears in the Koran about the meaning of suffering: 'The Jews and Christians have said: "We are the sons of God and his dearly beloved." Ask them: "Then why does he torture you for your sins? No! you are mortals, and creatures just like all others." He forgives whom he will, and he tortures whom he will. To God belongs the kingship of heaven and earth and all that is between them' (V, 21/18).

Quoting this text in his book *Bible et Coran* (Cerf, Paris, 1959), p. 97, Jacques Jomier writes: 'Suffering is presented in this verse of the Koran as a sign of divine rejection. Now the whole of the Bible is full of the idea that suffering may be a temporal chastisement sent by God in his love in order to set his people back on the right path. The New Testament, for its part, speaks often of the sufferings of Christ and Christians and shows the place of these sufferings in the divine plan of salvation. Islam, being greatly attached to an apologetic of force and victory, does not seem to share this way of seeing it; perhaps because seeing it in this way is only comprehensible from the point of view of love, and to suffer for the sake of love is not degrading, but rather the opposite. Sin alone is degrading. The Islamic ideal of greatness insists on the grandeur of force and power. For this reason Islam rejects the idea of the crucifixion of Christ (while admitting that many prophets have been put to death by the Jews).'

The Sufis owed their rediscovery of the price of love and redemptive suffering to the influence of a hidden grace coming to them mysteriously from the Cross of the Saviour. 'If an atom of what I have in my heart were thrown upon mountains, they would melt.' 'So when will the day of our new year come? Put in the pillory I shall be near to God.' 'They lead the victims (= the lambs) to the sacrifice, but I bring the sacrifice of my veins and my blood.' 'I shall die confessing the Cross ... So kill this cursed one (= his own person).' *Hosein Mansûr Hallâj, Dîwân* (translated from the French version by Louis Massignon (Cahiers du Sud), pp. xvi-xxi).

status termini, our exile, not our fatherland, the time for questions, not for answers. The sufferings of the exodus into the desert had no meaning without its hope of the promised land; those of the present life are only explained by expectation of the second coming.

It belongs to time to build in order to destroy and then to build again. It allows bonds of closest affection to be forged because it is sure of its power to pull them apart. Each individual note must be done away with to merge into 'cet ardent sanglot qui roule d'âge en âge'. 'For everything there is a season, and a time for every matter under heaven : a time to be born, and a time to die; a time to plant, and a time to pluck up what is planted; a time to kill, and a time to heal; a time to break down, and time to build up; a time to weep, and a time to laugh' (Eccles. 3, 1-4).[69] Nothing is spared, things just or unjust, pure or impure, the reflected beauty of heaven or the ugly and deformed. The Son of Man was bruised and covered in blood. In Michelangelo's great *Deposition from the Cross,* constructed spirally, which is to be seen in Santa Maria del Fior, it is first of all the majestic peace of death spread over the Saviour's abandoned body which moves us; but if we come closer and look straight upwards at the group, the shock of the clashing, broken lines suddenly makes us grasp that violence has here struck heedlessly and has blunted itself so that it could lay low the most beautiful of the children of men.

Yet something is made out of these ruins : two cities arise, God's and the Devil's, through the assent or refusal of creatures who appear and then disappear in order to be replaced by others.

The momentary passage of humanity on a short-lived planet

[69]'You may ask how we are to interpret a book as paradoxical as Ecclesiastes. What does it preach? "Vanity of vanities, says the Preacher, vanity of vanities! All is vanity ..." It is the most outstanding existentialist book ever written. It does not deny any of the moral values, but these are not its object ... With Aristotle, we are dealing with a *possible man*: contemplation, health, ease and friends constitute the happiness suited to human nature. But no one reaches this happiness. With Ecclesiastes, we are dealing with *man as he exists* ... What does this book mean? If we had a purely earthly existence, Ecclesiastes would be right. This purely earthly, and apparently naturalistic, view stems in reality from a sort of dark night, a burning intuition of the gift of knowledge, and faith in God not only remains vivid but is at the centre of this desolate thought. That is why its final conclusion is: "Fear God and keep his commandments; for this is the whole duty of man".' Jacques Maritain, *Neuf leçons ... ,* pp. 86-8.

could be nothing other than a futile, absurd and cruel adventure if we did not know that, visited once by the Word made flesh and Risen from the dead, this same humanity is drawn along behind him, with the whole visible creation as his train. The discord which has come between man and the material universe since the fall will not be resolved until the end of this painful travail: 'I consider that the sufferings of this present time are not worth comparing with the glory that is to be revealed to us. For the creation waits with eager longing for the revealing of the sons of God; for the creation was subjected to futility, not of its own will but by the will of him who subjected it in hope; because the creation itself will be set free from its bondage to decay and obtain the glorious liberty of the children of God. We know that the whole creation has been groaning in travail together until now' (Rom. 8, 18-22).

CHAPTER NINE

Evil in History

Evil made its appearance in the angels and then in man, where it called forth the Redemption. History develops in both good and evil, and is like a cipher.

I. CREATION HAS TO WORK TOWARDS ITS OWN FULFILMENT

God, as has already been said,[1] could have placed his free creatures, men and angels, immediately in their final condition in heaven, in the beatifying vision of his glory and so have created a world without evil. He did in fact place angels and men in the state of pilgrimage, with a fundamental respect for their natural status as free creatures, wishing to take account, in order to beatify them, of the law written in their own hearts by which they would wish to work together with God in the task of fulfilling the universe and themselves with it.

Only this testing-time in the state of pilgrimage could allow free creatures to bring their love to fruition in their free choice of their final end, in their free choice of God above all things, this love which is to be the most perfect flower in his paradise, to purchase which he is willing to run the risk of refusal by those of his creatures who wish to reject him.

2. THE DIVISION OF THE ANGELS, OR THE FIRST RENDING OF THE WORLD

It was in heaven that the first rending of the world was made, by the division of the angels.[2]

---

[1]Cf. above, p. 152.
[2]See my article 'L'aventure des anges', in *Nova et Vetera*, 1958, p. 127, et seq. And particularly the illuminating study by Maritain, *The Sin of the Angel* (Newman Press, Westminster, 1959).

a. *The first moment of the angels*

When God created the angels he poured into them supernatural grace and the theological virtues of faith, hope and charity. At the same time he gave them the initial impulse to act. By this first impetus, for which God alone was responsible, the angel's love goes out towards God, the author both of nature and of grace. But it is a spontaneous love, in which God is approached as first Cause of nature and of grace; it is not yet elective love, which is to be immediate and inspired by charity, freely-chosen love in which God will be approached directly in the transcendence of his own mystery.

b. *The severance of the angels*

After this came the angels' act of free choice, and the moment of their eternal severance.

The angels then did one of two things. Either amenable to the predisposing inspiration of grace, they acted so as to ratify it by the spontaneous, delegated, supernatural love which prompted them to love God more than themselves, God recognized as the supreme Source of all created good; and, confirming this love, suddenly extended and surpassed it by an act of free self-surrender to God thus preferred to themselves, that is to say by an act of pure charity flowing from the virtue of charity which was placed in them with grace at the first moment of creation. This meant that by abandoning themselves to the appeals of grace, the angels agreed to tear themselves away from their natural limits to lose themselves in the sacred darkness of God, being assured by their faith that the God of grace is also the God of nature, that by losing their being for his sake they thus saved it, and that his fire can burn the creature without consuming it. The angels who made this choice were saved and entered immediately and permanently into infinite beatitude : 'After a single act informed by charity, the angels entered into beatitude.'[3]

Or else, the angels turned their attention away from God's invitation and concentrated it upon their own nature, which in itself is good. They allowed themselves to be dazzled by their own beauty. They chose to love themselves not ordinately, in second place to God supremely preferred to themselves by an act of

[3]St Thomas, I, qu. 62, a. 5.

charity, but inordinately, refusing any free recognition of their dependence and setting up in themselves their final good and their ultimate refuge. By this rebellion they destroyed at once the virtues of faith, hope and charity, which were placed in them when they were first created. They even annihilated the spontaneous, delegated love, lifted high by grace, which, at the first moment, made them love God as the known Source of all created good. All that was left in them was the purely natural spontaneous love by which any creature, drawn irresistibly as it is towards its own happiness, naturally tends, whether it likes it or not, towards God himself. 'The contradiction and the conflict between this love-of-nature for God and the freely elicited hatred of God, the implacable natural necessity in the very dynamism of his being always to love—in each of the particular acts as well as in the radical tendency of his will—that same God whom he envies and detests in his heart, is one of the torments of the demon.'[4]

c. *In what way did the devil wish to be 'like God'?*

What is meant by the evil spirits desiring to be 'like God'?[5] His disordered love may be characterized either with regard to the *object* of this love, the immediate splendour of the angelic nature as preferred to the future beatitude proposed by God; or with regard to the *mode* of this love, that is, its independence. 'These two views,' says St Thomas, 'come to the same thing : in both cases the angel desired to have his ultimate beatitude by his own virtue, which belongs to God alone.'[6]

In the former instance it can be said that the angel's sin was 'to desire as the ultimate beatitude that to which he could attain by the resources of his *nature*, turning aside his desire of the supernatural beatitude which comes of the grace of God.'[7] It is for God to determine the final end of his creatures; by wanting to decide his final end for himself, the angel usurps a divine prerogative and wishes to be his own law; but to be a law to oneself belongs only to God.

In the second instance, it can be said, still with St Thomas, that the angel would not have refused the actual state of supernatural

[4]Maritain, *The Sin of the Angel*, op. cit., p. 93.
[5]St Paul says of Antichrist, the man of sin, that he will be 'proclaiming himself to be God', II Thess. 2, 4.
[6]I, qu. 63, a. 3.   [7]Ibid.

beatitude, but refused to receive it *ex misericordia*. He was interested only in a beatitude attained entirely by his own efforts; but the sole possibility he has to act as a first cause is to nullify in himself the divine influence of grace, and to do this is to sin.

d. *Of what good is the disaster of the angels the reverse side?*

The economy of God by which, in his subordinated power, he has arranged the present universe, and by which grace is normally given having regard to the treatment required by the nature of free and peccable beings, is just and good.

Other economies and other universes were possible. Of these universes, some would have been better than ours, and others not so good. But none of them would have represented the exact good ours does. Evil has its part in our universe, but it appears there as the reverse side of something good. This is the main answer given by St Augustine and taken up again by St Thomas.[8]

But of what good is the disaster of the angels the reverse side? The question has its sharpest point here : for since the angels have full self-knowledge and full self-possession, their first decision about their ultimate end committed them irrevocably, and if this decision was perverse, no redemption could be possible for them, nor could they ever desire it. What answer can there be to this?

Only one : the evil of the disaster and eternal damnation of the angels is the reverse side of that good which is represented by the economy of a universe arranged according to the subordinated power of God. That is to say, of a universe in which God normally gives his grace to free beings having regard to the treatment required by their fallible and peccable nature; of a universe, therefore, in which God desires to be loved with a freely-chosen love, and desires this so intensely that he allows himself to be freely rejected by some—for what can fail, sometimes does fail[9]—in order to be freely preferred by others. It is the reverse side—by no means inevitable, but arising entirely from the foolish and wilful free rebellion of certain angels—of an immense good intended and chosen only by God's transcendence.

e. *The perverse activity of the devil*

He is in a state of perpetual rebellion both against the trans-

---

[8]I, qu. 2, a. 3, ad 1.   [9]I, qu. 48, a. 2, ad 3.

cendent God and against the immanent created order of the universe. How could he fail to look for a way of sharing his resentment and his vindictive designs with those free beings which he hopes to win over?

He was to be seen in the earthly paradise proposing to our first parents the intoxicating idea of becoming autonomous, suggesting that they should be 'like gods' (Gen. 3, 5), deciding for themselves what is good and what evil. He came up to our Lord in the desert, still not understanding in what sense he was the Son of God, to try and make him swerve from the mission of which he guessed him to be the bearer (Matt. 4, 11). At the end of time he will raise up false Christs and false prophets 'so as to seduce, if it were possible, even the elect' (Matt. 24, 24).

But why does God leave him such freedom of action if not because he is good and powerful enough to make it an opportunity of some very great good? St Gregory the Great makes a very penetrating observation on this. On the words of Satan to God: 'Stretch forth your hand and touch his goods: I swear to you that he will curse in your face!' (Job 1, 11), he writes: 'It must be understood that the *will* of Satan is always wicked, but that his *power* is never unjust; he exercizes his will on his own account, but it is from the Lord that he takes his power. God permits in all justice the iniquities he seeks to commit. Thus it is with good reason written in the Book of Kings (I Kings 18, 10): *An evil spirit of the Lord assailed Saul.* Here it is, then, that one and the same spirit is described both as the spirit of the Lord and as the evil spirit; he is the spirit of the Lord, because he has licence to exercize a power which he justly retains; he is an evil spirit by the desire of his unjust will. Let us, therefore, have no fear of one who can do nothing without receiving permission.'[10] No one, after God, worked harder for Job's sanctity than the Devil, and no one could have wanted it less.

3. WHY WAS THE FALL OF THE FIRST MAN PERMITTED?

The only reason we can give for the fall of the angels is that God, 'to whom it belongs to conduct each being according to its

[10]*Magna Moralia*, lib. II, in cap. I Job (P.L., vol. LXXXV, col. 564).

nature'[11] wished to leave his spiritual creatures free to choose for or against him, and thereby run the risk of being rejected by them, rather than forgo the possibility of this freely-chosen love by which he sets the greatest store. The same reason applies to man and provides us with the first and immediate account of why the disaster came about in the earthly paradise.

But for this disaster there is yet another reason. Unlike the angels, who are simple and intuitive, made to involve themselves irreversibly by their first free act, man, complex and discursive, is able during his temporal existence to go back on his choice; hence the saying: 'Man's free will can be inclined in opposite directions before and after the choice; the angel's free will can be inclined in an opposite direction before the choice, but not after.'[12] Everything is over for the angel once he has sinned. But this is not so for man—he can still be forgiven. God, who leads his creatures, in his subordinated power, according to the treatment required by their nature, can turn even his sin into an opportunity to show him some great mercy. And so, to those who ask why God, who knew Adam's fall from all eternity, did not prevent it by a miracle, it must be answered with a second reason which did not exist in the case of the angels, that he would never have allowed the fall of the world of innocence, disastrous not only for Adam but for all his descendants, if he had not meant by it to bring us into what was, taken as a whole, the better world of the Redemption.

Strictly speaking, Christ did not come merely to re-establish man in the state from which he had fallen but to direct him towards a higher destiny. The early doctors were right to count the rehabilitation of humanity to its first condition among the benefits of the redemption: they were thinking of the sanctifying grace given by God, lost in Adam, and recovered in Christ. But they knew at the same time that the grace of Christ does not bring us back to the point we started from, but that it involves us in an unprecedented venture: 'The first age of human life,' writes St Cyril of Alexandria, 'was holy in the father of our race, Adam, who had not yet broken the commandments or transgressed the divine precepts; but holier still is the latter age, that of the second Adam, Christ, who regenerated our fallen race for a newness of

[11] St Thomas, *II Sent.*, dist. 23, qu. 1, a. 2.
[12] St Thomas, I, qu. 64, a. 2.

life in the Spirit.'[13] The same idea is to be found in St Leo the Great : 'The ineffable grace of Christ has given us better things than those which the envy of the evil spirit had taken away from us.'[14]

The Carmelites of Salamanca teach that God could only permit the fall in order to raise humanity to a higher state. Miracle for miracle, 'it would be a disorder and a sort of cruelty to permit evil with the sole intention of putting it right afterwards and return us to our original condition. But this is no longer the case when the permission of an evil is directed towards some very great good which by far and away surpasses this evil and blots it out . . . The case is this : If God permitted this disaster to man, it was not to limit himself to bringing a remedy for it, but because he foresaw the glory of Christ the redeemer, whose worth greatly surpasses the wickedness of the permitted fall . . . , and finally it is for a greater good of humanity itself, which by the blood of Christ receives a more abundant grace and a supreme nobility.'[15]

This view was exceptionally dear to St Francis de Sales. He tells us that God's good nature was not outdone by Adam's sin; that on the contrary where sin had abounded it made grace superabound; that our loss was a gain for us, since human nature has in effect received more graces by the redemption of its Saviour than it would ever have received by the innocence of Adam, should it have persevered in this; that as the rainbow, touching the aspalatus thorn, makes it more sweetly-smelling than the lily, so the redemption of our Lord, touching our wretchedness, makes it more useful and lovable than original innocence would ever have been; that the redeemed state is worth a hundred times more than that of innocence; that by our sprinkling with the blood of our Lord, using the hyssop of the Cross, we have been restored to a whiteness incomparably more excellent than that of the snow of innocence, so that the divine Majesty was not vanquished by evil but vanquished evil by good, as he has commanded us also to do; that his mercy, like a sacred oil, is held higher than his judgment; and that his compassion surpasses all his works.[16]

[13]*De adoratione in spiritu et veritate*, bk. XII (P.G., vol. LXVIII, col. 1076).
[14]*Sermo LXXIII*, no. 4 (P.L., vol. LIV, col. 396).
[15]*De incarnatione*, disp. 2, dub. 1, no. 36.
[16]*Traité de l'amour de Dieu*, bk. II, ch. 5.

This is the explication and development of a traditional view :
'Nothing,' writes St Thomas, 'prevents human nature being raised
to a higher state after sin.[17] God permits, indeed, that evils come
about so as to draw a greater good from them. Whence the words
of St Paul to the Romans, 5, 20 : "Where sin increased grace
abounded all the more." And the cry of the *Exsultet: O felix
culpa, O happy fault, that deserved so great a Redeemer!*'

And so there are two reasons which explain why the first sin was
permitted : one common to angels and men, the other proper to
man and reckoning with a free being living in time and the flesh.
To anyone asking why the divine power did not prevent the sin
of the first man by some miracle, it can be answered that he was
making ready to compensate for it abundantly by an even more
incredible miracle.

4. THE WORLD OF THE REDEMPTION

However holy the grace of Christ may be, it can be frustrated
by sin; and so arises the formation of two opposed cities, the one
of light, the other of darkness.

a. *It is in sum better than the world of creation*

The world of creation in the state of innocence was good. The
world of fallen and redeemed nature is good as well; following the
way pointed by the *Exsultet* we have gone one step further towards
affirming that it is in sum better than the original world of
creation.

But is this possible? The world which we have before our eyes,
laid low in the first place by sin, incessantly visited by pain, misery,
epidemics and disasters, full of scandals, betrayals and crimes, in-
habited by falsehood, imposture, violence, injustice, hatred and
cruelty, after hundreds of thousands of years, with fearful means
of destruction at its disposal, the world which has just invented
inter-continental wars, the extermination of six or seven million
Jews, the hunger- and death-camps, the gas chambers, the crema-
toria, and the enormous propaganda against God, is it possible that this world should be as a whole better than the world of
innocence would have been? We all know that a world touched

[17]III, qu. I, a. 3, ad 3.

by evil may in sum be better than a lesser world which was exempt
from evil. But does there exist some good, absent from the earthly
paradise, that our world can contain which could more than compensate for the limitless weight of our miseries?

Indeed, there is such a good. For we believe that the second
Adam, come to take the place of the first, is not purely man but
the eternal Son of God, and that his worth is infinite: this is our
supreme answer. We believe also that the holiness of the Blessed
Virgin, true Mother of God, in itself surpasses any holiness of the
original paradise; and that the grace of Christ, succeeding to that
of Adam, without doing away with suffering can throw a new
and wonderful light on it, and out of sin and the injustice inflicted
on the martyrs, can make acts of repentance which were unknown
in the earlier age and which, like those of the sinful woman at the
feet of our Lord or the thief on the cross, will be among the
splendours of eternity. We believe that incomprehensible mercies
flow down from the Cross of the Saviour of the world, and that
if he so greatly desires to join with himself in his sufferings the
disciples who are to be, with him, in him and through him, fellow
saviours, it is in order that the number of those to be saved in this
way by them may be inestimably great.

b. *The formation of the two mystical cities*

The hypothesis of a *massa perditionis,* a human race abandoned
to its eternal damnation because of one original sin, should be
looked on as purely theoretical and, in fact, unrealizable. The fall
would not have been allowed, even tolerated, had the Redemption not been foreseen in the undivided eternal moment of
God.[18] Immediately after the fall, the only thought God could
have was to go, in his unfathomable goodness, to the help of the
human race and make it ready to receive one day the visit of his
one and only Son who, born of the human race, would come to
compensate over and over again, by the bloody sacrifice of Calvary,
for the outrage of the first sin, draw all men to him (John 12, 32),
reconcile and 'pacify in the blood of his Cross all things both on
earth and in heaven' (Col. 1, 20) and restart and unite a new

[18]'In an identical decree,' say the Carmelites of Salamanca. *De incarnatione,* disp. 2, dub. 1, no. 36 (ed. Palmé), vol. XIII, p. 298. See Journet,
L'Eglise du Verbe Incarné (Desclée de Brouwer, Paris, 1951), vol. II,
p. 101.

universe (Eph. 1, 10). And so, at once and without any delay the first man, stripped irretrievably of original grace, in virtue of the redemption to come received the assistance of an even more mysterious grace, which by anticipation was already that of Christ.

Depending on whether it is accepted or refused, this grace of Christ which comes and knocks on the door of every heart will divide man into two opposite cities, both spiritual, mystical and transcendent—that is to say, their natures are determined by their immediate inclination, not towards the lesser ends of life on earth, but towards the supreme ends of eternal life. In the City of God, these supreme ends are desired; in the City of the Devil they are spurned. Both these cities cover the whole duration of time, and were there even before history started.

5. THE TWOFOLD MOVEMENT OF HISTORY

The two mystical cities hasten, in perpetual conflict, towards their end, leaving on history the marks of a twofold contrary movement, one upwards, the other downwards.

a. *The revelation of St Paul*

The first age of the world was that of the Gentiles, and it is called by theologians the age of the natural law. Thousands of millions of men lived under this dispensation. Absolutely speaking it has been done away with since the death of Christ, yet it survives, in certain aspects, in areas where the Gospel has not penetrated.

It is represented to us as a fresh start from the lowest point of the disaster. Yet it is not a return to what was lost but a journey through pain and darkness towards a mysterious redemption.

Running right through it is an upward movement towards the light, during which the first stage of the city of God was erected. For God did not abandon the Gentiles. 'He made from one every nation of men to live on all the face of the earth ... that they should seek God, in the hope that they might feel after him and find him. Yet he is not far from each one of us, for in him we live and move and have our being' (Acts 17, 26-8). If he desires 'all men to be saved and to come to the knowledge of the truth', he could hardly fail to make salvation possible for them (I Tim. 2, 4).

But a contrary movement of rebellion and descent into the

darkness also runs through the age of the Gentiles. In opposition to the world of light which is obedient to the natural law and forms the first stage of the City of God, there rises a world of darkness in revolt against the appeals of the natural law, which can be called paganism, and which forms the first stage of the city of evil. There is a conflict between these two spiritual worlds, these trans-cendent cities, in which are involved on the one side the watchful providence of God's grace, and on the other 'the Principalities, Powers and Rulers of the world of darkness, the spirits of evil which dwell in the heavenly places' (Eph. 6, 12).

The result of this conflict is invisible and unknown to us, con-cerning the souls which are saved or lost in the struggle—and doubtless many of those which might have been thought lost may have been saved at the last moment by some miracle of divine mercy.

There is also another result, a visible one, in which it is evil that gains the upper hand; for, by and large, the age of the Gentiles, with its often splendid spiritual, social and cultural structures, ends in disaster in relation to the things of God : 'Although they knew God they did not honour him as God or give thanks to him, but they became futile in their thinking and their senseless minds were darkened . . . they exchanged the truth about God for a lie and worshipped and served the creature rather than the Creator, who is blessed for ever! Amen' (Rom. 1, 21, 25).

But in spite of the outward failure of the dispensation of the natural law God did not turn away from humanity. He never takes away the light of grace which he destines for them, but if he sees it refused he transfers it elsewhere to other souls or other nations : 'Do the works you did at first,' said our Lord to the Angel of the church in Ephesus, 'if not, I will come to you and remove your candlestick from its place' (Apoc. 2, 5). Openly ignored by the Gentiles as a whole he decided to raise up a small nation, to be given birth through Abraham, which was to be his own. They were to be brought to greatness and possess 'the sonship, the glory, the covenants, the giving of the law, the worship, and the promises; to them belong the patriarchs, and of their race, according to the flesh, is the Christ. God who is over all be blessed for ever. Amen' (Rom. 9, 4-5). That was the dispensation of the Mosaic law, run-ning parallel to that of the natural law which continued to be valid for the Gentiles. It was a dispensation with blessings and privileges. But even within the time of Israel the two cities were to be opposed to each other again. For those of the Jews whose hearts, following the example of Abraham (4, 3), were open by faith to the hidden anticipations of Christ's grace, the law could be holy and just and good (7, 12): in the posterity of Abraham they were the children of the promise (9, 8). But for those who closed their hearts to God's predisposing grace and trusted in their own righteousness, the law became an accuser and the cause of death (7, 13): in the posterity of Abraham they were only children of the flesh (9, 8). As a whole, which of these two groups will have the upper hand in the eyes of the world? Only 'a remnant' of Israel was faithful (11, 5), but the mass let itself be led astray until the time when, in its turn, it was to receive mercy (11, 31).

The failure of the dispensation of the Mosaic law is linked with the failure of the dispensation of the natural law. In both the same fruit was borne by the downward movement of humanity into the darkness: 'Jews and Greeks are under the power of sin, as it is written (Ps. 14, 1-3): none is righteous no, not one; no one understands, no one seeks for God' (3, 10-11).

But the straying of the Gentiles was once the occasion for the choosing of the Jews; and later the defection of the Jews was to be the occasion for the choosing of the Gentiles. Since his mercy was not accepted, God, who had transferred it from the Gentiles to the Jews, made it return from the Jews to the Gentiles, so that even in the course of history men could clearly see the supreme law of the salvation of humanity, by which he tolerates rebellion only in order that his forgiveness may be made more evident: 'Just as you (the Gentiles) were once disobedient to God but now have received mercy because of their (the Jews') disobedience, so they have now been disobedient in order that by the mercy shown to you they also may receive mercy. For God has confined all men to disobedience, that he may have mercy upon all' (11, 30-2).

In the face of these shiftings of the light, these intersections of sin and grace and these reciprocal victories of human wickedness and divine goodness, of the city of evil and the city of God, what can we do but keep a reverent silence? 'O the depth of the riches and wisdom and knowledge of God! How unsearchable are his judgments and how inscrutable his ways! "For who has known the mind of the Lord, or who has been his counsellor?" "Or who has given a gift to him that he might be repaid?" For from him and through him and in him are all things. To him be glory forever. Amen.' (11, 33-6).

In a slightly earlier passage St Paul had compared the two follies : that of men who could not recognize their God either in creation in the age of the natural law, or in the prophets in that of the Mosaic law; and that of God who persistently wishes to save them by showing them his love. 'For since, in the wisdom of God, the world did not know God through wisdom, it pleased God through the folly of what we preach to save those who believe' (I Cor. 1, 21). St Thomas comments on this with his usual penetration : God had made the world in his wisdom, so that all creatures were as words describing the first revelation of God's wisdom; but in the vanity of his heart man became deaf to these voices and swerved from the truth. And so God sought to draw believers to himself by introducing more urgent revelations into the world; but since these were not made of the stuff of the world they in their turn would be disregarded and thought foolish by those who only want to know the things of this world : to all this, *faith bears witness*. Therefore, continues St Thomas, a master who is not understood tries to find other words to express what is in his heart.[19]

Christ came to gather the Jews and the Gentiles in his name and provide that henceforward there should no longer be Jews and Greeks in matters of faith (I Cor. 12, 13; Gal. 3, 28). To the Ephesians, lately Gentiles, Paul wrote : 'But now in Christ Jesus you who once were far off have been brought near in the blood of Christ. For he is our peace, who has made us both one, and has broken down the dividing wall of hostility . . . that he might create in himself one new man in place of the two, so making peace, and might reconcile us both to God in one body through the cross, thereby bringing the hostility to an end. And he came and preached peace to you who were far off and peace to those who were near; for through him we both have access in one Spirit to the Father' (Eph. 2, 13-8).

But the tragedy of the twofold development in opposite

---

[19]*I ad Corinth.*, lect 3, (ed. Marietti), no. 55. Cf. M. E. Boismard, O.P., *The Prologue of St John* (Blackfriars Publications, London, 1957), p. 86: 'Men would not recognize God from creation, they knew not how to read the Word of God written in the book of Creation, as St John also says in verse 10 of the Prologue: "He was in the world, and the world was made by him, and the world knew him not." '

directions of darkness and light was not at an end—it was unfortunately to take other, more terrible, forms.

When we consider, as the Epistle to the Romans invites us to do, the downward movement towards evil, we shall conclude that Christ appeared at the darkest moment of history, after the collapse of dispensations of salvation founded successively on the aid of the natural law and then of the Mosaic law. Certainly humanity was to experience and will experience situations which under certain aspects are much more fearful; but since being touched by the mystery of the Incarnation, and to the extent of its awareness of this, it cannot forget that it is saved in hope and that it bears in itself the fullness of Christ's grace with all its power to transfigure. And so in the perspective of the progress made by evil and of the Epistle to the Romans, it will be said that 'the fullness of time'—the phrase used in Galatians 4, 4—chosen by God for sending his Son, is the fullness of the distress of our world.

But we might also consider the simultaneous upward movement towards deliverance. In Pisidian Antioch Paul explained that God had chosen the Israelites and protected them in their wanderings, in order to give birth among them to the Saviour, proclaimed for the last time by John the Precursor (Acts 13, 17-41). The Epistle to the Hebrews shows, in the worship of the old Law, the outline and main figure of the worship of the new Law; it starts with the reminder that God, in many and various ways, spoke by the prophets before speaking to us in these last days by his Son (Hebr. 1, 1-2). Paul's disciple, Luke, tells how the Saviour himself opened the meaning of scripture on the road to Emmaus 'beginning with Moses and all the prophets' (Luke 24, 27). Following on this, we should read the passage in which St Paul teaches that being children we had first to come under the rule of guardians and trustees, but that, 'when the time had fully come, God sent forth his Son, born of woman, born under the law, to redeem those who were under the law, so that we might receive adoption as sons' (Gal. 4, 4-5). And so the 'fullness of time' becomes that of the prophetic grace announcing the Messiah.[20]

[20]On God's design to recapitulate all things in Christ when the 'fullness of time' (Eph. 1, 10) had come, P. Benoît writes: 'The fullness of time represents the coming of the messianic or eschatological era, which brings to an end the long expectation over the centuries, coming to fill to overflowing a measure already full.' *Épître aux Éphésiens* (Cerf, Paris, 1949), p. 83.

b. *The thought of the early doctors*

It has been pointed out[21] that the two possible interpretations of St Paul's phrase 'the fulness of time', one 'pessimistic' and the other 'optimistic', were known to the early doctors and are both traditional and should not be regarded as incompatible.

St Thomas endeavours to set them together. Having posed the question about the time of the Incarnation, he first answers that humanity had to undergo beforehand, under the natural law and the Mosaic law, the experience of its wretchedness so as to cry out to its Saviour, *ut clamaret ad medicum* : and then also that a long line of prophets was needed to prepare for such a visit.[22]

Further on[23] he says that it is by appealing to the twofold simultaneous movement in history, upwards and downwards, that he will explain the various phases of the economy of the sacraments. On the one hand, he says, 'as time went on, sin began to dominate men more and more; the precepts of the natural law were soon insufficient to show the right path to the reason which was now clouded; there was felt a need for a written law and a determination (by God) of certain sacraments of faith'; therefore the further man descends, the more God's mercy lowers itself to lift him up again. On the other hand, 'as time went on men's knowledge of their faith had to become more explicit; St Gregory the Great[24] said that with the progress of time there also operated a progress of the knowledge of God, and at the same time a progress in the economy of the sacraments; under this second aspect, God's acts of condescension are no longer called forth in any way by the shortcomings of man, but by God's desire to make him grow in the light.

Thus in the view of the early doctors, humanity before the coming of Christ was carried irresistibly along by two currents : one towards the life of grace and the other towards the death of sin.

What is the situation since the Saviour's coming?

[21]Henri-Irénée Marrou, *A Diognète* (Cerf, Paris, 1951), pp. 204-7. This is the second interpretation adopted in the Letter to Diognetus, ix, 2: 'When perversity was at its height and it had become completely obvious that the recompense to be expected was punishment and death, God's appointed time came for manifesting from then onwards his goodness and power: what superabundance of God's charity and his love for man!'
[22]III, qu. 1, a. 5 and 6.   [23]III, qu. 61, a. 3, ad 2.
[24]St Gregory the Great, *Homil. in Ezech.*, lib. II, Homil. IV, no. 1, (P.L., vol. LXXVI, col. 980).

c. *The era of the new law*

The double drift of humanity towards heaven or hell, so far from getting less, has rather increased its violence in the last age of the world. The tragedy only becomes more aggravated as people become more conscious of it. 'If I had not come and spoken to them they would not have sin; but now they have no excuse for their sin' (John 15, 22).

The irreducible opposition of the two loves, that of the world and that of God, fills the New Testament. 'Do not love the world or the things in the world. If any one loves the world, love for the Father is not in him' (I John 2, 15). 'We know that we are of God, and the whole world is in the power of the evil one' (I John 5, 19). 'If the world hates you, know that it has hated me before it hated you. If you were of the world, the world would love its own; but because you are not of the world, but I chose you out of the world, therefore the world hates you' (John 15, 18-19). 'Woe to the world for temptations to sin' (Matt. 18, 7).

'For the mystery of lawlessness is already at work; only he who now restrains it will do so until he is out of the way. And then the lawless one will be revealed, and the Lord Jesus will slay him with the breath of his mouth and destroy him by his appearing and his coming' (II Thess. 2, 7-8). 'For we are not contending against flesh and blood, but against principalities, against the powers, against the world rulers of this present darkness, against the spiritual hosts of wickedness in the heavenly places' (Eph. 6, 12). 'For whatever is born of God overcomes the world; and this is the victory that overcomes the world, our faith' (I John 5, 4).

The conflict will increase with the passing of time and will only come to an end at the moment of the second coming. ' "Sir, did you not sow good seed in your field? How then has it weeds?" He said to them. "An enemy has done this." The servants said to him "Then do you want us to go and gather them?" But he said, "No, lest in gathering the weeds you root up the wheat along with them. Let both grow together until the harvest; and at harvest time I will tell the reapers, Gather the weeds first and bind them in bundles to be burned, but gather the wheat into my barn" ' (Matt. 13, 27-30).

'When the Son of Man comes in his glory, and all the angels with him, then he will sit on his glorious throne. Before him will be gathered all the nations, and he will separate them one from

another as a shepherd separates the sheep from the goats . . .'
(Matt. 25, 31-2).

The whole Apocalypse speaks of nothing but the unfolding,
the vicissitudes and the issue of the terrible battle which—throughout the whole Messianic era from the first coming when Christ
came to save the world, to the second when he will come to judge
it—sets against one another, alternately victorious, the two powers
or spiritual worlds, the one of light, the holy city, in which God
and Christ reign, and the other of darkness in which Satan, the
two beasts and their worshippers reign. At the end of it all comes
the judgment: 'Then Death and Hades were thrown into the lake
of fire. This is the second death, the lake of fire; and if anyone's
name was not found written in the book of life, he was thrown into
the lake of fire. Then I saw a new heaven and a new earth; for
the first heaven and the first earth had passed away, and the sea
was no more. And I saw the holy city, the new Jerusalem, coming
down out of heaven from God, prepared as a bride adorned for
her husband . . .' (Apoc. 20, 14-22, 2).

Why does history continue after the coming of Christ, and
when will his return, announced and hoped for, come to bring it
to an end? We know, writes Henri Marrou in a study of St
Augustine, with what pathetic acuteness the question was put to
the first generation of Christians. He answers that the centuries
after Christ constitute properly the time of the Church as a com-
pleted act; 'the delay of the second coming is very exactly
measured by the delay necessary for the building up of the
Church's numbers; history will stop, come to its end, when the
number of the saints is complete.'[25] He quotes St Augustine:
'If the Judge delays our salvation, it is through love and not
through indifference, by design, not lack of power; if he wishes he
could come at this very moment, but he is waiting until the number
of our fellowship may be filled in to the very last one.'[26] Like 'a
single man spread out over the whole universe and growing
gradually with the course of time', the Church must come, in
the phrase of the apostle, 'to mature manhood, to the measure of
the stature of the fullness of Christ' (Ephes. 4, 13).[27]

---

[25]Henri Marrou, *L'ambivalence du temps de l'histoire chez saint Augustin*
(Vrin, Paris, 1950), pp. 21-2.
[26]*Enarr. in Ps. XXXIV*, II, 9.
[27]*Enarr. in Ps. CXVIII*, XVI, 6.

And so we should remember that it is not the undertakings of the city of evil but the achievements and accomplishments of the city of God which will give the signal for the last hour of the world.[28]

6. MARITAIN'S VISION OF THE DRAMA OF HISTORY

A clear statement of the tragic conflict of good and evil which makes up the fabric of human history will be found in contemporary works in the writings of Jacques Maritain, from which a few passages are quoted here.

a. *Ambivalence of the progress of history*

One of the first questions to be asked concerns the progress of history. If the world had a beginning and is destined to attain some transcendent end, even if this end is rejected by the sin of free creatures, why does God make it last, and how is its progress to be conceived? To this question a truly all-embracing answer, taking in both the spiritual and temporal planes, was given in *St Thomas Aquinas*: 'I think that two immanent tendencies intersect at every point in the history of the world and affect everyone with their momentary complexes: one tendency draws upward everything in the world which participates in the divine life of the Church, which is in the world but not of the world, and follows the attraction of Christ, the Head of the human race. The other

---

[28]'The religious view of the history of the world in the Koran is totally different from that of orthodox Judaism and of Christianity ... For Islam there is no progress in the revelation of the mystery of God. Religion ... is periodically brought back to men's minds by the prophets. Communities have been visited in succession, with no other connection between them than juxtaposition in time. The great Koranic law of history is that peoples rebellious towards those sent them by God have been annihilated, and subsequently replaced by others who took over the succession.' Jacques Jomier, 'Bible et Coran' (Paris, Cerf, 1959), pp. 140 and 143. 'Between the beginning and end of the world, the only landmarks in the gloomy desert of history (men being born, suffering, dying) are the oases of prophecy: Noah, Abraham, Moses, Christ. There is discontinuity between one prophet and the next, it is a mere series of broken words which shake up the times without transfiguring them.' Jules Monchanin, 'Islam et Christianisme', in *Bulletin des Missions*, vol. XVII, 1938, p. 21. Cf. also J.-M. Abd-el-Jalil, 'Aspects intérieurs de l'Islam' (Seuil, Paris, 1949), p. 37, et seq.

tendency draws downward everything in the world which belongs to the Prince of the world, the head of all the wicked. History suffers these two internal strains as it moves forward in time, and human affairs are so subjected to a distension of increasing force until the fabric in the end gives way. So the cockle grows up along with the wheat; the capital of sin increases throughout the whole course of history and the capital of grace increases also and super-abounds. As history draws nearer to Antichrist and suffers in all its visible structure transformations preparing the way for the advent of Antichrist, so also it draws nearer to him whom Antichrist, preceded and who conceals beneath that same concatenation of events in the world the holy task he continues to pursue among his own.'[29]

b. *The two sources of history*

How are we to resolve the fundamental problem of the relations between the two sources of history, the defectible freedom of man and the eternal freedom of God.

'The true conception is that the divine plan is immutable *once fixed* from all eternity. But it is only fixed from all eternity *with account taken of the free default of man,* which God sees in his eternal present. Man enters thus into the eternal plan. Not in order to modify it! To say this would be an absurdity. He enters into its very composition and its eternal fixation by his power of saying: No. In the line of evil, it is the creature who is the first cause. Thus we may interpret in two ways the Gospel saying, "Without me you can do nothing." It may be interpreted as relating to the line of good, and then it means: without God we can do nothing, i.e. without God we cannot do the slightest act in which there is being or goodness. Or it may be interpreted as relating to the line of evil, and then it means: without God we can do nothingness, i.e. without God we can make the thing which is nothing, we can introduce into action and being the nothingness

[29]Maritain, *St Thomas Aquinas* (Sheed & Ward, London, 1933), p. 87. This idea of a twofold progress in opposite directions is valid only on the cultural level. Cf. Maritain, *The Rights of Man and the Natural Law* (Geoffrey Bles, London, 1944): 'This is the idea of progress which, in my opinion, must replace both the illusory notion of necessary progress conceived after the manner of Condorcet, and that denial or dislike of progress which prevails today among those who have lost faith in man and freedom, which is in itself a principle of historical suicide.'

which wounds them and which constitutes evil. The first initiative always comes from God in the case of good, and then the initiative of created liberty itself arises from the divine initiative. But because of the power of refusal, which naturally forms part of all created liberty, the first initiative always comes from the creature in the case of evil.

'Thus we can form some idea of the drama of history, or rather the drama of the superior, the sacred regions of history. Whatever is the part of the visible material which conditions it in the world of nature, history is made up above all of the crossing and inter-mingling, of the pursuit and conflict of uncreated liberty and created liberty. It is, as it were, invented at each moment of time by the accorded or disaccorded initiative of these two freedoms—one in time, the other outside of time and knowing, from the heights of eternity, to which all moments of time are indivisibly present, the whole succession in a single glance. And the glory of the divine liberty is to create an even more beautiful work the more it allows the other liberty to unmake it, because from the abundance of destructions it alone can draw a superabundance of being. But we, who are lodged in the tapestry, see only the obscure entanglement of the threads which are knotted in our heart.'[30]

c. *Pessimism or optimism?*

Christianity 'is pessimistic in the sense that it knows that the creature comes from nothingness, and that everything that comes from nothingness tends of itself towards nothingness. But its optimism is incomparably more profound than its pessimism, be-cause it knows that the creature comes from God and that every-thing that comes from God tends towards God.'[31] It knows by reason, but this would not be enough for anyone with eyes to see evil in the world and God's terrible fair play which lets evil bring forth more evil. 'Fortunately, there is also the order of grace, and the virtue of the blood of Christ, the sufferings and prayers of the saints, and the hidden operations of mercy. All these, without in-fringing the laws of divine fair play, introduce into the most secret recesses of the plot factors which transfigure it . . . and in spite of everything guide history to its accomplishment. A more than

[30]Maritain, *On the Philosophy of History* (Geoffrey Bles, London, 1959), pp. 95-6.
[31]Ibid., p. 41.

human grandeur is dissembled in our creeping destinies. A sense
is given to our wretched condition, and this is probably what
matters most to us. It remains a wretched condition—but the
existent who vegetates in it is cut out to become God by participation.'[32]

A moving passage drawn from another context, shows how far
the views of evolutionism and its extrapolations have been surpassed: 'Indeed, reason demands us to have faith in man. Let us
turn from the present world of man and look at the world of
nature—and by this I mean an unbiased look. We see that,
despite the law of struggle and conflict which dominates everywhere, nature is penetrated in its depths by a measureless peace,
going above the individual and impossible to evade, which is constituted by the basic goodness and universal force of being. And
man, as a part of nature, has an essence which in itself is good.
We see that the evolution of the cosmos is a steady movement,
although constantly hindered, towards higher forms of life and
consciousness, attaining a final victory in the human species and,
within the limits of the latter, is taken in charge by human freedom; the slow and painful progress of the human species from the
cave onwards bears witness to energies in man which make all
scorn for the human race childish and presumptuous. Give a little
loving consideration to any individual in the common and anonymous mass of poor humanity: the more you know him, the more
you discover in him hidden resources of goodness which evil has
been incapable of destroying. The difficult condition of man
comes from the fact that he is not merely a creature of nature but
also one of reason and freedom—elements which are weak in him
and yet are his indestructible strength and the tokens of his unalterable dignity. Neither shortcomings nor blemishes can efface
his original greatness.

'We do, of course, see that we must have faith in man. But we
cannot. Our experience holds our reason in check. The actual
world of man has been a revelation of evil for us and shattered
our confidence. We have seen too many crimes for any sanction
to be able to give compensation, too many deaths in despair, too
sordid a debasement of human nature. Our vision of man has
been obliterated by the unforgettable picture of the bloody spectres

[32]*Existence and the Existant,* op. cit., pp. 127-8.

of the extermination camps. The totalitarian will to power, Nazi as well as Communist, nourished on our moral weakness, has let devils loose everywhere. Everything we used to love seems to have been poisoned; everything we had confidence in seems to have broken down. Our very being is threatened with mental and moral atomization. Our language itself has been perverted: its words have become ambiguous and no longer seem capable of anything but misleading us. We are living in the world of Kafka. Where is there a faith by which we may live?

'Perhaps we have chosen the wrong path. Perhaps we should have done better to attach ourselves to a faith for which a man may live and die ... If our humanism has turned bad, it may be because it was centred on man alone and was utilitarian rather than heroic; because it sought to relegate death and evil to oblivion, instead of looking them in the face and surmounting them by a raising of the mind to eternal life; because it has put its trust in techniques instead of love, that is to say, evangelical love ... Faith in man is reborn when it takes root in the supra-human. Faith in man is saved by faith in God.'[33]

d. *The way of the world*

It is to the repercussions of the perpetual conflict between good and evil on the world of culture that Jacques Maritain as a philosopher has devoted his attention. On this level also history is ambivalent: in the happiest periods of history evil was darkly at work in the flowering of our delicate and ephemeral gardens; in the darkest ages, good was busy with its invisible preparations for unforeseeable conquests. We should not be 'astonished that Christian civilizations perish as do other ones; and by the same abandonment to the fatalities of matter. New births will come to be. It is also a statistical law that those difficult discoveries which history has most need to grow are seldom made without the help and the energy of error and disaster. The purifications which would have saved everything come after all has gone to ruin, and begun to bloom again. "So runs the world away." ... Worlds which have risen in heroism lie down in fatigue, for new heroisms and new suffering to come in their turn and bring the dawn of

---

[33]'Une foi par quoi l'on vit?' in *Le philosophe dans la cité* (Alsatia, Paris, 1960), pp. 171-3.

another day. Such is the growth of human history, which is not a process of repetition but of expansions and progress : it grows like an expanding circle, so stretching out to its double consummation —in that absolute from below where man is a god without God, and the absolute on high where he is God in God.'[34]

7. CONCLUSION : HISTORY IS A CIPHER

'Can we recognize a value, a fruitfulness, a meaning to this pilgrimage of humanity, alternately triumphant and defeated, throughout the length of its history?' Once asked, says H. I. Marrou,[35] this question can never more be evaded.

The earth is three thousand million years old, and men have been on it for five or six hundred thousand years. At first sight two points are obvious. For one thing, there are too many precious things which start to pour forth afresh with each generation—the passionate search for the truth, longing for beauty, and above all holiness, shown in its fullness in Gospel times—for us ever to despair of the human adventure as a whole. And for another, there is too much wickedness, too many monstrous things, insolent victories of pride and tyranny, for the idea of a justice immanent in time to be anything but an inadequate, often derisible, answer to the anxious questionings of our minds.

God, it has been said, wrote two books : one with language which is the Bible, and the other with deeds, which is the history of the world. And in these two books, in which good and evil are mixed, the share of evil is such that it is likely to be a stumbling-block for us.

'To understand the meaning of an author, all the contrary passages must be harmonized,' said Pascal;[36] and he added : 'How much to be esteemed are those who reveal to us the cipher and teach us to know the hidden meaning.'[37]

[34]Maritain, *True Humanism* (Geoffrey Bles, London, 1938), p. 287. It is needless to remind oneself that a humanism is only integral if it opens itself to the values of both reason and faith. It is surprising to think that Marxism has been seen as an 'integral' humanism.
[35]Henri-Irénée Marrou, '*De la connaissance historique*' (Seuil, Paris, 1954), p. 16.
[36]*Pensées,* ed. Brunschvicg, no. 684.
[37]Ibid., no. 678.

To discover the cipher of sacred history as well as that of the world, to break the seal and harmonize opposites there is only one possibility. It is the mystery of a God who 'would never permit any evil to exist in his works if he were not powerful enough and good enough to make good come out of the very evil.'[38] With this the absurdity vanishes: good and evil, holiness and sin, being and non-being are no longer set on the same level.

History, which would be a stumbling-block because of the, in a sense, infinite evils which it spreads out before our eyes, only ceases to be one in the presence of the absolutely infinite holiness of God. It must be read from this exalted viewpoint. Only the divine darkness can throw light on it, overcome the discrepancies and give us to understand that the conflict of the two transcendent cities has a meaning. Not, indeed, because hell, where hatred of God lasts for ever, is a structural element of the universe (Teilhard de Chardin); nor because God, to realize himself over the course of history, needed evil to surmount and reconcile (Hegel). But because the divine omnipotence and goodness can take occasion of the ravages of evil to compensate abundantly for them by good things of which we can have no idea here on earth.

Father de Caussade also spoke of the Bible and the world as two books which are only explained by contact with the divine darkness: 'The written word of God is full of mystery; and no less so his word fulfilled in the events of the world. These are two sealed books, and of both it can be said "the letter killeth". God is the centre of faith: all that emanates from this centre is hidden in the deepest mystery. This word and these events are, so to say, the feeble rays from a sun obscured by clouds...

'The Sacred Scripture is the mysterious utterance of a God yet more mysterious; and the events of the world are the obscure language of this same hidden and unknown God. They are mere drops from an ocean of midnight darkness.'[39]

Taking the words of Hebrews 13, 8: 'Jesus Christ is the same yesterday and to-day and for ever,' de Caussade connects the Saviour's own life as told in the gospels with his mystical life carried on in his saints, which is, he says, like a gospel of the Holy Spirit:

[38] St Augustine, *Encheiridion*, III, 11.
[39] J. P. de Caussade, S.J., *Abandonment to Divine Providence* (English trans. from 10th complete French edition, by E. J. Strickland, The Catholic Records Press, Exeter, 1921), pp. 20-21.

'O! great history! grand book written by the Holy Spirit in this present time. It is still in the press. There is never a day when the type is not arranged, when the ink is not applied, or the pages are not printed. We are still in the dark night of faith. The paper is blacker than the ink, and there is great confusion in the type. It is written in characters of another world, and there is no understanding it except in heaven . . .

'Mysteries can neither be seen nor felt; they are objects of faith. Faith judges of their virtue and truth only by their origin, for they are so obscure in themselves that all that they show only serves to hide them and to blind those who judge only by reason.'[40]

Against the city of God stands the mystery of iniquity. It 'is the very inversion of the order of God : it is the order, or rather, the disorder, of the devil. This disorder is a mystery, because under a false appearance of good it hides irremediable and infinite evil . . . ancient history, sacred and profane, is but a record of this war.' Finally, 'all that is opposed to the order of God renders it only the more to be adored. All workers of iniquity are slaves of justice, and the divine action builds the heavenly Jerusalem on the ruins of Babylon.'[41]

But this absolute trust in God in the face of all the contrary events of history, this total surrender of oneself, of one's life and death, into the hands of his omnipotence and goodness—are these a grace which may be found anywhere among men? In answer to those who could see among primitive peoples only the 'prayer of self-interest', a contemporary ethnologist, Father Goetz, quotes a prayer of pure abandonment composed among the Gallas on the day after a war which had been disastrous for them : 'O God of earth, my Lord, you are above me, I am beneath you . . .

'When I see one or two men, I see them with my own eyes and I know them. But you, although you do not see them with eyes, you see within yourself.

'A wicked man has hunted all the menfolk from their homes, he has scattered the children and their mothers like chickens. The wicked enemy has torn the children from their mothers' hand and killed them. All this you have permitted. Why did you do that? You alone know.

[40]Ibid., pp. 23-4.
[41]Ibid., pp. 91-2.

'You made the corn grow, you have made it come up before our eyes; the hungry man was cheered at the sight of it.

'When the wheat was in flower you sent locusts and insects, locusts and pigeons. All this came from your hand. Why did you do that? You alone know.

'My Lord, spare the men who pray to you. As the owner of the grain binds him who steals the grain, so bind us, my Lord. If you have bound the one you love, you unbind the one you love. Since you love me, unbind me, who begs you from the depths of my heart.

'If I do not cry to you from my heart, you do not hear me. If I do cry from my heart, you know it and listen to me.'[42]

For those who know its cipher, how could the spectacle of the world's history, or the spectacle of what is improperly called the history of the Church—in truth the history of the Christian world, in which the only lights are of Christ and the only degradations are of the devil—how could the spectacle of history as a whole be anything but the spectacle of the infinite patience of the divine Goodness?

[42]Joseph Goetz, S.J., *Les religions des primitifs* (Fayard, Paris, 1958), p. 108.

CHAPTER TEN

The Right Attitude
to Evil

'O Godhead, Godhead, eternal Godhead! . . . Ocean of Peace!'
exclaimed St Catherine of Siena.[1] Peace which is not made up of
what we, in our human words, call impassibility or indifference;
Peace which is Love, burning Love: when the Word Incarnate
spoke it was to say that he came to cast fire upon the earth, and
would that it were already kindled (Luke 12, 49); Peace which
is pity and tenderness: 'O eternal and unfathomable Trinity!
O unspeakable Love! If you call me your daughter, I may say
that you are my Father . . .'[2] and yet which could never be disturbed within itself by the eternal disaster of the angels, or by the
downfall of the earthly paradise, or even by the suffering of Christ
and the agonizing cry which he raised on the cross: 'My God,
my God, why hast thou forsaken me?' (Mark 15, 34).[3]

From all eternity God sees the work of his creation and the
redemption of the world in the fullness of this unalterable and
infinite Peace which is Love. The elect, borrowing God's eyes, will
in their turn see the whole unfolding of the history of the world
in the very depths of this Peace. All questionings will cease for
them then, the veil will be lifted, and what we could not see here
below in our condition as pilgrims, and what was an occasion
either of scandal or of adoration for us, will suddenly become for
ever clear; the problem of the meaning of creation, of why an all-
powerful and infinitely good God could allow so many evils, will
be resolved in this light: 'And I heard a great voice from the

---

[1] *Les oraisons de sainte Catherine de Sienne*, ed. de l'Art Catholique (Paris,
1919), p. 21.   [2] Ibid., p. 41.
[3] On our Lord's words: 'My soul is very sorrowful, even to death,' (Matt.
26, 38), Kierkegaard wrote: 'It seems to me even more terrible for God to
have heard these words than for Christ to have uttered them. To be unchanging even to this point and yet be love, deep, limitless and inexhaustible solicitude!' Quoted by Jean Wahl, *Études Kierkegaardiennes* (Vrin,
Paris, 1949), p. 372.

throne saying, "Behold, the dwelling of God is with men. He will dwell with them, and they shall be his people, and God himself will be with them; he will wipe away every tear from their eyes, and death shall be no more, neither shall there be mourning nor crying nor pain any more, for the former things have passed away. And he who sat upon the throne said, "Behold, I make all things new" ' (Apoc. 21, 3-5).

Peace, in the great words of St Augustine, is 'the tranquillity of order', which may be expressed as the victory of the love that gathers together scattered activities to make them all converge on their supreme End.

Peace reigns at the point where this convergence is made, and it will pass into the hearts of those who are then able, from these heights, to look upon the universe and its history.

But is there not a world, the world of freedom and morality, in which God may be frustrated, where he in fact suffers the eternal resistance of his rebellious free creatures? And can peace be there where resistance is experienced?

The answer is that the order of freedom and morality is a particular order made to return, by one path or another, into the universal order. In those who refuse the inflowing of creative Love, the privation which they choose for their share is in its own way a perpetual admission that fullness is in God, and a proof of the intimate superabundance proper to Love. To see this is to see how the evil of sin and hell itself returns into the universal order, certainly not as a component, a structural part, but privatively, as a hollow witness, in an inadequate and finite way, to the infinite fullness of God. Such a perception of evil will disturb no one's inner peace. We know that this will be the privilege of the elect; but, for us who are on this side of the veil, these things are only known in the darkness of faith.

It is the gift of knowledge which permits faith, even in the midst of its darkness, to be enlightened about the depths of evil, and pours over the world's tragedy the tears which are one of the Gospel beatitudes. And it is the gift of wisdom which again permits faith to be enlightened, still in the midst of its darkness, about the fact that evil is only allowed so that it may be the occasion for pure and hidden good, and communicates to it the peace of the children of God which passes all understanding, and which is another of the beatitudes.

There was a deep understanding of evil in St Thomas Aquinas, who analyzed all the forms of sin and human wickedness; and yet an unshakable peace, which finally reduced him to a silence in which all words were mere straw.

We have already quoted the passage from Angela of Foligno, in which she says that God's goodness was shown to her as intensely in the damned who refuse it as in those who accept it.

St John of the Cross, in a maxim whose truth seems necessarily to grow in greatness as time goes on, assures us that the more the evil of the world is intensified, the more clearly the divine goodness reveals itself: 'The Lord has ever revealed to mortals the treasures of his wisdom and his spirit; but now that wickedness is revealing her face more and more clearly, he reveals them in large measure.'[4]

The obscurities remain for the servants of God. But an invincable certainty grows in their hearts. The preaching of the Gospel to the Canadian Indians was set back by an epidemic, which caused the people to dread the missionaries as the greatest sorcerers on earth. Father Lalemant wrote: 'It must be said that there is every excuse for these unfortunate people; for it often happened, and was remarked on a hundred times, that where we were better known and baptized more people was where most people died; while in the huts to which entry was forbidden us, people who were sometimes in the last extremities of sickness could be seen at the end of several days happily cured. We shall in heaven see the secret but always adorable judgments of God.'[5] To which Mary of the Incarnation, with her wonderful spirit added 'wherever they went God allowed death to accompany them in order to purify the faith of those who were converted.'[6] It is enough to re-read a few pages of this servant of God, who thought that missionaries ought to have 'more love than the seraphim', to understand that when fervour reaches a certain vehemence in souls, the certainty of God's love for men becomes for them so absolute that any questions, or even hesitations, seem blasphemous to them, and disasters which affect what is dearest to them can only make them worship the more.

[4]'Spiritual Sentences and Maxims' No. 1, in *Complete Works*, trans. and ed E. Allison Peers (Burns Oates, 1943), vol. III, p. 241.
[5]Quoted in 'Mary of the Incarnation', *Ecrits spirituels et historiques*, (Desclée de Brouwer, Paris, 1935), vol. III, p. 204.   [6]Ibid., p. 204.

A faith illuminated by the gift of wisdom is the only light which allows the mind to plumb the depths of evil without foundering. The gift of wisdom, with that of knowledge, belonged to the Blessed Virgin when, after hearing the Angel of the Annunciation, she realized that the time of the Messiah had come, and that she must give her assent to the Word who was asking to take flesh from her. But she would have gradually to learn, and with how much heart-break and at what price, how the evil of the world was to be overcome.

Her time came suddenly at Bethlehem 'where there was no room for them at the inn'; it was in destitution that she had to bring forth into the world the one whom she knew to be the Son of God. With what amazement she looked into the mystery of the liberality of the Lord who, as St Paul was later to say to the Corinthians, though he was rich, yet for our sake became poor, so that by his poverty we might become rich (II Cor. 8, 9). But was it possible that God, if this little Child was his Son, more precious than the whole universe, should abandon him to the hazards of such a confinement and entrust him to such weak supports?

And then came the flight on the road of exile. A sudden departure in the night was necessary to snatch the Child away from death, then a journey, without resource or protection, to a far-off, unknown land, where another language was spoken. The Blessed Virgin's heart must have been troubled at each peril on this long journey. If this Child really meant anything to God, could he not have saved him by safer, less precarious means? But God remained silent; even when his own Son was caught up in it, he let the pitiless course of events unfold.

The Quattrocento depicted the Blessed Virgin fainting either at the foot of the cross, or at the later moment of laying Christ in the tomb. But unconsciousness only comes on us when anguish is too intense to be borne. It is not true that the Blessed Virgin fainted; she remained united with her Son by contemplating his bloody Passion; she knew the greatest agony a creature can know —though less than that of Christ, who did not lose consciousness either; she bore absolutely the whole weight of anguish which was laid on her, the terrible weight of the co-redemption of the world. 'Standing by the cross of Jesus was his Mother . . .' says the Gospel (John 19, 25); and the Church sings *Stabat Mater dolorosa*.

In the clearness of the vision of heaven all darkness will be dispelled; but here on earth, as long as we are on the road of exile, the mystery of evil only begins to get lighter in the darkness of faith : the veil has not been lifted for anyone, even for the saints or the Blessed Virgin. But it was not the same for the humanity of Christ. From the first moment of his life, his understanding was illuminated by the immediate vision of the Godhead; he did not *believe*, he *saw* the great good for which an all-powerful and infinitely good God could permit evil to come upon his work. Because of this he had the peace of paradise in him; but throughout his mortal life this was concentrated, as it were, in the high point of his soul, and the lower spheres of his being, his heart, his feelings, his body, could be overwhelmed by sorrow, trouble and agonies. With one part of himself he was with the Father, with another in exile; already at his goal but still on the way, *Comprehensor et viator*. From this arises the unfathomable mystery of Christ's encounters with evil. It is for each one to try and penetrate it in his own heart. Only a few poor words can be said about it.

Christ saw man ravaged by the evil of physical suffering. Suffering is not eternal, but is destined in the divine plan to be overcome and eliminated. And so, to mark the precariousness of its reign and the fact that physical evil has not always been man's lot but rather was forced upon him, Christ on certain occasions cast it out with a single word : 'And behold, a leper came to him and knelt before him saying, "Lord, if you will, you can make me clean." And he stretched out his hand and touched him, saying, "I will; be clean" ' (Matt. 8, 2-3). He knew that a first sin lies at the origin of human sufferings and that in this sense they bear witness to a momentary victory of the devil : 'And there was a woman who had had a spirit of infirmity for eighteen years; she was bent over and could not fully straighten herself. And when Jesus saw her, he called her and said to her, "Woman, you are freed from your infirmity." And he laid his hands upon her, and immediately she was made straight, and she praised God' (Luke 13, 11-13). And to those who reproached him for healing on the Sabbath, he replied : 'You hypocrites! Does not each of you on the sabbath untie his ox or his ass from the manger, and lead it away to water it? And ought not this woman, a daughter of Abraham whom Satan bound for eighteen years, be loosed from this bond on the sabbath day?' (Luke 13, 15-16). Yet Christ's immediate purpose was not to remove suffering but to take it upon himself and light it up from within.

Christ encountered death, which itself has not always been definitively man's lot; it is the wages of sin (Rom. 6, 23), the last enemy to be destroyed (I Cor. 15, 26). It was to testify to its usurping and temporary character that Christ was to triumph three times over it, even before his own glorious resurrection. There is a tenderness in each of these three evangelical accounts of resurrection; it might be said Jesus was troubled by the humiliation inflicted by death on the poor human nature which it dislocates. At Naim, seeing the mother whose only son was being taken to his burial, 'He had compassion on her and said to her, "Do not weep!"' (Luke 7, 13). He would take the hand of the little daughter of Jairus, who was twelve, and having made her sit up, saw that she had something to eat (Mark 5, 42-43). He wept over the tomb of Lazarus. This was the hour of his solemn meeting with death. He allowed it to carry out all its ravages even to the decomposing of the corpse. They sent him the message quickly : 'Lord, he whom you love is ill' (John 11, 3). He contented himself with the answer : 'This illness is not unto death; it is for the glory of God, so that the Son of God may be glorified by means of it' (John 11, 4). It was indeed unto death, since Lazarus died; but death was no longer to have the last word, nor ever will again. Christ was stronger than death, and he showed this then by the raising of Lazarus to this mortal life on earth and shortly afterwards by his own glorious resurrection to the eternal life of heaven, in the wake of which all the elect will ultimately be drawn. But at the sight of the tomb Christ was 'deeply moved' and 'wept' (John 11, 33 and 35). He wept over Lazarus, over what has become of human life, through men's own works, over the unspeakable disaster of original sin. Jesus deeply moved and weeping in the face of death and commanding it with a single word! What serenity he had, what power and greatness, but also what tenderness! Who will ever understand death as Christ did?

Above all Christ came to take away sin, which is the real evil. He could take it away as a surgeon removes a cancer and its adhesions. A paralysed man was brought to him and everyone waited to see what he would do. But Christ saw what no one else saw : not his disease, but the drama of sin and despair going on in his heart. 'Take heart, my son; your sins are forgiven' (Matt. 9, 2). He would cure the paralytic as he would raise Lazarus; but these evils were secondary.

The moment a heart opens itself to repentance, Christ is ready to forgive. He is not insistent about its sin—he used infinite delicacy. It is true that he gave the Samaritan woman a salutory shock by telling her of her husbands. She did not excuse herself, she knew that he was right. She simply tried to change the subject. He followed her lead and answered her new questions.

At the house of Simon the Pharisee he did not have a word of blame for the woman known in the town as a sinner who was now overwhelmed by repentance, only these words which each of us would wish to hear from him at the moment of death : 'Her sins, which are many, are forgiven, for she loved much' (Luke 7, 47). This is already the same as : 'To-day you will be with me in Paradise' (Luke 23, 43).

To the woman taken in adultery and waiting in terror for the moment when she would be stoned, but who at the end remained alone in front of him, all he had to say was : ' "Woman, where are they? Has no one condemned you?" She said, "No one Lord." And Jesus said "Neither do I condemn you; go, and do not sin again" ' (John 8, 10-11).

Sin, which was to lead Christ to his agony, was the everlasting torment of his life. He had to confront the horror of hell at the outset of his preaching, with the three temptations in the desert. The Gospel is full of revealing flashes : 'When he was in Jerusalem at the Passover feast, many believed in his name when they saw the signs which he did; but Jesus did not trust himself to them, because he knew all men and needed no one to bear witness of man; for he himself knew what was in man' (John 2, 23-25). Nothing of the rottenness and inconstancy in our hearts was hidden from him. He wept over Jerusalem : 'O Jerusalem, Jerusalem, killing the prophets and stoning those who are sent to you! How often would I have gathered your children together as a hen gathers her brood under her wings, and you would not!' (Matt. 23, 37). Was he weeping for his country, as is sometimes said? It goes deeper than that. He was weeping because most of the chosen people disregarded the great prophecy of the Old Testament: all the helping graces of God over nearly two thousand years, sent down like dew upon this cherished people, were to end in a betrayal. He was weeping for Jerusalem's sin, the Jerusalem which is the image of each of our souls.

The terrifying freedom God allows to evil appears nowhere more tragically than in the Gospel accounts of the Saviour's agony, Passion and death. How could God hand over this only Son, in whom he was well pleased, to the savage devices of the wickedness of men who seem scarcely to realize of what invisible powers they are the tools? How could he suffer the one whom he had sent into the world to bear witness to the truth to be buffeted, spat upon in the face and crowned with thorns? How could he remain silent when a plea went up to him like that of the agony: 'Abba, Father, all things are possible to thee; remove this cup from me; yet not what I will but what thou wilt' (Mk. 14, 36) or that of the crucifixion: 'My God, my God, why hast thou forsaken me?' (Mk. 15, 34).

And at the same time nowhere outside these Gospel accounts is there such powerful proof of the infinite patience of the divine Goodness towards sinful humanity, or of the unforeseeable designs of his omnipotence, which brought about the deliverance and redemption of the world amid such impious evils and so fatal a disaster.

Christ's sinless soul was situated at the meeting-place of the unleashed onslaughts of hell and the outrageous freedom of action granted to evil by heaven. The seven divine words from the Cross might offer some openings into the depths of this mystery.

Although God puts before each one of us, in ever more harrowing ways, the question of evil, not in order to shake our faith and trust but to make them truer and more intense, his goodness has already helped us to answer it through the words of the Lord's Prayer:

OUR FATHER, WHO ART IN HEAVEN—For a child the word Father means the wonderful alliance of power and tenderness. We are not orphans. We have a Father whose power and tenderness are infinite and who watches over us every moment of our lives, even the most desolate. He is waiting for us in the place where there is, not evil, but what is beyond evil. The words of Plotinus: 'Let us fly towards our beloved fatherland ... For we have a fatherland from which we come and a Father who waits for us there,'[7] held a great fascination for St Augustine, because a Christian can never read them without thinking of the Gospel revelations.

HALLOWED BE THY NAME—May thy name of Father be recognized, and acknowledged even in the darkness of the greatest trials. Job was innocent, and it was not true that the misfortunes which overwhelmed him were punishments. Yet all he had to look forward to was death and the comfortless descent to sheol. At the time when he lived he could not even begin to suspect what we call eternal life. Why, then, his sufferings? He had no glimpse of any answer. Yet it was then that he made his sublime and selfless act of faith : 'I know that my Redeemer lives, and at last he will stand upon the earth; and after my skin has been destroyed, then without my flesh I shall see God, whom I shall see on my side, and my eyes shall behold, and not another' (Job 19, 25-26). Similarly by hoping against all hope Abraham began to believe in the promise of descendants (Rom. 4, 18); and when Isaac, the only son of the promise, had grown up, God demanded that he be sacrificed. To believe, with boundless trust, even against all appearances, that God is the Father, is what God expects from the best among us, and this is the love which even here on earth dispels the problem of evil.

THY KINGDOM COME—May thy kingdom start to come when thy love ceaselessly comes down into the very midst of the world to set up thy Church; and may it come fully when thy love overturns the works of evil so as to transfigure the universe. I remember a visit to what remains today of the death-camp at Majdanek, near Lublin, where two million human beings perished. In grim huts encircled by electric fences and watchtowers pathetic human vestiges are piled up, wretched canvas shoes, women's footwear, children's boots, and here and there the remains of dolls. And there is the oven, a monstrous cauldron brought from Berlin. Then the central building in concrete, with showers on the way to the gas-chambers, the great parallel ovens. each charged with batches of six corpses, and the channels for collecting the fat and potash. Technically everything is seen to, even the cement slab on which gold was taken from the teeth of the corpses. Outside it was evening and the setting sun was veiled

[7]Enneads, I, 6, 8.

by a pink cloud—there was a great silence over the Polish plain. Several yards in front of me the square brick chimney, constructed by the prisoners themselves, towers over the building, rising into the sky like a sort of steeple. So many frantic, terrified eyes have looked at it and seen the red flames burn up, then die away in dark smoke. Is it possible that these emaciated beings, waiting for their horrible end in the death-camp, did not turn towards the all-powerful and infinitely good God to call him to witness and implore him to help them in their atrocious anguish with some miracle. Yet no answer came. I in my turn tried to say the Lord's prayer, to call upon the Father in heaven who has seen all this and remained silent. It is a mystery. To what depths God requires us to trust him and believe in his Love! May thy kingdom come, and hasten to destroy this devilish apparatus and cleanse the earth of such fearfulness.

THY WILL BE DONE—Thy will to choose among the infinite number of possible worlds one in which evil was to have a part, and such a terrible part. Thy will to allow the tares to grow with the wheat until the end of history. Thy will to allow evil to triumph while giving us the command to fight it; and allow thy City to be constantly checked by the onslaughts of the spirits of darkness. All this is thy will and good pleasure. For there is a will of God which is *proposed* or made known to us by his commandments, counsels and inspirations, and in which we are required to acquiesce freely with love, a love of conformity to the divine will as made known to us. And there is a will of God which is *imposed* on us, which no one can hinder, and which is known to us only by effects which, once they have come, show us that God has willed them if they are good or allowed them if they are evil. It may cut across our most legitimate desires, tear away from us by death the ones who are dearest to us and whose defence was entrusted to us, and overwhelm us with pain or calumny. We may well ask to be spared—Christ did: 'Abba, Father, all things are possible to thee; remove this cup from me,' (Mk. 14, 36). But when all is said and done, our submission, not merely resigned, but loving, is expected. This is God's 'good pleasure'.

GIVE US THIS DAY OUR DAILY BREAD—Give us your grace, the bread without which the soul cannot live; give us the inner strength to carry out whatever you want of us. Give us every day sufficient faith and love to be able to acquiesce in this world in which evil is in such conflict with good, even in our own hearts. I need this bread of the soul, I beg it, not only for myself, but for every free creature on earth. In your goodness, grant that they may say in all circumstances : May your holy will be done! Grant that each of us may carry our share of trials without being broken by them.

FORGIVE US OUR TRESPASSES—Forgiveness, as we well know, is the bread of which we first have need—without it we cannot live. And we cannot look on the future or on death without raising our eyes to you. The worst evil of all, sin, has entered us, and works secretly at our unconscious being. The seven deadly sins are coiled up in us like sleeping serpents. But the power of the divine forgiveness is infinite; a single drop of the blood of Christ is enough to wash away the stains of the world, a single word from him to open paradise to a thief. He himself prayed on behalf of us all : 'Father forgive them, for they know not what they do.' They do not know the offence they commit against Love, nor the depth of this Love; they do not even know the evil they do to them-selves, or that the rejection of Love is the hell on earth which they establish in themselves. Forgive us even as we forgive . . . better than we forgive. And put something of your own open-handedness into our forgiveness; ours will remain limited, but it is an un-limited forgiveness we ask of you.

AND LEAD US NOT INTO TEMPTATION—This can mean two things. You could in all justice allow the imprudent things I do a dozen times a day to take their inevitable course. One infidelity would bring on the next and so on till disaster. Do not let this happen—shatter this fatal logic. I am the foolish man who built on sand (Matt. 7, 26). Do not send the winds and the rains and the floods.

But also do not submit us to a trial of strength. Do not allow the temptation I come up against today—and I shall ask the same thing tomorrow—to be above my powers of resistance. Or, rather, make my love greater. May the words of St Paul be true of us all : 'God is faithful and he will not let you be tempted beyond your strength, but with the temptation will also provide the way of escape, that you may be able to endure it' (I Cor. 10, 13).

BUT DELIVER US FROM EVIL—Deliver us from the Evil One and his snares, and from all forms of evil in so far as they might be fatal for us; deliver us especially from the evil of sin. This last request is a renewal, although a negative one, of all that which comes before it. The Lord's Prayer ends up with an appeal for deliverance. May all evil which has so greatly oppressed humanity be one day driven out, and the time of the Kingdom, our heavenly country, come at last.

The question of evil can never be side-stepped, for God sets it before every man from the time he first comes into the world. Not to make us lose our faith and love, but to allow them to grow in us to the very end. Such an answer must be formed in the silence of our hearts, and it may take shape in an unrelieved darkness lasting till death. It may also come in a flash from the eternal Wisdom transfiguring our anguish, reducing all our doubts and objections to nothing. Every soul must go by the path God has prepared for it.

If the tares and the wheat, evil and good grow together throughout history, we believe that as a whole, even in our days and until the end of time, good is stronger than evil, and Christ stronger than Belial. When evil takes the fearsome proportions which we have seen during the first and second world wars and which others may yet see at other times, it is a sign that God is rousing in the secrecy of men's hearts the wonderful acts of love which will 'make the most of the time' (Eph. 5, 16), and bring once more to life that mysterious beauty of the Church on which it is said that the angels long to look (I Peter 1, 12). We know that evil is more evident to the eye than good; but good is more lasting than evil, and undermines the structures of evil which will topple down on one another. We believe that if ever evil, at any time in history, should threaten to surpass the good, God would annihilate the world and all its workings.

Index

F

F

R
F